Sustainable Tourism Development

Sustainable Tourism Development

Edited by **Lucas Weber**

WILLFORD PRESS
New York

Published by Willford Press,
118-35 Queens Blvd., Suite 400,
Forest Hills, NY 11375, USA
www.willfordpress.com

Sustainable Tourism Development
Edited by Lucas Weber

International Standard Book Number: 978-1-68285-151-7 (Hardback)

Printed in the United States of America.

Contents

Preface

The main aim of this book is to educate learners and enhance their research focus by presenting diverse topics covering this vast field. This is an advanced book which compiles significant studies by distinguished experts. This book addresses successive solutions to the challenges arising in the area of application, along with it; the book provides scope for future developments.

Tourism is synonymous with travel. Travel often leads to adverse environmental impacts due to the modes of transportation. This has given rise to the relatively nascent concept of sustainable tourism. This extensive book collaborates researches from across the globe in this field. Some of these studies revolve around tourism development with sustainability, eco-agritourism, medical tourism, rural tourism, ecotourism, infrastructure, etc. The exclusive content of this book will provide an in-depth analysis of this field. It will be beneficial for students, academicians and anyone else who wishes to delve deeper into this field.

It was a great honour to edit this book, though there were challenges, as it involved a lot of communication and networking between me and the editorial team. However, the end result was this all-inclusive book covering diverse themes in the field.

Finally, it is important to acknowledge the efforts of the contributors for their excellent chapters, through which a wide variety of issues have been addressed. I would also like to thank my colleagues for their valuable feedback during the making of this book.

Editor

1

Potential of Homestay Tourism Based on Seaweed Cultivation from the Views of Seaweed Cultivators in District of Semporna Sabah, East Malaysia

Rosazman Hussin[1], Suhaimi Md. Yasir[2] and Velan Kunjuraman[3]

[1, 3] The Ethnography and Development Research Unit, Faculty of Humanities, Arts and Heritage, Universiti Malaysia Sabah, 88400 Kota Kinabalu, Sabah, Malaysia.
[2] Seaweed Research Unit, Faculty of Science and Natural Resources, Universiti Malaysia Sabah, 88400 Kota Kinabalu, Sabah, Malaysia.

Abstract. Community participation in tourism development especially among fisherman and farmers has begun to given serious attention by the government whereby the communities are given opportunities to engage in tourism development programmes in order to enhance their quality of life. In order to encourage local community participation in tourism development in rural areas, participants' perceptions regarding tourism activities are important aspect to be sought. Good or bad perceptions from the community towards tourism development are important because it can determine the success of the programme. Firstly, this paper aims to explore the views or perceptions of seaweed cultivators towards homestay tourism which is based on seaweed cultivation in the District of Semporna, Sabah. Qualitative and quantitative research approaches have been applied in this study, such as the usage of the face to face interviews survey using survey questionnaires and field observation as primary methods. The findings show that the majority of the respondents have a positive perception of homestay tourism based on seaweed cultivation, such as the acceptance of visits by the tourists to their working place. Seaweed cultivators agreed that this tourism activity bring additional income to them. Activities that can become tourist attractions include tying seaweed seeds on a casino table. Moreover, the tourists have an opportunity to take a boat to see the seaweed farm, and take pictures of seaweed activities and so on. These findings also revealed that the majority of the respondents assumed that the visits of the tourists would motivate them to carry out the activity with more enthusiasm. This shows that seaweed cultivation could become a new tourism product which has great potential to develop in the district of Semporna, Sabah.

1 Introduction

Tourism sector is considered as an important asset in a country [1] and developing countries began to give serious attention to the tourism industry in their respective countries. Developing countries basically utilize tourism as an important mechanism to increase domestic and foreign investment [2-3], development of infrastructure [4] as well as employment opportunities [5-6], through the exchange of currencies [6-7]. Malaysia is no exception in this regard. Tourism sector in Malaysia can be categorised as at a decent level. This can be proved by the number of tourist arrivals in the country which have increased by 25.03 million, registering a total expenditure of MY60.6 billion (USD 46.26 billion) in 2012 differing from the previous year which only recorded a turnover of 24.71 million tourist arrivals and total expenditure of 58.3 billion [8]. Therefore, tourism has the same potential compare to other sectors such as the manufacturing and agricultural sectors.

2 Tourism in Sabah

The government is highly concerned about the development of the tourism industry in every state of Malaysia and ensures that the development in all of the states are at par with one another. Sabah is rich in natural resources which have the potential to fuel the country's economy. Natural resources such as forests, peaks and islands became important elements in eco-tourism. Moreover, the unique culture in Sabah's community attracts tourists to Sabah [9]. In terms of economy, the tourism industry in the state has a significant impact on the revenue. The number of tourists who visited the state, either domestic or international tourists is constantly increasing. This is supported by the statistical data issued by the Minister of Tourism, Culture and Environment. Datuk Seri Panglima Masidi says that Sabah tourism is income in 2013 was recorded at RM6.35 million, becoming the main source of income in the state. In addition, domestic tourism has contributed 68 percent or 2.29 million to the country's income, an increase of 18.6 percent of the total domestic tourism in 2012 [10].

Sabah has many popular tourist destinations such as Tunku Abdul Rahman Park, Kinabalu National Park, Poring Hot Springs, and the Sepilok Orang Utan Rehabilitation Centre. In 2000, the Kinabalu National Park has been listed in the World Heritage Sites, and that indicates the state has vast potential in strengthening Malaysia's position as an attractive tourist destination. In addition to the above listed tourist destinations, Sabah is also well known with its cultural tourism such as NunukRagang and homestay tourism [11]. There are several tourist homestays run by the local community in the state such as Atamis Homestay in Kundasang [1], Village Homestay in Kiulu Pukak [12], Miso Walai Homestay in Batu Puteh, Kinabatangan [13], and Walai Tokou Homestay in Kundasang [14]. Homestay programme has also has the ability to generate income for the Malaysian economy. For example, a total of 133,689 people had visited the homestay from January to May 2012. This include 110,322 domestic tourists and 23,367 foreign tourists, an increase of 70.7% over last year which was only 78,333 people. The total income from the homestay programme for the first five months of 2012 was RM 7,376,446.50 (+53.1%). This total is higher than the total in the months of January to May of 2011 which was only MY4, 817,158.30.30 [15]. So, certainly homestay programme in Malaysia has the potential to grow and stay competitive.

3 Homestay Tourism Based on Seaweed Cultivation Activities in Semporna: An Introduction

Semporna is one of the areas that are close to Tawau. In Semporna, there are several tourist attractions such as islands of Mabul and Sipadan. Semporna became the centre for marine tourism activities and is still under development. Marine tourism is usually known for its beautiful beaches and coral reefs. Boat Transport is one of the special transports where travellers have to take the boat to go to islands near Semporna. Moreover, tourism in Semporna became popular when there are constructions of new hotels and restaurants in the area. These help Semporna to be known as a tourist destination, thus leisure travellers will be keen to visit Semporna. Semporna is a busy district which receives tourists every day. One of the key factors that attracks tourists to visit Semporna is the unmatched sea water clarity. Therefore, the many water activities are carried out such as diving, snorkelling, swimming and fishing. The tourists may enjoy the beauty of nature with a visit to nearby islands such as Sipadan Island, Mabul Island, Kapalai Island, Mataking Island and Sibuan Island. A marine specialty in Semporna District has prompted the government to introduce measures which strategies can help to develop the tourism industry in the area. According to Prabahkaran, et al. [16], Semporna District has a diverse marine motivate the visitors to visit remote destinations in the state. Elements like these are sure to develop a tourism industry based on natural resources such as seaweed cultivation. Stakeholders as Semporna District Office has identified 10 reasons tourists visited Semporna [17]: (1) Scuba diving, (2) Island shopping, (3) Picnic area, (4) Water villa, (5) Archaeological sites, (6) Fishing, (7) Water festival (*Regatta Lepa*), (8) honeymoon, and (9) Seafood Heaven.

Apart from the above, Semporna is also popular with seaweed cultivation by fishermen communities along the coast. Semporna is one of the locations where it undertakes seaweed activities on a large scale in Malaysia. In Southeast Asia such as the Philippines, Indonesia and Sulawesi seaweed species that is commonly cultivated are *Kappaphycus* and *Eucheuma* and exported abroad [18]. There are many different species of seaweed was cultivated by coastal communities in Malaysia. In Peninsular Malaysia, the species of seaweed such as *Caulerpa*,*Sargassum*, *Ulva*, and *EnteromorphaAcanrophora* are typically undertaken by communities in coastal especially fishermen community [19]. In Sabah, seagrass species such as *Eucheumaspinosum* and *Kappaphycusalvarezili* is the only type of seagrass cultured by fishermen community [20]. Seaweed cultivation activity has a great potential to serve as a unique tourism product in Semporna since it is cultivated on a large scale by fishermen communities as their main or side income. Seaweed cultivation activities in Sabah are concentrated in Semporna, Lahad Datu, Kudat and Kunak covering 7,535 hectares of the sea area. Semporna has been a tremendous interest because the fishermen community in most of the islands in the location carry out seaweed cultivation activities although seaweed is relatively new in the tourism industry, in collaboration with stakeholders and fishermen community, this activity can be used as a tourism product in the future, contributing to the country's economic income and improve the socio-economic level of the communities that are working on the seaweed cultivation.

The homestay programme is identified as a mechanism to promote seaweed cultivation tourism which can be used as one of the tourism products to attract tourists. The packages offered through the homestay programme are one way to promote seaweed cultivation as a unique tourism product. The seaweed cultivation activities attract the interest of tourists to witness the activities that are run in the seaweed industry. There are several islands near Semporna where seaweed cultivation activities are actively conducted and this may attract tourists to pay for a visit namely to Omadal Island, Selakan Island and Sebangkat Island. It is very important to ensure that the seaweeds participate in the process of developing as a tourism product. Without the participation of the local communities, the tourism projects will definitely not succeed. Err [21] argues that without the participation of local communities, sustainable tourism in Malacca would not be realised. The concept of participation by Scheyvens is closely-related to the neopopulist and sustainable development approach. Neopopulist approach focuses on people in the context of small-scale, local, and bottom-up approaches to achieve development. However, sustainable development approach emphasizes the environment as the main priority in achieving development [22].

For Tosun [23], community participation in development is a voluntary act of an individual to take a chance and social responsibility. This process requires the cooperation of the community in all aspects of development planning so that the projects are implemented properly. In the process of tourism development, community participation can be viewed from two perspectives, namely the decision-making process and the resulting benefits of such a development [24].

4 Studies on the Views or Perceptions of the Local Communities on the Development of Tourism

Tourism involving local communities often needs the support of the communities that occupied the destination. Without their support, the tourism activities might not achieve the goal of the development. This is often related to the extent of the impact that tourism can fulfil the needs of the communities with their perception to move forward in life. Studies related to the perceptions of communities on tourism are done by foreign scholars in their geographic areas in the country [25-29]. However, there are some studies done by local scholars [30-33].

Studies done by Perdue et al. [27] and Akis et al. [28], confirm that local communities gain benefits in terms of the economic aspect and enable them to support the tourism development in their area. Studies by Wall [29] in Bali, Indonesia found that the local community has a positive outlook when they receive benefits from tourism development. Aside from the economic benefits, socio-cultural and environmental aspects of the trade-off are also important factors for the development of the community tourism [27]. For example, from the socio-cultural perspective, tourism can develop or increase the demand for cultural products such as handicrafts which maintain traditional ideas and culture [34].In studies by Oviedo-Garcia et al. [35] on tourism in Santipoce found that people have a positive view on the high level of tourism that benefits them. This gives them the confidents to support the development of the tourism in their area. A review by Marzuki [30] in Langkawi found that people in the area receive the benefits and negative impacts of tourism development. The study found that residents receive more benefits than negative effects in the socio-economic aspect of the area such as offering opportunities for employment, business and infrastructure facilities. The study also shows that the development of tourism in Langkawi benefits the population in terms of the opportunity to be engaged in entrepreneurial activities. However, the study also showed the negative effects of the social and environmental aspects. Residents in the area found that there was a monopoly by traders from the mainland for accommodation, goods and transport businesses.

5 Community-Based Tourism Planning Approach

Community-based tourism planning approach is an approach that emphasizes community participation in tourism development [36]. In other words, community-based tourism planning approach also has the same meaning with a "bottom-up" approach which emphasizes community participation. Community participation in tourism development and planning has received a profound attention from many tourism researches [37-40]. This approach emphasizes community participation in tourism development and that benefit from tourism to be distributed to all [41].

According to this approach, there should be appropriate measures when planning a tourism development involving the community so that the community agrees with the planning that is going to be carried out in their area. Therefore, in this study the researchers highlight the potential of seaweed cultivation as a new tourism product in Semporna, Sabah and identify views of the seaweed cultivators in the area. There are two objectives in this study. They are as follows:

i.   To identify demographic backgrounds of seaweed cultivators interested in becoming homestay operators;

ii. To identify views of the seaweed cultivators on seaweed cultivation activities homestay based tourism; and to identify the monitoring method on the expected number of tourist arrivals in the seaweed cultivation site.

6 Methodology

The study was conducted on three islands located in Semporna namely Selakan Island, Omadal Island, and Sebangkat Island. Initial field survey was conducted on the three islands in Semporna to identify seaweed cultivation activities conducted by seaweed cultivators in September 2012. The Islands were chosen because the majority of the fishing communities are involved in seaweed cultivation as their full or part time job. In addition, these islands also have the potential to become tourist destinations because of the seaweed cultivation which is a unique way to serve as a tourism product that can attract the tourists. This study uses a quantitative approach to get the data which is by using face to face interview survey [42]. A total of 80 local communities were selected based on non-probability purposive sampling as respondents from the three islands located in Semporna District. Non-probability purposive sampling in this study is considered as suitable for a group of subjects that have certain characteristics selected as the respondents. In this study, the respondents were selected based on the purpose of the study in which respondents must have experience in the kelp industry on seaweed cultivation activities as a full or part time job. Aside from face to face interview survey method, the researchers also performed field observations in order to get the data. A questionnaire of 12 close-ended questions was used by the researchers to survey the respondents. The close-ended questions are intended facilitate the respondents answering the questions, as well as to save the respondents' and researchers' time [43]. In addition, measurements on a Likert scale responses were used. According to Likert Resis [84], data that is collected through a Likert scale have higher reliability compared to other scales. There are some scale of measurement used in a study which are 1-3, 1-5, 1-7 or 1-9. This study used eight options, 1 = highly disagree, 2 = disagree, 3 = not sure, 4 = agree, 5 = strongly agree, 6 = no response, 7 = not relevant, 8 = do not know to measure items that have been built. The data were analysed using Microsoft Excel 2007 and involves a descriptive analysis.

7 Data Analysis and Research Findings

Table 1. Demographical Analysis of the Respondents

Information	N=80
Gender (%)	
Male	65.0
Female	35.0
Education (%)	
No School	33.8
Primary School	35.0
Secondary School	18.8
Diploma	2.5
Bachelor's	1.2
Others	7.5
No answers	1.2
Residential location (%)	
Selakan Island	37.5
Sebangkat Island	47.5
Omadal Island	15.0
Age (%)	
17-27 years	38.8
28-38 years	30.0
39-49 years	13.8
50-60 years	8.8
61-71 years	1.2
No answers	7.5
Income (%)	
<500	58.8
501-1000	16.2
1001-2000	1.2
2001-3000	1.2
Not determine	5.0
Not sure	2.5
Not relevant	8.8
No answers	6.2
Maritial Status (%)	
Unmarried	32.5
Married	65.0
Widowed/divorced	2.5

Source: Research Analysis, 2014

Based on Table 2, the results of this study shows that as many as 80 seaweed cultivators were interviewed in the three research area namely Selakan Island, Sebangkat Island and Omadal Island. There are 52 respondents (65.0%) consisting of men and 28 respondents (35.0%) consisting of women. The survey shows that there are more male than female respondents at 30 percent. The findings showed 35.0 percent of the respondent had their primary school education while 33.0 percent of the respondents never attended school. Since the majority of the respondents had low level of education, this made them less likely to have the knowledge and skills in tourism planning process in the region. In addition, they are also lack of understanding on the process of tourism development that will be carried out by the authorities in the area. The majority of the respondents have jobs as a seaweed cultivator earning less than RM 500, that is by the percentage of 58.8 percent. Next, a total of 13 respondents receive a monthly income of between RM501 to RM1000. Therefore, it can be concluded that the majority of the respondents are earning less than RM500. This makes it hard for them to improve their living standard. The study also found that 38.8 percent of the respondents are between the ages of 17 to 27. Secondly, 24 of the respondents are from the ages of 28 to 38 which is a total percentage of 30.0 percent. In addition, this study also found that 52 (65.0%) of the seaweed cultivators are married. A total of 32.5 percent of the respondents in this study are not married and 2.5 percent are widows/widowers. Overall, most of the seaweed cultivators are married and are considered as having appropriate jobs. Thus, they are the right participator for the homestay tourism programme.

7.1 Seaweed Cultivators' Outlooks on Tourism Activities and the Monitoring Method on the Tourist Arrivals

This section is divided into two themes, namely (1) Seaweed cultivators' outlook on offerings for tourism activity related to seaweed cultivation, and (2) Monitoring method on the expected tourist arrivals.

Table 3. Seaweed Cultivators Outlooks on Tourism Activities Based on Seaweed Cultivation

Variables Examined		Scale (%)							
		1	2	3	4	5	6	7	8
Theme 1:Seaweed Cultivators' outlooks on tourism activities based on seaweed cultivation									
1.	I feel a sense of pride upon visitors coming to see our work	3.8	3.8	7.5	58.8	20.0	3.8	1.2	1.2
2.	Tourist arrivals would bring additional income to us.	11.2	16.2	21.2	37.5	7.5	3.8	1.2	1.2
3.	Activities of tying seaweed seeds is interesting to see by the tourists.	1.2	-	12.5	56.2	25.0	3.8	1.2	-
4.	Tourists are to be allowed for a practical experiences in tying seaweed seeds, thus giving valuable experience.	1.2	2.5	15.0	52.5	22.5	3.8	1.2	1.2

Source: Data Analysis, 2014
Note: *1= highly disagree, 2=disagree, 3=not sure, 4=agree, 5=strongly agree, 6= no response, 7=not relevant, 8=do not know*

Table 4. Monitoring Method of the Tourist Arrivals

Variables Examined	Scale (%)							
	1	2	3	4	5	6	7	8
Theme 2: Monitoring method of the tourist arrivals								
5. Tourists must obtain permission from the kelp industry before visiting the seaweed cultivation sites	5.0	3.8	22.5	42.5	17.5	6.2	1.2	1.2
6. Only three groups of tourists should be allowed to visit the site in one day for every company	7.5	11.2	38.8	33.8	2.5	3.8	1.2	1.2
7. Tourists are not allowed to granting some money to the cultivators	10.0	6.2	41.2	27.5	8.8	3.8	1.2	1.2
8. A group of tourists visiting session should be between 30 to 45 minutes	5.0	13.8	33.8	35.0	6.2	3.8	1.2	1.2
9. Tourists are allowed to take pictures of seaweed cultivation	1.2	-	8.8	62.5	21.2	3.8	1.2	1.2
10. Tourists are encouraged to visit the seaweed cultivation sites around 10am until 4pm only	1.2	16.2	28.8	42.5	5.0	3.8	1.2	1.2
11. Tourist arrivals must be in a small group	10.0	8.8	21.2	45.0	7.5	5.0	1.2	1.2
12. Presence of tourists can disrupt our work processes	16.2	26.2	18.8	28.8	3.8	3.8	1.2	1.2

Source: Data Analysis, 2014
***Note**: 1= highly disagree, 2=disagree, 3=not sure, 4=agree, 5=strongly agree, 6= no response, 7=not relevant, 8=do not know*

Table 3 displays cultivators' outlook on offerings for tourism activities related to seaweed cultivation. The study found that the majority of the respondents which is 47 respondents (58.8%) agreed with this statement. About 20 percent of the respondents strongly agreed that they have higher motivation when tourists came for a visit to see them doing their job at their working site and these findings suggest that the respondents welcomed tourists to pay for a visit to their seaweed cultivation site. The results show that the majority of the respondents, which is 30 respondents (37.5%) agreed that the arrivals of tourists could bring them additional income. In addition, a total of 17 respondents (21.2) are not bound by it and doubt it. However, the majority of the respondents has a positive perception of tourist arrivals to their place and feels what it is a good chance for them to improve their socio-economic development through tourism. In addition, it was found that a total of 45 respondents (56.2%) agreed with the statement that seaweed seedlings binding activity is a very interesting activity for tourists viewing. There were 20 respondents that strongly agreed with this statement. Findings of this study support the objectives that seaweed cultivation can be used as a tourism product in the area and the respondents have a positive opinion in this regard. In addition, it was found that the majority of the respondents in the survey which is by 42 respondents (52.5%) agree with the view that tourists are allowed to try to tie the seaweed seed in the casino tables. A total of 18 respondents strongly agreed with this view and this is considered as they want to promote seaweed cultivation as a tourism product in the area.

Based on Table 4, a total of 34 respondents (42.5%) agreed that tourists must obtain permission from the kelp industry before visiting the seaweed cultivation site. However, 33.8 percent of the respondents agreed that only three groups of tourists should be allowed to visit the site in one day for every company. Table 4 also describes the information related to the issue of granting some cash to the seaweed cultivators. Findings showed that a total of 33 respondents (41.2%) were not identified in the issue of granting the seaweed cultivators in the form of cash. They have doubts in this regard and it is beyond the knowledge of the respondents. In addition, the study found that a total of 22 respondents agreed with this. If tourists are allowed to grant cash to the cultivators, it is likely that it can increase revenues and motivate them to continue to be seaweed cultivation activists. Seaweed cultivators also agreed (35%) that a group of tourists visiting session should be between 30 to 45 minutes. As shown in Table 4, it was found that a total of 31 respondents (38.8%) were not sure on the procedures of seaweed cultivation tourists visits. In this case, it can be categorized that these respondents have little knowledge on the procedures of tourist visits in their area and there are still some respondents who have no knowledge on this case.

Thus, the findings of this study found that almost all of the respondents which is by 50 people (62.5%) agreed that tourists are allowed to take pictures of seaweed cultivation. It is also important for cultivators to feel that seaweed cultivation is something unique and should be known by the tourists. A total of 17 respondents (21.2%) also strongly agree in this respect and encourage tourists to take pictures. From the aspect of time duration for the sightseeing session at the cultivation site, the results show that a total of 34 respondents (42.5%) agreed in this case. This is because it is the appropriate time for photo taking on seaweed cultivation activity. During the sightseeing session, the travellers will have the opportunity to see the seaweed cultivation process from the early stages until the end. With this, they get to know and understand the real seaweed cultivation process. Additionally, there were also some respondents which is by 28.8 percent who were not sure in this case. The study also found that 36 respondents (45.0%) agreed with this view. This is considered as important because the cultivators are not interested when their jobs are affected by the arrivals of large numbers of tourists. In addition, the space factor is also taken into account where the space provided only have the ability to cultivate seaweed and it is difficult to place a large number of tourists. Finally, a total of 23 respondents (28.8%) agreed with the details at a lot of seaweed cultivation at any given time. Therefore, they do not agree with the presence of tourists which can disrupt their work processes. This is because they have targets to complete tasks in the area. However, a total of 21 respondents responded that it will enhance their motivation level indirectly when tourists come and see their hard work.

8 Conclusion and Discussion

Overall, this study was able to achieve all three objectives. The first objective of which is to identify the demographic backgrounds of the seaweed cultivators. In this study a total of 80 respondents participated which consisted of 52 men and 28 women. The majority of men tend to carry out seaweed cultivation activity compared to women in the three islands namely Selakan Island, Sebangkat Island and Omadal Island. The study found that most of the respondents had primary school education by 35.0 percent, followed by respondents who have never attended school amounting to 33.0 percent. The majority of respondents working as seaweed cultivators are earning less than RM500 at the percentage of 58.8 percent. Thus, it can be concluded that the majority of respondents earn less than RM500 a month and this causes them to not be able to improve the socio-economic development.

Through the findings of this study, it can be concluded that the majority of the respondents had a positive view towards making seaweed cultivation as a tourism product in their area. The study also found that the cultivators agreed that tourism activities based on seaweed cultivation can improve their socio-economic status. This situation is supported by previous studies by [27-28, 30, 35]. Review by Oviedo-Garcia et al. [35] found that the local population of Santipoce giving their views positively rather than negatively in which they receive benefits from tourism activities in their area while supporting the development project. Western scholar also stressed that local population positive outlook on the development of tourism is an important point and may have a positive impact on the planning of tourism development [35, 45-47]. Murphy [38] has emphasized that community input and participation in tourism planning should be taken into account so that the mission of the tourism project can be achieved.

The results of this study concluded that the majority of the respondents had positive views on the offerings of seaweed cultivation as a tourism product in their area. This is a good thing where they realise that this offerings will not only provide additional income but would also increase their potential to become entrepreneurs in the field of tourism when they set up a homestay programme in their area as well as making seaweed cultivation as a unique tourism product. Development of rural areas, particularly Semporna can be developed if the coastal communities are also engaged in business activities. Besides, business activities help to improve their standard of living in terms of their socio-economic. In addition, the tourism industry in the state began identifying seaweed cultivation as a tourism product in Semporna and other locations where seaweed cultivation is performed on a large scale. This could indirectly increase the state income itself and help to increase the country's Gross Domestic Product (GDP). This study is proposed to all the stakeholders, particularly the tourism industry in the state of Sabah. The Ministry of Tourism, Culture and Environment Minister should introduce measures that would encourage rural communities to participate in the tourism business particularly in the homestay programme. They can provide some incentives or capital for the coastal communities to participate in the homestay business. This is because it appears that the majority of fishermen community in Semporna receives less than RM500 and financial constraints pose an obstacle for them to set up a homestay programme in their area. Therefore, the responsible parties should take concrete steps so that the fishermen community can change or improve their lives by engaging in business activities such as the establishment of a homestay programme. Through this study it was found that seaweed cultivation has the potential to become a tourism product. Thus, it is job of the responsible parties such as Semporna District Fisheries Department in Sabah to promote the communities in the area. If this happens, offerings on seaweed cultivation as the first tourist product in the country will become a reality. The study is only a preliminary and comprehensive study for the needs of the future. Future studies should focus on the reaction or other points of view such as tour operators, government officials, NGOs and village chiefs in promoting seaweed cultivation as a tourism product.

References

1. V. Kunjuraman, R. Hussin, Satisfaction of Domestic Tourist with the Homestay Programme in Mesilou Village, Kundasang, Sabah. *Proceedings of the 3rd Regional Conference on Tourism Research,* 29-31 Oct, 2013, Langkawi, Malaysia. 18-27 (2013)
2. J. S. Akama. *The role of government in the development of tourism in Kenya.* Int. J. Tou. Resea **4**, 1-13 (2002)
3. C. L. Jenkins. *The use of investment incentives for tourism projects in developing countries.* Tou Manage **3**, (June), 91 (1982)
4. T. Nimmonratana. Impacts of tourism on a local community: A case study of Chiang Mai. In K. S. Chan. (Ed). *Tourism in Southeast Asia: A new direction,* 6. New York: Haworth Press. (2000).
5. E. de Kadt. *Social planning for tourism in the developing countries.* Annals Tou Resea **6**, 1, 36-48 (1979)
6. M. A. H. Bhuiyan, C. Siwar, S. M. Ismail. *Tourism development in Malaysia from the perspective of development plans.* Asi Soc Sci **9**, 9, 11-18. (2013)
7. A. Nankervis. Dreams and Realities: Vulnerability and the tourism industry in Southeast Asia: A framework for analyzing and adapting tourism management toward 2000. In K. S. Chan. (Ed). *Tourism in Southeast Asia: A new direction*, 49-61. New York: Haworth Press. (2000)
8. Tourism Malaysia. www.MOTAC.gov.my accesed on 2 May 2013
9. S. Ghazali, M. Sirat. *Global Ecotourism and local communities in rural areas.* Pulau Pinang: Universiti Sains Malaysia Press. (2011)

10. Tourism Minister's speech. www.theborneopost.com accsed on 3 March 2014.
11. T. M. Tangit, A. Adanan, S. A. Kibat. *Tourism development and its impact on residents' quality of life: A case study on Malaysia's First World Heritage Site, Kinabalu Park, Ranau, Sabah.* Proceedings of the 3rd Regional Conference on Tourism Research, 29-31 Oct, 2013, Langkawi, Malaysia, 275-283 (2013)
12. P. L. Yong. *Projek Miso Walai Homestay dan Penyertaan Komuniti Tempatan: Satu Tinjauan di Mukim Batu Putih, Hilir Kinabatangan, Sabah.* Unpublished Academic Practice. School of Social Sciences, Kota Kinabalu: Universiti Malaysia Sabah. (2004)
13. R. Hussin. *Ecotourism and Community Participation in the Homestay Programme of Sukau Village: Long-term or Limited Benefits? Jur Sarj* **23**, 72-86 (2008)
14. A. Adrianna, J. Cindy, O. Nor'ain. *Study of tourists' expectation and perception towards products and services offered by Walai Tokou Homestay Kundasang Sabah.* In N. Othman & M. Jamaludin (Eds.). The 3rd Tourism outlook conference & global events Congress II, Heritage & Tourism: Alliance & Network relationship, Event management & Event Tourism, Shah Alam: UITM (UPENA). (2007)
15. Ministry of Tourism Malaysia (MOTOUR) (2012a), *ETP: Transforming tourism to the new heights.*
16. S. Prabhakaran, V. Nair, S. Ramachandran. *Marine waste management indicators in a tourism environment.* Worldwide Hospitality and Tourism Themes, Emerald Group publishing. **5**, 4, 365-376 (2013)
17. District Office Semporna. *Tourism: 10 reasons to visit Semporna*, District Office Semporna, Sabah. (2014)
18. L. Sievanan, B. Crawford, R. Pollnac, C. Lowe. *Weeding through assumptions of livelihood approaches in ICM: Seaweed farming in the Philippines and Indonesia.* Oce & Coas Manage **48**, 297-313 (2005)
19. S.M. Phang. *Seaweeds of Cape Rachado Port Dickson.* Nature Malaysiana, **10**, 9-15 (1989)
20. C. R. Kaur, & M. Ang. *Seaweed culture and utilization in Malaysia: Status, challenges and economic potential.* Paper was presented at MIMA Seminar on Developing the seaweed aquaculture sector, 27 October 2009, Kuala Lumpur: MIMA. (2009)
21. A. C. Err. Pembangunan pelancongan lestari di Melaka: Perspektif pelancong. Mal Jour of Soc and Spa **9**, 3,12-23Available at www.geografia online. (2013)
22. R. Scheyvens. *Tourism for Development: Empowering Communities.* Harlow: Prentice Hall. (2002)
23. C. Tosun. *Limits to Community Participation in the Tourism Development Process in Developing Countries.* Tour Manage **21**, 6, 613-633 (2000)
24. D. J. Timothy. Tourism and Community Development Issues. In R. Sharpley & D. J. Telfer (Eds.), *Tourism and Development: Concepts and Issues.* England: Channel View Publications. (2002)
25. K. Andereck, K. Valentine, R. Knopf, C. Vogt. *Residents' perceptions of community tourism impacts.* Annals of Tou Res **32**, 4, 1056-1076 (2005)
26. C. Jurowski, M. Uysal, R. Williams. *A theoritical analysis of host community resident reactions to tourism.* Jour of Tra Res **36**, 2, 3-11 (1997)
27. R. Perdue, P. Long, L. Allen. *Resident support for tourism development.* Annals of Tourism Research, **17**, 4 586-599 (1990)
28. S. Akis, N. Peristianis, J. Warner. *Residents' attitudes to tourism development: The case of Cyprus.* Tou Manage **17**, 7, 481-494 (1996)
29. G. Wall. *Perspective on tourism in selected Balinese Villages.* Annals of Tou Res **23**, 1, 123-138 (1996)
30. A. Marzuki. *Resident attitudes towards impacts from tourism development in Langkawi Islands, Malaysia.* World Applied Sciences Journal 12 (Special issue of Tourism and Hospitality) 25-34(2011)

31. K. Kayat. *Power, Social Exchanges and Tourism in Langkawi: Rethinking resident perceptions.* Int. Jour. of Tou Res, **4**, 171-191 (2002).

32. F. Aref, M. Redzuan. *Community capasity building for tourism development.* Jour of Hum Eco, **27**, 21-25 (2009).

33. F. Aref, M. Redzuan, S. S Gill. *Community Perceptions towards Economic and Environmental Impacts of Tourism on Local Communities.* Asi Soc Sci, **5,** 7, 130-137 (2009)

34. R. Kumar, S. S. Gill, P. Kunasekaran. *Tourism as a poverty eradication tool for rural areas in Selangor, Malaysia.* Glo Jour of Hum Soc Sci **12,** 7, 21-26 (2012)

35. M. A. Oviedo-Garcia, M. Castellanos-Verdugo, D. Martin-Ruiz. *Gaining residents' support for tourism and planning.* Int. Jour. of Tou Res **10,** 95-109 (2008)

36. E. Inskeep. *Tourism Planning: An Integrated and Sustainable Development Approach.* New York: Van Nostrand Reinhold. (1991)

37. W. Goudy. *Evaluations of Local Attributes and Community Satisfaction in Small Towns.* Rur Soci **42,** 3, 371-382 (1977)

38. P. E. Murphy. *Tourism: A Community Approach.* London: Routledge. (1985)

39. T. B. Jamal, D. Getz. *Collaboration Theory and Community Tourism Planning.* Annals of Tou Res **22,** 1, 186-204 (1995)

40. B. Bramwell. *Participative planning and governance for sustainable tourism.* Tou Rec Res **35,** 3, 239-249 (2010).

41. R. Sharpley. *Travel and Tourism.* London: SAGE Publications Ltd. (2006)

42. R. K. Yin. *Case Study Research: Design and Methods.* (3rded). Thousand Oaks: Sage Publications. (2003)

43. K. D. Bailey. *Methods of social research.* New York: Free Pr. (1984)

44. Y. P. Chua. *Kaedah Penyelidikan.* Kuala Lumpur: McGraw Hill Education (Malaysia). (2006)

45. D. Gursoy, C. Jurowski, &, M. Uysal. *Residents attitudes: A structural modelling approach.* Annals of Tou Res **29,** 79-105 (2002)

46. D. Ko, W. Stewart. *A structural equation model of resident's attitudes for tourism development.* Tou Manage **25,** 521-530 (2002)

47. D. Gursoy, D. G. Rutherford. *Host attitudes toward tourism: An improved structural model.* Annals of Tou Res **31,** 3, 495-516 (2004)

Sustaining Tourist Satisfaction on Mount Kinabalu, Sabah

Hamimah Talib[1] , Jennifer Chan Kim Lian[2], Timothy Ajeng Mereng[3]

[1,3]Faculty of Science and Natural Resources, Universiti Malaysia Sabah, 88999 Kota Kinabalu, Sabah, Malaysia
[2]Faculty of Business, Economics and Accountancy, Universiti Malaysia Sabah, 88999 Kota Kinabalu, Sabah, Malaysia

Abstract. An increase in demand specifically for Mt. Kinabalu climbing activity has seen a significant influx of tourist to the Kinabalu Park. The main purpose of this study is to determine the tourist satisfaction level and to identify issues that might affect tourist satisfaction while participating in mountain climbing activity on Mt. Kinabalu, Sabah. Data collection was conducted using a structured questionnaire around the Kinabalu Park headquarter complex. There were 24 items listed out in the questionnaire on which tourists satisfaction level measurement were based on – resource (mountain trails, facilities, scenery), activity (climbing experience), guide and staff service performance as well as satisfaction towards crowding. This study found that respondents rated their satisfaction "towards their achievement" the highest. Items with the lowest ratings were satisfaction "towards the facilities at Laban Rata" and "facilities along the trail". This finding suggests that, although the tourists are generally satisfied with their experience in Mt. Kinabalu, there is room for improvement in the aspects of facilities. This study has also identified "water insufficiency" and "traffic congestion" as alarming issues which could also serve as indicators for satisfaction. This study serves as the pilot study to come out with the baseline indicators for tourist satisfaction issues.

1 Introduction

Past studies have shown that tourists' satisfaction is one of the most important determinants in the quality management of an industry [1]. As for the Kinabalu Park in Sabah, Malaysia, there has been an increasing demand for Mt. Kinabalu climbing activity and although high visitation has marked substantial revenue generated through tourism activities at the park, it has also caused rapid influx of tourist to this world heritage site. Mt. Kinabalu is located in the Kinabalu Park which was designated a world heritage site by UNESCO in 2000 for its outstanding universal values and its role as one of the most important biological sites in the world. The most commonly done activity at the Kinabalu Park is mountain climbing related activities other than sightseeing. The current number of daily climbers is approximately 190 climbers with the only limiting factor being the available accommodation on the mountain. There has been limited information about key indicators used to monitor the park impacts such as the level of visitor satisfaction in relation to park attractions and facilities, the amount of budget allocation for nature park conservation activities and staff training. According to UNWTO [2], indicators are measures of the existence or severity of current issues, signals of upcoming situations or problems, measure of risk and potential need for action and means to identify and measure the results of a specific action for a destination. Hence, a major challenge for Kinabalu Park is to ensure the world heritage site is managed sustainably while at the same time making sure that tourists are still satisfied with their experience.

To deliver a quality tourism experience without compromising the integrity of the resources, a better understanding of visitors and a proper visitor management framework to structure and guide decision-making is necessary. Level of satisfaction, perception/motivation value for money and tourist complaints are the baseline environmental responsible indicators [3]. This study serves as a pilot study to come out with the baseline indicators for tourist satisfaction issues, as part of a bigger effort to come up with the environmental responsibility and management framework for Mt. Kinabalu. The main purpose is to determine the tourist satisfaction level as well as to identify issues that might affect tourist satisfaction while they participate in mountain climbing activity on Mt. Kinabalu. Thus, data concerning tourist satisfaction indicators would be specific for mountain climbing activity only.

1.1 Mountain tourism

There is no coherent definition of mountain tourism [4]. Thus, mountain tourism is best generalized as visits to places of interest or operation of holidays in the mountains. The mountains are second only to coasts and islands as popular tourism destinations, making up 15 to 20 percent of annual global tourism, or US$70 to 90 billion per year [5]. Tourists are attracted to mountain destinations for many reasons, which include the cool climate, clean air, unique landscapes and wildlife, scenic beauty, local culture, history and heritage, and the opportunity to experience snow and participate in snow-based or nature-related activities and sports. While modern forms of transportation have made even remote mountain areas accessible to an increasing number of visitors, mountain tourism tends to be very unevenly distributed, with only a small number of locations having significant tourism infrastructure. For example, in the European Alps, where tourism now exceeds 100 million visitor-days per year, 40 percent of communities have no form of tourism whatsoever, whereas 10 percent have extensive and specialized tourism infrastructure [6].

According to the United Nations Environment Programme (UNEP) handbook [7], the most common activities done in the mountains are nature walk (canopy walk, nature interpretation programme), land-based adventure activities (cycling, mountain biking, quad-biking, horseback riding, canyoneering, rock climbing, ice climbing, hand gliding and caving), freshwater-based recreational activities (river tours, canoeing, sailing, windsurfing, kite surfing, kayaking, rafting and freshwater fishing) and snow-dependent recreation activities (cross country, downhill and glacier skiing, heli-skiing, snow scootering, snowboarding, snowshoe walking and sledding). Generally, mountain tourism offers subsidies for community development projects, especially those concerning communications, roads, water pipes and treatment, waste disposal, schools, professional training, leisure, public health, culture, and sports [5]. All mountains have one major common characteristic: rapid changes in altitude, climate, vegetation and soil over very short distances that lead to dramatic differences in habitat and high levels of biodiversity. Mountain weather can be unpredictable, and rainfall varies significantly. Mountains usually comprise a montane, subalpine and alpine zone. In terms of Malaysian tourism, although the term "mountain tourism" is not yet a mainstream, but the fact that Mt. Kinabalu has been one of the icon to Malaysia's tourism especially in the state of Sabah, has made it too important to be ignored.

1.2 Sustaining tourist satisfaction

Customer satisfaction is a psychological concept that involves the feeling of well-being and pleasure that results from obtaining what one hopes for and expects from an appealing product or service [8]. Customer satisfaction is the leading criterion to determine the quality delivered to customers through the product and by the accompanying servicing [9]. Over the years, countless studies have explored a destination's performance through tourist satisfaction analysis where results suggest that overall tourist satisfaction and a tourist's decision whether to return is partially determined by one's assessment of the destination's different characteristics [10]. This shows that in order for a destination to be sustainable, it is vital to understand visitors' perception and satisfaction factor for the destination.

Tourist satisfaction is one of the important determinants in the quality management of organizations [1]. Hence, this study attempts to establish an empirical data for tourist satisfaction that will lead to the identification of the current situation at the world heritage site in order to achieve sustainability in terms of tourist demand as well as resource availability. Yoon and Uysal [11] stressed the importance of tourist satisfaction that "tourist satisfaction has an important role in planning marketable tourism products and services for destinations and its assessment must be a basic parameter used to evaluate the performance of destination products and services".

WTO [12] outlined two main components of issue to guide identification of indicators for tourist satisfaction that should be tailored to the needs of a particular destination. The two components are "determining whether tourists were satisfied upon leaving", and "measuring the impact of satisfaction levels on the industry and destination". As for the purpose of this study, only the first component, which is "determining whether tourists were satisfied upon leaving" was used as a guide. Outlined under this component are 3 indicator categories namely the level of satisfaction by visitor on exit; perception of value for money; and complaints received, as shown below.

Component of the issue	Indicators
Determining whether tourists were satisfied upon leaving	- Level of satisfaction (including specific question/s to key activities and attractions) - Perception of value for money - Complaints received

2 Study method

The population of interest for this study is the tourists or climbers of Mt. Kinabalu. Data collection was conducted between 23 December 2013 and 14 January 2014. Interviews using a structured questionnaire were conducted mainly around the Kinabalu Park headquarter complex, intercepting climbers who have just descended from the summit. Fifty nine respondents participated in this pilot study. The total amount of respondents was considered sufficient particularly for a pilot survey. Roscoe [13] and Sekaran [14] contended that a sample size of between 30 to 500 samples would be sufficient for most studies, depending on the types of analysis to be performed on the data [15].

The questionnaire comprises two main sections. The first section is for the purpose of collecting background information of respondent. The second section is regarding satisfaction level based on experience in the park, using a 5-point Lickert scale, ranging from 1 indicating "bad" to 5 indicating "excellent". The baseline indicators for tourist satisfaction issues were elicited based on the construct adapted from WTO [12]. Attributes of a product can influence consumer satisfaction [16]. As such, for construct validity, discussions with the park management were done to ensure all important park components were included. There were 24 items listed out in the questionnaire on which the tourist satisfaction level measurement were based on under four main elements, namely the resource (mountain trails, facilities, scenery), activity (climbing experience), guide and staff service performance as well as satisfaction towards crowding. Additional questions were also included to find out whether respondents experienced traffic congestion and water insufficiency as well as open ended questions to gauge visitor complaints other than open ended questions. Finally questions regarding visitor's willingness to pay were asked to elicit respondents' perception of value [17].

3 Result

Table 1 is a summary of respondents' background. A majority of the respondents are in the age group of 31-40 years old (41%), followed by age group of 21-30 (37%). Slightly more than half (58%)

were male. In terms of nationality, majority of the respondents were non-Malaysian (66%). In terms of education level, majority of the respondents hold Diploma or Bachelor degree (60%), followed by those who have postgraduate degree (36%). About 75% of the respondents stated that they are in a packaged tour. Asked whether the payment they made for the activity was expensive, reasonable, or cheap, majority (61%) stated that it was reasonable. The majority of the respondents were also on their first time visit (83%).

Table 1. Demographic Characteristics of Respondents

Variables	Frequency	%	Variables	Frequency	%
Age			**Education Level**		
Below 20	2	3	Master / PhD	21	36
21 -30	22	37	Diploma / Bachelor	35	60
31 - 40	24	41	Secondary Education	2	4
41 – 50	8	14	Primary Education	0	-
Above 50	3	5			
			Tour Package		
Gender			Yes	37	75
Male	34	58	No	12	25
Female	25	42			
			Perception on Tour Package		
Nationality					
Malaysian	20	34	Expensive	15	37
Non-Malaysian	39	66	Reasonable	25	61
			Cheap	1	2
			First Visit		
			Yes	47	44
			No	10	56

Before the data were analysed for satisfaction rating, items' reliability measurement was extracted using Cronbach's Alpha reliability coefficient. The reliability measurement shows that the reliability coefficient for all items ($r = 0.949$) was well above the minimum acceptable standard for reliability ($r = 0.60$) [18].

Table 2 shows the respondents' satisfaction level rated based on a 5-point Lickert scale and issues identified from the study. Overall, the satisfaction level rating for all items ranges from 3.64 to 4.65, which indicates that tourists are generally satisfied with their experience involving specified items (approaching scale 4.0 and well above 4.0). The highest rating for satisfying experience is the satisfaction "towards their achievement" with a mean score of 4.65. The next highest items were satisfaction "towards the scenery at the summit" (4.39) and "towards scenery at Laban Rata" (4.30). Items with the lowest ratings were satisfaction "towards the facilities at Laban Rata" and "facilities along the trail" with mean scores 3.64. With regard to traffic congestion and water insufficiency, slightly more than half of the respondents indicated that they did not experience such problems, where about 55% stated no traffic congestion and about 56% stated they did not experience water insufficiency.

Question concerning visitors' willingness to pay were inquired on the amount they are willing to pay for entrance fee as the indicator to respondents' perception of value for the resource. It is found that the majority (43%) of the respondents stated that they are willing to pay RM10 to enter the park, followed by about 39 percent willing to pay a premium of RM30. The five-point Lickert scale was also used to find out the motivation for willingness to pay, with 1 indicating the main motivation and 5 the least motivation. It is found that the main motivation for the willingness to pay is "to conserve and preserve this national park for future generations", while the least motivating factor is "I get satisfaction from paying to help Kinabalu Park".

Table 2. Satisfaction Ratings and Issue

Variables	Mean score	Variables	N	%
Level of Satisfaction				
		Traffic Congestion	25	45
Towards your achievement		Yes	30	55
Low's peak scenery	4.6545	No		
Laban Rata scenery	4.3889			
Towards your whole experience	4.3036	**Experience Water Insufficiency**		
Trail to summit scenery	4.2679			
Towards park staff service	4.2545	Yes		
Towards mountain guide service	4.1964		23	44
Headquarter scenery	4.1607	No	29	56
Trail to Laban Rata scenery	4.1455			
Timpohon Gate scenery	4.1296	**Willingness to Pay**		
Towards park operation and management	4.1250	RM3		
Towards the trail condition	4.0179	RM10	11	21
Crowding at Timpohon Gate		RM30	23	43
Crowding at the trail to Laban Rata	4.0175		19	39
Crowding at headquarter	3.9074			
Towards sufficiency of water supply	3.8214	**Motivation of Willingness to Pay**	**Mean score**	
Towards the facilities at the park headquarter area	3.8214			
Crowding at Laban Rata	3.8036	To conserve and preserve this national park for future generations	1.4390	

Crowding at Low's Peak	3.7818	To use the recreational facilities and to enjoy the scenery	
Towards waste management			
Towards the travel agency services	3.7778	I feel responsible for the local community	1.9535
Crowding at the trail to summit	3.7778	I want better facilities	
Towards the facilities along the trail	3.7091	I get satisfaction from paying to help Kinabalu Park	
Towards the facilities at Laban Rata	3.6923		2.2571
	3.6909		
	3.6379		
	3.6364		2.3684
			2.9187

4 Discussions and Conclusion

The state of Sabah, Malaysia has been widely promoted as a prime tourist destination for those seeking to experience unique nature, culture and adventure due to its unique natural and cultural resources as well as pristine landscape and environment. In view of the importance of environmentally-responsible tourism, especially in the context of Sabah, it is important to identify the key indicators and a holistic environmental responsible framework that can be applied to mountain tourism destinations in Sabah, in particular the world heritage site Kinabalu National Park. Tourist satisfaction has been supported by many researchers as one of the important indicators in the quality management of organizations [1], to determine the quality delivered to customers [9], and that its assessment must be a basic parameter used to evaluate the performance of destination products and services [11].

The findings of this study show that although tourists are generally satisfied with their experience on Mt. Kinabalu, there is room for improvement in the aspect of facilities especially at the Laban Rata rest house and along the mountain trail. The Laban Rata rest house is located 3,272 metres above sea level and is where the climbers would normally stay overnight before proceeding to the summit. Although crowding is one of the issues thought to have effect on tourist satisfaction, it is evident through this study that the more critical issues to look into are the facilities on the mountain and along the trail. Apart from satisfaction levels, this study also identified "water insufficiency" and "traffic congestion" as worrying issues which could also serve as indicators for satisfaction. Although the results indicated that slightly more than half of the respondents did not encounter problems with the two issues, they were experienced by almost half of the total respondents and therefore should not be left out.

This study serves as the pilot study to come out with the baseline indicators for tourist satisfaction issues in Mt. Kinabalu involving only mountain climbing activity. Thus, the findings are restricted to indicators for tourist satisfaction specifically on the mountain and along trail. Further study to include all aspects in this world heritage site is needed to be used for future reference to facilitate a proper tourist management framework.

References

1. M.C. Lo, P. Songan, A.A. Mohamad, A.W. Yeo, Rural destinations and tourists' satisfaction, J. Serv. Res. **11**(2) (2011).
2. S.K. Nepal, Mountain tourism and climate change: Implications for the Nepal Himalaya, Nepal Tourism & Dev. Rev. **1**(1) (2011).
3. Seminar on Tourism Sustainability and Local Agenda 21 in Tourism Destinations and Workshop on Sustainability Indicators for Tourism Destinations. Jeddah, Saudi Arabia. (2006)
4. P.F. Keller, Conf. On Chang. Paradigms of SMT. (2012)
5. O.J. Lynch, G.F. Maggio, Mountain Forum. CIEL. Washington, DC, USA. (2000)
6. "People and Mountains," People and the Planet website, http://www.peopleandplanet.net/doc.php?id=966&section=11
7. United Nations Environment Programme (UNEP). *Tourism And Mountains : a Practical Guide To Managing The Environmental And Social Impacts Of Mountain Tours*. (2007)
8. World Tourism Organization (WTO). *Identification and Evaluation of those Components of Tourism Satisfaction and which can be Regulated and State Measures to Ensure Adequate Quality of Tourism Services*. (1985).
9. T.G. Vavra, Improving your measurement of customer satisfaction: a guide to creating, conducting, analysing, and reporting customer satisfaction measurement programs, ASQ Quality Press. (1997).
10. J. Alegre, J. Garau, Tourist satisfaction and dissatisfaction, Annals of Tourism Res.**37**(1) (2010) 52-73
11. Y. Yoon, M. Uysal, An examination of the effects of the motivation and satisfaction on destination loyalty: A structured model, Tourism Manage, **26**(1) (2005) 45-46
12. World Tourism Organisation (WTO). *Indicator of Sustainable Development for Tourism Destinations. A Guidebook*. (2004)
13. J.T. Roscoe, *Fundamental Research Statistics for the Behavioural Sciences (2nd edition)*(2011) 281-285.
14. U. Sekaran. *Research Methods for Business : a Skill-Building Approach. Research Methods for Business Students(4th edition)*(2000) .
15. M. Saunders, P. Lewis, A. Thornhill, *Research Methods for Business Students (4th edition)* (2007)
16. K. Matzler, E. Sauerwein, The factor structure of customer satisfaction: an empirical test of the importance grid and the penalty-reward-contrast analysis, Int. J. of Serv. Ind. Mgmt. **13(4)**(2002) 314-332
17. S. Zaiton, Willingness to pay in Taman Negara: a contingent valuation method, Int. J. of Econ. and Manage.**2**(1) (2008) 81-94
18. S. Coakes, L. Steed, *SPSS version 14.0 for Windows: Analysis Without Anguish*. (2007)

3

International Tourists Interest in Street Vendors Souvenirs: A Descriptive Study

David Yoon Kin Tong[1]

[1]Faculty of Business, Multimedia University, 75450 Melaka, Malaysia

Abstract. The aim of this study is to analyse international tourists' interests on street vendors souvenirs sold in Melaka UNESCO sites. Their interests are then matched with the actual souvenirs sold by the vendors. Selling the wrong types of souvenirs creates a misfit between buyers and sellers and will neither benefit the tourists nor the vendors. The study was implemented in two phases. In the first phase, using judgmental sampling the survey questionnaires was distributed to international tourists walking around Christ Church and A Formosa. Of the 181 data collected, only 127 tourists expressed that they were interested in street vendors' souvenirs. This cohort of tourists and their interests were analysed using SPSS. In the second phase, using structural observations, the researcher used smart phone digital camera to capture pictures of street vendor's stores items. The photographs were uploaded in computer and the details of the items sold were zoomed in for analysis. The latter was then compared with international tourists' interests. The findings indicated that only two categories of souvenirs fulfilled the tourists' interests. This implies that the vendors have room for enhancement to include different categories of souvenirs to capture the tourists' attention.

1 Introduction

In 2011, Malaysia was ranked 9th as the most popular tourist destinations in the world and 3rd in Asia after China and Turkey. This achievement was made possible when UNESCO announced Melaka as a World Heritage City in July 7, 2008. With the proclamation by the government that 2014 is the 'Visit Malaysia' year, more tourists are expected to visit the country. In conjunction with this declaration and the Melaka state government's vision of 'Visiting Malacca means visiting Malaysia' past tourism records from 1999 to 2012 indicated that Melaka had 85.2 million tourists, comprising 75.7% domestic tourists and 24.3% international tourists. In 2012, the tourism statistics showed an increase of 12.9%, totalling 3.7 million in one year [1]. Tapping on the previous records, there was 3:1 ratio of domestic and international tourists in Melaka and reflecting on the income brought to tourism industry, it provides substantial income that spread across the product and service sectors.

Focusing on sale of souvenirs in the tourism industry, we revealed most souvenirs are sold in permanent outlets. For examples, the specialty store, departmental shop, merchandise retailers, duty-free shops, gift shops, and other retailers [2]. Contrasting these outlets are street vendor stores. Street vendors are mobile and can position their stores at the vicinity or close to the tourist sites. Previous studies on souvenir items sold by fixed retail stores are well-investigated [2-3]. Currently, there is a dearth of study on vendor souvenirs sale [4-5] and we are uncertain on the demand of souvenirs by international tourists. The demand of the souvenirs is the combined result of attractions, prices, and quality to tourists. The key issue here is whether the local street vendors can satisfy the specific requirements of the tourists [6]. Based on this inquiry we raised two research questions for this exploratory study: 1) What types of souvenirs international tourists are looking for from the street vendor stores? 2) According to international tourists' interests, are street vendors selling the right souvenir items to them?

To answer the research questions, this study was organised in two phases. In the first phase, primary data was collected from international tourists. In the second phase, structural observation on the street vendors' stores was carried out. Photographs were taken on the displayed items in the stores. The photographs details were analysed and inferred. The outcome of this study will provide an insightful of souvenirs product purchase-selling fit. Understanding this fit will improve the revenue of these low income group traders. Finally, the study is briefly concluded.

2 International tourists in Melaka

2.1 International tourists' demographic profile

To identify international tourists' interests on street vendor souvenirs, a judgmental sampling was deployed. Judgmental sampling permits the researcher to differentiate domestic tourists from international tourists [7]. The survey questions were distributed by research assistants (RA) to international tourists that wondered around Christ Church and A Formosa.

A total of 181 valid data were collected within one month on January 2014. Of them, 127 (70.17%) tourists expressed their interest in purchasing street vendors' souvenirs while other tourists 54 (29.83%) were keen to shop in specialty or departmental stores. The latter group was excluded in the analysis. The types of souvenirs they expected from the street vendors were categorised into five product classes with references to Wilkins' study [8]. The findings indicated that 63 (49.6%) of the tourists were interested in the category of photographs, paintings, postcard category; 32 (25.2%) expressed they were keen on caps, hats, clothing category; 35 (27.6%) indicated they were keen on Melaka small accessories; 49 (38.6%) said that they would purchase the carving, jewellery, glassware, antiques category. Lastly, few were interested in the local specialty dry food products (see Table 1).

Table 1. Demographic profile of international tourists

Descriptive statistics results					
Gender			*Marital status*		
	Frequency	*%*		*Frequency*	*%*
Male	93	51.4	Married	78	43.1
Female	88	48.6	Single	93	51.4
			Separated	4	2.2
Is this your first visit to Melaka?			Widowed	1	0.6
Yes	163	90.1	Divorced	5	2.8
No	18	9.9			
Purpose of visit			*Tourists' Nationality by Countries by Continents*		
Pleasure	145	80.1	Europe	134	74.0
Relaxation	14	7.7	Asia/Middle East	10/3	5.5/1.7
Visiting	7	3.9	Oceania	22	12.2
Business	4	2.2	North America	11	6.0
Others	11	6.1	South America	1	0.6
Age group					
20 – 30	89	49.2			

31 – 40	51	28.2			
41 – 50	15	8.3			
Above 50	26	14.4			
Employment			***Preferred shop for souvenir***		
Employed	113	62.4	Street vendor	127	70.2
Unemployed	40	22.1	Specialty	40	22.1
Self-employed	14	7.7	Departmental shop	6	3.3
Retired	14	7.7	Others	8	4.4

2.2 International tourists' interest in street vendors' souvenirs – Primary data

When asked about the main purpose of souvenirs purchase from the international tourists, 99 (78%) of them stated that they purchased it for gift giving, and 88 (69.3%) mentioned they would buy it for their own. Probing on their interests on the souvenirs, they preferred locally made souvenirs (Mean = 4.32; SD = 0.95) and it should of reasonable quality (Mean = 4.09; SD = 0.93). Next, what would arouse them was 'value for money' (Mean = 3.82; SD = 0.89). Lastly, souvenirs should be attractive (Mean = 3.61; SD = 0.81) (see Table 2).

Table 2. International Tourists Interest in Street Vendors' Souvenirs

Types of souvenirs to purchase	No (%)	Yes (%)	Purpose of purchase of souvenirs purchase	No (%)	Yes (%)
Photos, paintings, postcard	64(50.4)	63(49.6)	Gift giving	28 (22)	99 (78)
Caps, hats, clothing	95(74.8)	32(25.2)	Own use	39(30.7)	88(69.3)
Melaka small accessories	92(72.4)	35(27.6)	Assisting others	126 (99.2)	1 (0.8)
Carving, jewellery, glassware, antiques	78(61.4)	49(38.6)	Conscious	117 (92.1)	10 (7.9)
Local specialty dry food products	92(72.4)	35(27.6)	Resale	127 (100)	0
Others	119(93.7)	8(6.3)	Other purpose	123 (96.9)	4 (3.1)

Tourists interest	Mean	SD
Locally made souvenirs interest me.	4.32	0.95
Street vendors' souvenirs with reasonable quality interest me	4.09	0.93
Street vendors' souvenirs that are reasonably priced interest me.	3.37	0.92
Street vendor's souvenirs that are of value for money interest me.	3.82	0.89
Street vendors selling souvenirs at a high pedestrian area interest me.	3.44	0.97
Street vendors selling souvenirs in or near tourists' area interest me.	3.31	0.93
Street vendors' stores assortment souvenirs interest me.	3.39	0.86
Street vendors' stores attractive souvenirs interest me.	3.61	0.84

3 Observation on street vendor operations

In the second phase, structural observation was used for the study. This observation is a unique information gathering technique by observing participant, event or situation. Structured observation means the observer has planned and streamlined what to observe. Observation can be either participant observer or non-participant observer. Participant observer involves some intervention or process in the event, whereas non-participant observer simply observes without being bias [9]. In this study, the non-participant observation was adopted. The observation started by walking around on early February 2014 at the vicinity of the UNESCO tourist sites of Christ Church, St. Paul's Church and A Formosa. Using Nokia Lumia 1020 with 41 Megapixels camera photographs were taken on the displayed items of vendor stores. The digital pictures allow the researcher to zoom in for analysis of the items sold. The details were studied and inferred.

3.1 Souvenir product origin

Close scrutiny of the pictures taken on a street vendor stores items, we identified some items were locally made and some were imported goods. Figure 1(a)shows the souvenir products were made in Malaysia. The souvenirs consisted of curios such as key chains, Malay kris, the Twin Towers bells, magnets, and others. In Figure 1(b), the imported items were the rubber snakes, harmonica, plastic binoculars, catapult, whistle, etc. The origins of the products were concurred by observing the items' tags. Imported items were mainly made in China.

(a) Locally-made souvenirs   (b) Imported souvenirs
Figure 1. Souvenir Product Origin

3.3 Souvenir Price, Quality, Value, Assortment and Attractiveness

Based on the souvenirs' price tags, most of the souvenirs sold by the vendors were of reasonable prices. For example, in Figure 2(a), the T-shirts were sold at RM 20.00 [10]. For some vendors, the items could be bargained for lower prices. However, on the perceptions of whether the souvenirs are value for money, we found some souvenirs prices did not match its quality. They were flimsy and made of inferior materials. In Figure 2(b), it shows the name tags were made of inferior plastic quality affecting its value for money. On matching the tourists' expectations of souvenirs assortment and attractiveness, Figure 2(c) shows there were sufficient assortments but they were of different product line. For example, a vendor store has mixture of bracelets, key chains, wooden cars, and bikes. As regards souvenirs attractiveness, the miniature ships, cars, and bikes have little appeal to tourists.

(a) Value of souvenirs

(b) Quality of souvenirs

(c) Assortment and attractiveness of souvenirs

(d) Melaka small accessories

Figure 2. Souvenir Price, Quality, and Value

3.4 Street Vendor Location

In Figure 3, the pictures show three main locations of the street vendors at St. Paul's Church. At the entrance from A Formosa, there were three stores. At mid stairs climb to St. Paul's Church, there were four stores. Surrounding St. Paul's Church, there were three stores and around the Church, there were at least six souvenir stores. These stores set up met the expectation of the tourists that it should be at high pedestrian area or near tourists' sites (see Figure 3).

(a) Vendor stores location next to A Formosa

(b) Vendor stores at mid stairs to St Paul's Church

(c) Vendor stores surrounding St. Paul's
Church

(d) Vendor stores around St. Paul's Church

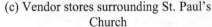

Figure 3. Street Vendor Location

3.5 Types of Souvenirs

Lastly, we examined the types of souvenir categories that match the international tourists' interest. In the category of photograph, painting, and postcard, we found no vendor was selling those items, except three local artists were promoting their paintings on the floor. Nevertheless, for the category of caps, hats, and clothing, these items were available. As for Melaka small accessories category, Exhibit 2 P4 shows a local vendor was selling some Melaka wooden key chains, porcelain plates, cutty sark, and others. For the carving, jewellery, glassware, antiques and the local specialty dry food products categories, there was no vendor selling these items. Overall, we found similar items were sold by few vendors.

4 Discussion and Conclusion

In most developing countries, street vendors selling souvenirs are aplenty especially in famous tourists' sites. Whatsoever, these front line merchants play significant role in tourism industry by promoting sale of souvenirs to tourists.

The international tourists are eyeing for quality and authentic locally made souvenir products. While some souvenirs are locally made, its quality remains elusive. The vendors should consider selling items of reasonable quality to attract the tourists. Quality products attract and satisfy buyers and results in profitability [11]. In price expectation, souvenirs sold in high concentration of vendors remain competitive. Tourists delighted in bargaining will enjoy imploring for discounted price from the vendors. The lack of carving, jewellery, glassware, antiques and the local specialty dry food products categories imply that vendors should consider including these product class or category. The photograph, painting, and postcard, the pictures product class was unrepresented suggesting those local artists could display their artworks like the street vendors. These artworks should be displayed at certain height to attract the attention of buyers [12]. Vendors should also consider selling souvenirs of same product lines with real assortments; cooperate to lower the levels of duplication as it affects the value to sale [13]. Finally, the location of the stores set up met the tourists' expectations.

Street vending creates employment and income to this group of traders. Analysing their goods sold and tourists' demand contributes to the knowledge and understanding of souvenir products purchase-selling fit or misfit. However, observations on the vendors' items implied some misfit and stiff competition among another with similar items displayed for sales. Since there is a demand for locally-made souvenirs, the local craftsman can contribute to provide unique products for sale. Additionally, there are room for enhancement for vendors to sell other categories of products that are in demand by international tourists. If these items are sellable it could contribute substantially to vendors' income and local tourism sector's revenue.

References

1. Asmaliana.com tourism blog, *Melaka at a glance*, (n.d.), http://asmaliana.com/blog/2013/03/27/melaka-in-a-glance/ (accessed: June 23 2014).
2. K.S. Kristen, P.E. Horridge, 2004, *A Structural Model for Souvenir Consumption, Travel Activities, and Tourist Demographics*, J. Travel Research, **42**, 4, 372-80 (2004)
3. D. Thang, B. Tan, *Linking consumer perception to preference of retail stores: an empirical assessment of the multi-attributes of store image*, Journal of Retailing and Consumer Services, **10**, 193-200 (2003)
4. D.J. Timothy, G. Wall, *Selling to tourists: Indonesian street vendors*, Annals of Tourism Research, **24**, 2, 322-340 (1997)
5. K.S. Kristen, D.J. *Timothy, Souvenirs: Icons of meaning, commercialization and commoditization*, Tourism Manage., **33**, 489-499 (2012)
6. D.M. Valles, Tourism and Employment: Improving the quality of tourist product (2011), http://ec.europa.eu/enterprise/sectors/tourism/files/working_groups/finalreportc_june2001_en.pdf (accessed: August 28 2014).
7. W.L. Neuman, *Social Research Methods: Qualitative and Quantitative Approaches*, (6th Ed., Pearson International Edition, USA, 2006)
8. H. Wilkins, *Souvenirs: What and why we buy*, Journal of Travel Research, **50**, 3, 239-247 (2011)
9. B.N. Flagg, *Formative evaluation for educational technologies*, (Hillsdale, NJ: Erlbaum, 1990)
10. Spohia, *Haggling tips*, StreetDirectory Malaysia (2014), http://www.streetdirectory.com/travel_guide/malaysia/Travellers_Guide_&_Tips/247/haggling_tips.php (accessed: August 28 2014).
11. P. Kotler, K.L. Keller, *Marketing Management*, (13th Ed., Pearson International Edition, Pearson Prentice Hall, 2009)
12. X. Drĕze, S.J. Hoch, M.E. Purk, *Shelf Management and Space Elasticity*, J. of Retailing, **70**, 4, 301-326 (1994)
13. R.R. Burke, 2005, *Retail shoppability: A measure of the world's best stores* (2005), https://kelley.iu.edu/CERR/files/shoppability.pdf (accessed: June 23 2014).

4

Analysis of Tourism Resource Dependency on Collaboration among Local Governments in the Multi-Regional Tourism Development

Dong-Won Ha[1], Seung-Dam Choi[2], Yeon-Kyung Kwon[3], Hyun-Jung Kim[4]

[1,2,3,4]Department of Tourism, Hanyang University, Seoul, South Korea

Abstract. The purpose of this study was to derive the multidimensional attributes of resource dependency of local governments in multi-regional tourism development. The questionnaire was designed based on resource dependence theory and related literature, and five factors of resource dependency were derived by analysis of the questionnaire for the civil servants who participated in the Jirisan area tourism development project which is a representative multi-regional tourism development project of Korea. The measured values of the derived possession, importance, discretion, alternative, and connection were found in various ways according to the project characteristics such as project scale and visitors in the Jirisan area tourism development project. This shows that a variety of variables have an effect on resource dependency.

1 Introduction

There is an increasing need for cooperation among local governments in tourism development [12, 16-18, 29]. It is necessary to understand the important factors related to this. One of these important factors is the resource dependency of organizations. This is defined as the dependency on other organizations for resources required for survival and operation of the organization. This is an important concept for understanding cooperation between local governments because it determines organizational cooperative behavior [23].

The aim of this study was to derive multidimensional attributes of preferentially required resource dependency for understanding the resource dependency of local governments in multi-regional tourism development cooperation. For this purpose, this study aims to derive the factors of resource dependency based on the analysis of the resource dependence theory and related literature and a questionnaire for the local governments involved in the Jirisan area tourism development project which is a representative multi-regional tourism development project of Korea. In addition, it aims to analyze the measured values of each derived factor and to explore the implications of the results of the empirical analysis.

2 Theoretical Considerations

2.1 Resource Dependence Theory and Resource Dependency

The resource dependence theory proposed by Pfeffer & Salancik [24] descries the relationship between organizational resource dependence and cooperation between organizations [20]. They have become increasingly dependent on external resources by obtaining or using insufficient resources from the outside in order to achieve their goals because organizations never can be self-sufficient in all resources required for survival and operation. As a result, interorganizational collaboration is implemented in the form of exchange of information, strategic alliance, partnership, and merger. This theory has been actively studied in interorganizational collaboration. Skinner, Gassenheimer & Kelley [30] confirmed that there was a positive correlation between dependency and cooperation by using variables such as dependency, power, cooperation, conflict, and satisfaction for dealers of agricultural and electrical equipment.

Park, Jung, & Lee [22] clarified the relation between resource dependency and cooperation by analyzing that manufacturers' dependence on private brand (PB) had an effect on the long-term relationship between them and distributors. Moreover, in studies on cooperation between governmental organizations, Aldrich [2], Scharpf [27] analyzed the resource-dependent characteristics of organizations by classifying them as interdependence, general dependence and mutual independence according to the level of interorganizational dependency with the use of an interorganizational dependency model [6, 14].

On the other hand, the resource dependence theory suggests the importance of resources, discretion over their use and distribution, their alternative possibility, and their possession as a component of resource dependency [20, 27]. In particular, first, the importance of resources is a measure that an organization places emphasis on resources of the other. Second, the discretion over the use and distribution of resources can be described as control over resources and is the authority for the use and distribution of organizational resources. When one organization has the ability to access its own resources, control them, and make regulations, the organization that needs these resources comes to depend on the organization that possesses them.

Third, the alternative possibility of resources can be expressed as a concentration of resource control and is an alternative measure of the ability of organizations to substitute one source of resources for another. This is related to the number of other organizations that provides the organization with resources. When the number is small, the organization becomes highly dependent on resources of the other because it has less resources to substitute. Finally, the possession of resources is the resource possession of the organization. The organization becomes highly dependent on resources of the other because when it possesses less resources.

2.2 Tourism Development and Resource Dependency

The resource dependency in tourism development of local governments has similarities with the resource dependency of companies and also has significant differences. First, it includes resource dependence factors theory applied to the corporate sector such as the importance of resources, discretion over their use and distribution, and alternative possibility. This is because the common organizational characteristics are reflected in local governments and companies. In particular, the prerequisites for organizational resource dependency in the corporate sector suggested by resource dependence theory, which are mutual exchange of interorganizational resources, resource constraint, incomplete transfer and imitation of resources, recognition of resource value by other organizations [24 - 27] correspond to local governments to implement tourism development [5, 16, 29].

Subsequently, the most significance difference between the corporate sector and the tourism developments of local governments is the connection of resources. Unlike manufacturers, local governments need resources such as natural and cultural resources for their tourism development [7, 21, 23]. Therefore, the obtained resources are frequently shared with other local governments. For successful tourism development, local governments have recognized the need for geographical and spatial connections [12-13] and cultural connection [17] and become highly dependent in connection with the other local governments.

Furthermore, the level of possession of resources is an important factor in tourism development of local governments as well as in resource dependence theory. According to the study by Sohn & Kim [29], the level of possession of resources was set as an organizational environment factor and had an effect on the interaction of local governments.

3 Research Methods

3.1 Measurement of the Resource Dependency

In order to measure the resource dependency of tourism development, this study derived a total of 17 measurement items based on resource dependence theory and literature related to tourism development and resource dependency (see Table 1).

3.2 Respondents and Analysis Methods

The questionnaire respondents were 22 civil servants of the seven local governments that participated directly in the Jirisan area tourism development project. This study aimed to derive the factors of resource dependency based on an analysis of the results to an attitude survey. This was the only source of data since it was not possible to collect secondary data to measure resource dependency. Furthermore the respondents had enough knowledge related to the primary factor, which was cooperation.

In consideration of the relationship between the local governments related to the Jirisan area multi-regional tourism development, the questionnaire consisted of a total of 17 items so that the civil servants of local governments could indicate the level of dependency. The number of the questionnaire that the civil servants responded to varied according to the number of detailed projects they participated in. They responded to seven items on average.

180 questionnaires were collected out of the distributed 264. Out of these a total of 166 were used in the analysis.

Table 1. Measurement Items of Resource Dependency

Measurement Items	related literature
Possession level of tourism development resource	Ahn [1],
Possession level of tourism resource	Kim, Chae, Choi & Kim [11],
Possession level of tourism resource facilities	Sohn & Kim [29],
Possession level of tourism financial resource	Pfeffer & Salancik [24],
Possession level of tourism organizational resource	Ring [25],

Proportion of tourism project	Skinner, Gassenheimer & Kelly [30]
Utility of tourism project	
Necessary of tourism project success	
Actual use authority	
Access control authority	
Norms-making authority	
Alternative to local government	
Alternative to other local government	
Difficulty of tourism project	
Similarity	Kim [9],
Complementarities	Kim & Shin [12],

4 Analysis Results

4.1 Derivation of Resource Dependency Factors

In this study, a factor analysis was conducted to derive factors of resource dependency. As a result, a total of five factors were derived. Based on previous studies on resource dependence theory, the derived factors of resources were named as possession, importance, connection, discretion, and alternative. The total variance explanatory power of the five factors was 76.69%, and the KMO value was 0.651. According to Bartlett's test of sphericity, the validity was demonstrated ($x2=1439.545$, p<.000). All Cronbach's alpha values were more than 0.6, and the reliability was examined (refer to Table 2).

Table 2. Factor Analysis Results of Resource Dependency

Factor	Variable	Factor's Loading	Commun-ality	Eigen Values	Variance Explanatory Power	Cronbach's α
Possession	Possession level of tourism resource	.902	.894	3.927	25.122	.894
	Possession level of tourism resource facilities	.877	.806			
	Possession level of tourism development resource	.870	.840			
	Possession level of tourism	.775	.689			

	financial resource					
	Possession level of tourism organizational resource	.743	.716			
Importance	Proportion of tourism project	.865	.809	2.961	16.041	.839
	Necessary of tourism project success	.860	.794			
	Utility of tourism project	.841	.756			
Connection	Ease of use in common	.814	.758	1.140	11.023	.663
	Complementarities	.738	.753			
	Similarity	.724	.640			
Discretion	Norms-making authority	.876	.812	1.949	12.369	.791
	Access control authority	.862	.816			
Alternative	Difficulty of tourism project	.824	.693	1.526	12.130	.626
	Alternative to other local government	.809	.727			

4.2 Analysis of Resource Dependency Level in the Multi-Regional Tourism Development

Based on the results, the level of resource dependency in the Jirisan area tourism development project is shown in Table 3. Although the mean value of resource dependency is at a low level, 2.84 points, possession (3.26 points) and connection (3.13 points) that highly reflect the main characteristics of tourism development are relatively high.

This study examined differences in resource dependency according to tourism development project scale. It was found that there was no significant difference in resource dependency between large- and small-scale products. However, there are significant differences in the detailed factor importance of resources, and large scale projects show greater importance of resources than small scale ones.

This study examined differences in resource dependency according to visitor scale. As a result, there was no significant difference in resource dependency between local governments with large and small visitors. However, there are significant differences in the detailed factor analysis. With regard to the possession and importance of resource dependency, local governments with more visitors show higher dependency. With regard to the alternative of resources, local governments with fewer visitors show higher dependency (see Table 3).

Table 3. Resource Dependency Mean Comparison according to Project and Visitor's Scale

	total (n=166)	Project Scale			Visitor Scale		
		Small (n=118)	Large (n=48)	t-value(p)	Small (n=71)	Large (n=95)	t-value(p)
Possession	3.26	3.26	3.25	.100	2.98	3.46	-4.036**
Possession level of tourism development resource	3.40	3.36	3.50	-.878	3.14	3.60	-3.347**
Possession level of tourism resource	3.39	3.36	3.48	-.745	3.01	3.67	-4.619**
Possession level of tourism resource facilities	3.28	3.35	3.10	1.246	2.85	3.60	-4.446**
Possession level of tourism financial resource	2.96	2.92	3.06	-1.032	2.56	3.26	-6.313**
Possession level of tourism organizational resource	3.24	3.31	3.08	1.523	3.35	3.16	1.454
Importance	2.78	2.71	2.94	-2.304*	2.57	2.93	-3.926**
Proportion of tourism project	2.64	2.51	2.98	-3.975**	2.31	2.89	-5.622**
Utility of tourism project	2.89	2.87	2.94	-.605	2.82	2.95	-1.338
Necessary of tourism project success	2.80	2.75	2.92	-1.363	2.59	2.95	-3.171**
Discretion	2.63	2.58	2.76	-1.852	2.58	2.66	-.856
Access control authority	2.72	2.65	2.90	-2.156*	2.66	2.77	-1.018
Norms-making authority	2.54	2.50	2.63	-1.180	2.51	2.56	-.522
Alternative	3.04	3.02	3.08	-.545	3.44	2.74	7.948**
Alternative to other local government	3.19	3.17	3.25	-.570	3.63	2.86	6.718**
Difficulty of tourism project	2.89	2.87	2.92	-.348	3.25	2.61	6.185**
Connection	3.13	3.11	3.17	-.575	3.13	3.13	.051
Similarity	3.43	3.53	3.19	2.663**	3.55	3.35	1.673
Complementarities	3.13	3.08	3.25	-1.137	2.93	3.28	-2.712**
Ease of use in common	2.82	2.71	3.08	-2.538*	2.92	2.75	1.235

**: $p < 0.01$, *: $p < 0.05$

5 Conclusions & Discussions

The purpose of this study was to derive multidimensional attributes of resource dependency of local governments in multi-regional tourism development. The measurement items of resource dependency consisted mainly of the analysis of resource dependence theory and related literature. The factors of resource dependency were derived by analysis of the questionnaire for the civil servants who participated in the Jirisan area tourism development project which is a representative multi-regional tourism development project of Korea. The five derived factors consisted of possession, importance, discretion, alternative, and connection. Among them, connection is the factor that is most characteristic of resource dependency for tourism projects. This finding differentiates this study from the results of previous studies on resource dependency between companies.

The measured values by factor vary according to project scale and visitors in tourism development projects. Local governments with large scale projects and visitors show higher measured values than those with fewer visitors. On the other hand, in the alternative factor, local governments with fewer visitors show higher measured values than those with more visitors. These results suggest that various variables have an effect on resource dependency.

These results extend the application of resource dependence theory in tourism development. Specifically, this study revealed that connection among resources should be added to factors of resource dependency suggested in corporate sector [24].

This study is significant in that it empirically demonstrates the relevance of resource dependency theory, previously only applied to private companies, to the domain of tourism projects conducted by local governments. In the future, it will be necessary to find methods capable of compensating for the lack of attitude surveys by the analysis of secondary data drawn from a greater variety of sources related to resource dependency. It would also be beneficial to draw responses from a larger pool of respondents.

References

1. J. S. Ahn, *Determinants of Governance Structure in International Joint-Ventures*, Korean Academy of International Business, 367-390 (1996)
2. H. Aldrich, *Resource Dependence and in Terorganiza Tional Relations Local Employment Service Offices and Social Services Sector Organizations.* Administration & Society, **7** (4) ,419-454 (1976)
3. S. S. Andaleeb, *Dependence Relations and the Moderating Role of Trust; Implications for Behavioral Intentions in Marketing Channels.* International Journal of Research in Marketing, **12,** 2, 157-172 (1995)
4. S. S. Andaleeb, *An Experimental Investigation of Satisfaction and Commitment in Marketing Channels; The Role of Trust and Dependence.* Journal of retailing, **72,** 1, 77-93 (1996)
5. J. E. Choi, *Exploratory Research on the Policy Suggestions of Multi-Regious Tourism Development Plan.* Northeast Asia Tourism Research, **7,** 2, 69-90 (2011)
6. J. W. Choi, *Evolutionary Process Analysis of Government-Firms Relationship in Korea*, Journal of Public Administration, 37, 1, 137-174 (1999)
7. C. A. Gunn, *Tourism Planning* (2nd ed.). New York: Taylor and Francis, (1988)
8. S. D. Jap, S. Ganesan, *Control Mechanisms and the Relationship Lifecycle: Implications for Safeguarding Specific Investments and Developing Commitment,* Journal of Marketing Research, 37, 2, 227-245 (2000)
9. K. C. Kim, *The Change of 4S's Economics Concept and Linkage Competitiveness,* Korean Journal of Marketing, **1,** 1,C1-C26 (1998)
10. B. M. Kim, *Tourism Resource*, Seoul: BaekSan Press, (1995).
11. S. E. Kim, W. H. Chae, J. H. Choi, & S. K. Kim, Study of Cooperation among Local
12. Y. Y. Kim, Y. S. Shin, *Exploratory Research on Network-Centric Tourism Development as an Alternative to Multi-Regional Tourism Planning,* Seoul City Research, **11,** 3, 123-138 (2010)

13. W. J. Kim, H. C. Hong, *The Spatial Linkage and Behavior Characteristics of Multi Destination Trip in the Eastern Part of the Gyeonggi Province,* Journal of Tourism Sciences, **30**, 3, 267-291 (2006)

14. J. K. Kim, *A Model of Government-NGO Relationship: From the Resource Dependency Perspective,* Journal of the Korean Association for Policy Studies, **9**, 2, 5-28 (2000)

15. K. D. Kwon, S. H. Lee, *An Empirical Study on Cooperation between Business and Large Firms: Focused on the Dependence, Power and Trust,* The Journal of Entrepreneurship and Venture Studies, **6**, 2, 53-75 (2003)

16. Y. J. Lee, S. D. Choi, *Conceptual Study on the Characteristics of Tourism Industrial Clusters,* Journal of Tourism Studies, **15**, 47-66 (2003)

17. H. J. Lee, *The Connection Method between Local Festival and Cultural Tourism Resource,* The Research Institute of Paekche Culture, **27**, 139-152 (1998)

18. Ministry of Culture, Sports and Tourism, T*he Third Tourism Development Master Plan,* (2011),.

19. Ministry of Culture, Sports and Tourism, *Annual Report according 2012 Tourism Trends,* (2013),.

20. W. Nienhueser, *Resource Dependence Theory–How Well Does It Explain Behavior of Organizations. management revue.* The International Review of Management Studies, **19**,1, 9-32 (2008)

21. S. H. Park, *New Tourism Resources*, Seoul: DaeWang Press, (2012)..

22. H. H. Park, G. O. Jung, S. C. Lee, *A Study of the Factors Influencing on Manufaturer's Private Brand Dependence and Long-term Relationship with Retailer,* Korean Marketing Review, **26**, 4, 77-106 (2011)

23. D. G. Pearce, *Tourist development.* London: Longman Group Limited, (1981)

24. J. Pfeffer, G. R. Salancik, *The External Control of Organizations: A Resource Dependence Perspective*, New York: Harper & Row, (1978)

25. P. S. Ring, *Networked Organization: A Resource-Based Perspective.* Uppsala: University press, (1996)

26. D. L. Roger, D. A. Whetten, Interorganization Relationships: Patterns and Motivations. *Administrative Science Quarterly*, **22**, 2, 220-234 (1982)

27. F. W. Scharpf, Interorganizational Policy Studies: Issues, Concepts and Perspectives In *K. Hanf W. Scharpf(ed.), Interorganizational policy making: limits to coordination and central control.* Beverly Hills, CA: Sage Publications, (1978).

28. R. W. Scott, *Organizations: Rational, Natural, and Open Systems.* Englewood Cliffs, New Jersey: Prentice-Hall, (1981)

29. D. H. Sohn, J. H. Kim, *The Study on the Inter-Organizational Relations of Local Government Tourism Administration,* Korean Journal of Tourism Research, **13**, 119-141 (1999)

30. S. J. Skinner, J. B. Gassenheimer & S. W. Kelly, *Cooperation in Supplier-dealer Relations.* Journal of Retailing, **68**, 2, 174-193 (1992)

5

Tourism Development from the Perspectives of Sustainability in Melaka State

A. S. A. Ferdous Alam[1], Er A. C.[2], Halima Begum[3]

[1]Institute for Environment and Development (LESTARI), Universiti Kebangsaan Malaysia (UKM), 43600 UKM Bangi, Selangor, Malaysia

[2,3]Faculty of Social Sciences and Humanities (FSSK), Universiti Kebangsaan Malaysia (UKM), 43600 UKM Bangi, Selangor, Malaysia

Abstract: Tourism is an important development tool and it is considered the second largest contributor to the Malaysian economy. Even though the visitors are satisfied by the prevailing facilities, a few shortcomings need to be addressed on sustainable tourism such as the lack of knowledge on sustainable tourism in different sectors, and the neglected local communities in making decisions on sustainability. The aim of this study is to realize the relationship between three factors namely economy, environmental impacts of tourism, and community satisfaction and perceptions on tourism development in Melaka, a UNESCO World Heritage site in Malaysia. In order to observe this relationship, 735 tourists were interviewed to get the tourists' responses. Here, the concepts on sustainable tourism development include the conservation of the environment, mitigation of pollution from tourism development, and support of local economies. Additionally, sustainable tourism is aimed at generating local employment for the community. Data from the interviews have been analysed using descriptive and simple statistical tools. It is found that the variables are suitable in this study due to the high Cronbach's Alpha values. The study found that there are positive significant influences between the three dimensions and their perceptions on sustainability and tourism development.

1 Introduction

In modern economy, tourism is the most significant leading source in the world. It has been declared as one of the main noteworthy service industries globally [1]. The definition of tourism includes "travelling to relatively continuous or uncontaminated natural areas with a focus on knowledge, appreciating and enjoying the scenery and its wild flora and fauna, and other prevailing cultural and historical aspects", as it consists of places of historical importance, archaeological and religious sites, sanctuaries, parks, hill resorts, clubs, beaches, etc. It is a multi-sector industry including a collection of industries, activities, and services that deliver travel experiences such as transportation, accommodation, eating and drinking businesses, retail shops, entertainment businesses, activities, facilities, and other hospitality services offered for individuals or groups travelling away from home [2].

The World Trade Organization [3] forecasted that by the year 2010, this sector would expand by an average of 4.1% a year over the next two decades, exceeding 1 billion total worldwide travelers and reaching 1.6 billion by 2020. In addition, socially, environmentally, and economically, sustainable tourism is really a crucial matter in numerous government agendas.

In the tourism industry, achieving competitive advantage refers to the notion where a destination must have an overall "appeal" and where the tourist experience offered is superior to that of alternative destinations competing for the same target tourists [4]. This study, therefore, is an attempt to understand the factors that attract tourists to visit Malaysia and consider it as a tourist destination.

2 Literature Review

The report of [5] mentioned that the innermost hypothesis of sustainable development (SD) is "that which meets the needs of the present without compromising the ability of future age groups to meet their own needs". As a development approach, this sector has achieved significant earnings and has provided substantial contribution to the local and national economy in many countries. It is also identified as one of the largest and fastest growing industries [6, 7, 8]. For some developed or developing countries, the tourism industry forms a critical component of the local, regional and national economy, contributing significantly to employment opportunities, GDP growth, and foreign exchange earnings. Tourism has turned out to be one of the very important sources of earnings for developed countries as well where it has already created a substantial foundation for a tourism based economy, for example in countries like Singapore, Maldives and Malaysia in which the total contribution of the Travel & Tourism sector to the GDP in 2011 was 8.2%, 70.5%, 15%, respectively.

Today, the tourism industry of Malaysia has moved with such rapidity to become the second income generator in the national economy whilst experiencing tremendous growth year by year. The total contribution of travel and tourism to the GDP was 15.8% in 2013 [9]. Even though the tourism industry is a latecomer in Malaysia compared to its neighbouring countries, namely Thailand and Singapore, it has recorded successful performance in terms of tourist arrivals and receipts [10]. For example, in 2010, Malaysia recorded 24.5 million tourist arrivals and RM55.6 billion in tourist receipts compared to 5.5 million tourist arrivals and RM8.5 billion in tourist receipts in 1998 [11]. Globally, Malaysia was ranked 9th in the top ten most visited countries in terms of international tourist arrivals in 2009 and 2010, achieving figures of 23.6 and 24.6 million tourist arrivals, respectively [12,13].

Malaysia can make an exceptional contribution to the tourism sector by attracting various researchers and academicians globally for support in this study. The government has declared sustainable tourism as an instrument of development giving precedence with least negative impacts to defend the environment and traditions [14]. In addition, it is generally used for increasing the economic growth of a country and tourism development should be encouraged [15].

Lying just north of the equator, Malaysia is located south of Cambodia and Vietnam and north of Singapore and Indonesia. More than one thousand islands are part of Malaysia with 38 designated as marine parks. Parts of the primeval rainforest are more than 100 million years old with a dazzling selection of birds and wildlife. Malaysia has wonderful golden beaches, lush vegetation, mountains, and fabulous shopping centres, which are associated with some magnificent hotels. This has made the country the fastest growing destination in South East Asia. The mix of the ancient and the ultra-modern makes Malaysia a fascinating place to visit, while the low cost of living and huge selection of choices for visitors make it an ideal holiday location. Malaysia experiences tropical climate throughout the year, enjoying warm days and mild evenings in all seasons. The country also offers a fascinating cultural mix with colourful festivals, unique arts and crafts, architecture, food and a rich array of dance forms. It is ideally placed to take advantage of its increased interest in the tourism industry, especially the ecotourism segment, as it possesses a wide variety of natural land and marine habitats. Therefore, the long term prospects of Malaysian tourism remain optimistic as a result of a strong government support and a relatively strong and stable political situation [16].

Admittedly, according to [17], foreign tourist arrivals and tourist expenditure on the basis of per capita and per diem are increasing year by year in Malaysia. Malaysia has targeted to capture a place within the top 10 countries in the world in terms of international tourist arrivals through various development plans. In this regard, less developed countries (LDCs) consider tourism as an important tool for their economic development [18].

3 Data and Method

This study collected primary data via interviews among 735 tourists based on a survey questionnaire and it was carried out between October and November, 2013. The non-probability convenience sampling technique was used for collecting data. Melaka was preferred as the research area because as mentioned by [19], "it has been chosen by tourists as a family holiday destination because there are a lot of national heritage and historical sites in the state". Heritage buildings such as the A-Famosa, Stadhuys, and traditional shop houses in the city are still protected by maintaining its aesthetic value. Similarly, the Kampung Morten culture is demonstrated through dance and traditional music as well as arts, batik, and puppet shows to attract tourists.

The data collection method used a questionnaire with a five-point Likert scale such as agree and disagree, etc. because it is a useful technique in a survey-based research; respondents choose one option that best aligns with their view. Therefore, the Likert-type rating scale has had great popularity among social science researchers [20, 21].

4 Conceptual Framework

Mainly, there are three pillars of sustainability namely environment, economic and community. These are shown below:

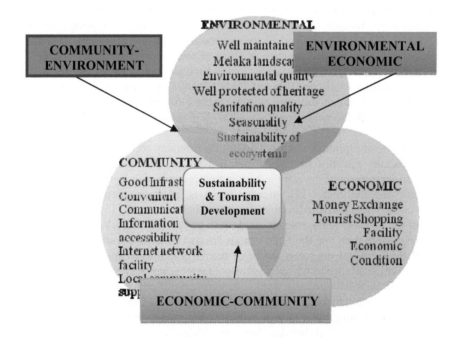

Figure 1. Conceptual Framework
Source: Adopted from sustainability assessment and reporting for the University of Michigan 200

5 Demographic profile of survey respondents

Table 1 illustrates that there are no differences in terms of gender and marital status among the respondents. In terms of age range, most of the respondents are categorized within the 21 to 30 years age group whereas the following group is the 31 to 40 years age group. Most of the visitors are also from the Malay ethnic group and the religion of most respondents is Islam. The majority of the respondents are self-employed, at almost 35.24%. Around 75% of the tourists are Malaysians; most of them are from Melaka at 17% while others are from Selangor (12.38%), Kuala Lumpur (10.48%), Johor Baru (8.57%), Negeri Sembilan (4.22%), Kelantan (4.22%), Kedah (3.53%), Pulau Pinang (3.4%), Perak (2.86%), Sabah (2.58%), Terengganu (2.04%), Pahang (1.49%), Sarawak (1.22%), Perlis (0.68%) and others (7.76%).

About 62% of them have higher degrees, as they reported being a diploma holder or a graduate. Around 28% of the families consist of 5-6 people while 33.47% of the families comprise of 3-4 members. Most of the respondents' incomes are below RM 1000 (about USD $300). 50% of the respondents stay for at least one night while visiting Melaka.

Table 1. Demographic profile of the Tourists'

Issues	1	2	3	4	5
Respondent's gender	Male (51.16)	Female (48.84)			
Respondent's age	11-20 (13.33)	21-30 (40.54)	31-40 (26.67)	41-50 (12.65)	50-< (6.81)
Ethnic	Malay (58.64)	Indian (7.21)	Chinese (14.69)	Others (19.46)	
Religion	Islam (64.9)	Hindu (7.21)	Buddha (10.61)	Christian (14.42)	Others (2.86)
Marital Status	Married (48.16)	Single (48.16)	Single Mothers (2.45)	Single Fathers (0.68)	Others (0.55)
Profession	Self Employed (35.24)	Government (25.85)	Private (26.94)	Others (11.97)	
Income P/M (RM)	Below 1000 (42.04)	1001-1500 (8.57)	1501-2000 (14.42)	2001-2500 (6.8)	2501< (28.16)
Level of Education	Diploma/Degree (61.91)	Primary school (14.15)	High school (20.68)	Not in school (1.22)	Others (2.04)
Respondents' nationality	International (17.41)	Malaysian (74.83)	Others (7.78)		
No of Households	Below 2 (24.22)	3-4 (33.47)	5-6 (27.76)	7 (8.44)	8-< (6.11)
Category of visits	Local (19.32)	Visitors (29.93)	Tourist* (50.48)	Others (0.27)	

Source: Authors' analysis on primary survey from Melaka 2013
Note: * Who stayed at least 1 night treated as tourist and rest are visitors;
Percentage in the parenthesis

6 Result and analysis

Tourism planning and development in terms of sustainability has become an important concept and topic [22- 24]. This focus is in part due to tourism's inherent nature to have both positive and negative effects on an economy, environment, and the community. [25- 27] indicated that, "if tourism development was planned improperly, it could destroy the very resources that are the foundation of tourism in a community (e.g. economic, environmental and social)".

6.1 Reliability and convergent validity

Cronbach's alpha was used to determine the reliabilities of the multi-item factors. The reliability level for attitude in the direction of economy, environment, and community met the critical value of 0.7 as suggested by [28]. All of the variables have high Cronbach's Alpha values such as 0.795, 0.886, and

0.872 for economy, environment and community, respectively. This proves that the variables are significant and suitable as all the variables used have higher than the suggested value.

6.2 Economic factors

The availability of adequate money exchange facilities is an important economic factor that allures tourists to visit Melaka as mentioned by 68.57% of the respondents (Table 2). This is followed by the attractive facilities for shopping and availability of gift and souvenir shops, which have attracted tourists to come to this place as mentioned by 67.62% of the respondents. Three main economic features that are important in developing countries for sustainable tourism are income generation, employment opportunity, and foreign exchange earnings. For instance, for many third world countries, tourism is the major income source of foreign exchange. Less developed countries (LDCs) have considered sustainable tourism as a vital tool for their economic growth [29] and tourism earnings reduce levels of reliance on exports of traditional primary commodities, providing an opportunity for many developing countries to diversify their economic bases [30, 31, 32]. Overall, the economic condition and its growing nature were mentioned by 68.03% of the respondents as another factor that attracts tourists to Melaka.

Table 2. Economic factors of tourism development for Sustainability in Melaka

Economic Issues	1	2	3	4	5	Mean (%)	SD (%)
Money exchange	2 (0.27%)	24 (3.27%)	205 (27.89%)	344 (46.80%)	160 (21.77%)	3.87	0.8
Tourist shopping	3 (0.41%)	32 (4.35%)	203 (27.62%)	331 (45.03%)	166 (22.59%)	3.85	0.83
Overall Financial conditions of the locality	8 (1.09%)	14 (1.90%)	213 (28.98%)	345 (46.94%)	155 (21.09%)	3.85	0.81

Source: Authors' analysis on primary survey from Melaka 2013
Note: 1=Very Unsatisfied; 2= Unsatisfied; 3= Neutral, 4=Satisfied; 5= Very Satisfied, Percentage in the parenthesis

6.3 Environmental factors

About 72.38% of the respondents were satisfied and very satisfied with the well-maintained heritage sites in Melaka (Table 3). Moreover, around 65.71% of the respondents agreed that they were satisfied with the quality of sanitation and hygiene facilities as the facilities are available and conveniently located around the city. Melaka's beauty in terms of landscape and the well-protected ecological heritage site were selected by 70.75% and 70.88% of the respondents, respectively. The eco-friendly environment and the good practices in the sustainability of the eco-system have contributed to visitors being attracted to visit Melaka as mentioned by 69.66% and 70.2% of the respondents, respectively. However, most of the visitors, namely around 63.95%, reported that they came based on the seasonality of the weather. For example, sustainability has become an important topic and concept in relation to tourism planning and development [33]. To support this, the World Wide Fund for Nature [34] indicated that sustainable tourism is like a fire; you can cook your dinner on it, but if you are not careful, it will burn your house down. However, this focus is in part due to tourism's inherent nature to have both positive and negative effects on the environment.

Table 3. Environment factors of tourism development for Sustainability in Melaka

Environmental Issues	1	2	3	4	5	Mean (%)	SD (%)
Well maintained	2 (0.27%)	19 (2.59%)	182 (24.76%)	388 (52.79%)	144 (19.59%)	3.88	0.75
Melaka landscape	2 (0.27%)	20 (2.72%)	193 (26.26%)	344 (46.80%)	176 (23.95%)	3.91	0.79
Environmental quality	4 (0.54%)	24 (3.27%)	195 (26.53%)	372 (50.61%)	140 (19.05%)	3.87	0.78
Well protected of heritage	2 (0.27%)	23 (3.13%)	189 (25.71%)	360 (48.98%)	161 (21.90%)	3.89	0.78
Sanitation quality	4 (0.54%)	34 (4.63%)	214 (29.12%)	336 (45.71%)	147 (20%)	3.82	0.8
Seasonality	2 (0.27%)	23 (3.13%)	240 (32.65%)	335 (45.58%)	135 (18.37%)	3.79	0.78
Sustainability of ecosystems	4 (0.54%)	22 (2.99%)	193 (26.26%)	339 (46.12%)	177 (24.08%)	3.9	0.81

Source: Authors' analysis on primary survey from Melaka 2013
Note: 1=Very Unsatisfied; 2= Unsatisfied; 3= Neutral, 4=Satisfied; 5= Very Satisfied, Percentage in the parenthesis

6.4 Community factors

All kinds of infrastructural facilities in Melaka are satisfactory as mentioned by around 69.53% of the respondents (Table 4). Around 58.78% of the respondents mentioned that the internet access facility is good. Information from the local people is also easily accessible at the same time, as mentioned by 60.28% of the respondents. Though sustainable tourism has been perceived as the industry of the future, it faces many challenges as it enters the new century. These challenges include a greater commitment by the communities that serve as hosts to the tourists with increased respect for the places [35, 36, 37], and a greater responsibility towards the tourists themselves [38, 39]. However, the ultimate challenge is in delivering tourism products that are appropriate and compatible with both hosts and guests. The community is also very supportive locally and this was mentioned by 64.08% of the respondents. Lastly, the convenience of the overall communication in Melaka has attracted tourists to visit Melaka, as mentioned by 62.31% of the respondents.

Table 4. Community factors of tourism development of sustainability in Melaka

Community Issues	1	2	3	4	5	Mean (%)	SD (%)
Good Infrastructure	1 (0.14%)	17 (2.31%)	206 (28.03%)	376 (51.16%)	135 (18.37%)	3.85	0.74
Convenient Communication	3 (0.41%)	34 (4.63%)	240 (32.65%)	344 (46.80%)	114 (15.51%)	3.72	0.79
Information easily accessible	5 (0.68%)	39 (5.31%)	248 (33.74%)	338 (45.99%)	105 (14.29%)	3.68	0.81
Internet network facility	10 (1.36%)	50 (6.80%)	243 (33.06%)	322 (43.81%)	110 (14.97%)	3.64	0.86
Local community supports	7 (0.95)	31 (4.22)	226 (30.75)	355 (48.30)	116 (15.78)	3.73	0.8

Source: Authors' analysis on primary survey from Melaka 2013
Note: 1=Very Unsatisfied; 2= Unsatisfied; 3= Neutral, 4=Satisfied; 5= Very Satisfied, Percentage in the parenthesis

7 Conclusion

Sustainable tourism is a development strategy that has already become noticeable as a dominant source of income and employment generation, and a global economic contributor to GDP in many countries. Tourism generates employment, attracts foreign investment, and represents a key source of earnings for developing countries that have an inadequate industrial sector and depend on foreign aid to a great extent. The overall picture of Malaysia as a tourist destination is positive and the findings of the study indicate that the tourists were satisfied with their visits given the sustainable tourism preservation in the city in Melaka.

Cooper et. al. [40] indicated that, "If sustainable tourism is dominated by the public sector, it is unlikely to be developed at the most advantageous proportion". Thus, the private sector can play a crucial role in managing tourism and its objectives. Profit as well as business survival in the long term depends on maintaining attractive facilities in tourism destinations whereas the role of customers (tourists) must not be ignored. Malaysia is perceived by international tourists as offering natural attractive beauty, especially its historical places, unique tourist attraction points, beaches, and good facilities such as providing quality restaurants and hotels. It was found that the overall economic issues are increased tourist activities such as increased tourist shopping which in turn increases money exchange.

The job opportunity in Melaka has increased as well in order to offer various tourist support services and the overall income from tourism has also increased. Additionally, Melaka is also perceived to be offering adequate facilities in meeting the tourists' needs for food and accommodation; tourist sites are well maintained, landscapes are nice, the community is friendly and the environment is well protected. Furthermore, the sound infrastructure, convenient communication, and adequate internet facilities are important catalysts for sustainable tourism in Melaka.

8 Acknowledgements

This work was supported by the Fundamental Research Grant under FRGS/1/2013/SS08/UKM/02/1 headed by Associate Prof. Dr. Er Ah Choy, Faculty of Social Sciences and Humanities (FSSK), Universiti Kebangsaan Malaysia (UKM) and Grant number DPP-2014-105 led by Prof. Joy Jacqueline Pereira, Southeast Asia Disaster Prevention Research Institute (SEADPRI), Universiti Kebangsaan Malaysia (UKM) are gratefully acknowledged.

References

1. H.J. Schumacher. Ecotourism. Business World, S1/6 (2007)
2. Bhargava Mohit. Raj Pub (2009)
3. World Tourism Organization *Madrid: WTO* (1999)
4. L. Dwyer and C. Kim. Determinants and Indicators. Current Issues in Tourism, 6, **5**, 369-414 (2003)
5. G. Brundtland G, OUP (1987)
6. M.L.Miller. *Proceedings of the 1990 Congress on Coastal and Marine Tourism* Newport, OR: National Coastal Resources Research and Development Institute Vol. **1** , 1–8 (1990)
7. C. Hunter. JST 3 (**3**), 155-65 (1995)
8. S. McMinn. The Environmentalist **2**, (1997) 135-141 (1997)
9. World Travel and Tourism Council, (2013)
10. Tourism Malaysia Tourism today. Ministry of Tourism (2011)
11. Mintel Country report no.2, Mintel International Group Ltd. (2011)
12. United Nations Study on the role of tourism in socio-economic development (2007)
13. World Tourism Organization UNWTO, Tourism Highlights (2011)

14. A. Liu, & G. Wall. Planning Tourism Employment: A Developing Country Perspective. Tourism Mgt, 27, **1**,159-170 (2006)

15. C.M. Hall . *Longman* (1995)

16. Malaysia Tourism Report Business Monitor International, **5** (2010)

17. M.A.H. Bhuiyan, C. Siwar, S.M. Ismail, S. M., ASS, **9**, (2013)

18. M. Taleghani. J Amer Sci, 6(**11**) 412-416 (2010)

19. A.C. Er. Geografia: Malaysian JSS 9, **3**, 12-23 (2013)

20. R. Likert, S. Roslow & G. Murphy. JSP, **5**, 228-238 (1934)

21. C-N. Wang, & L. Weng. Chinese Jour of Psy **44**, 239-251 (2002)

22. E. Inskeep, Van Nostrand Reinhold (1991)

23. C. Southgate & R. Sharpley. Tourism and Development: Concepts and issues, Channel View. (2002)

24. F. Yuksel, B. Bramwell and A. Yuksel. Tourism Mgt, **20**, 351–360 (1999)

25. H.C. Choi & E. Sirakaya. Tourism Mgt, **27**, (2006) 1274-1289 (2006)

26. S.F. McCool. National Recreation and Park Association 3-7 (1995)

27. J.C. Nunnally & I.H. Bernstein. McGraw-Hill. (1994)

28. T.V. Singh. Publishing Company, 30-41 (2003)

29. S.F. McCool. JTR, 40, **2**, 124-131 (2001)

30. G. Dann. Contemporary Issues in Tourism Development, Routledge (1999) 13-30 (1999)

31. WWF Tourism (2004)

32. C. Tosun. and D. Timothy. JTS 14, **2**, 2-12 (2003)

33. K. Meethan. Palgrave. (2001)

34. R. Sharpley. Tourism, JAPA, 54, **3**, 360-372 (1994)

35. T. Winter. JHT 4, **2**, 105-115. (2008)

36. C. Aas, A. Ladkin. and Fletcher, J. ATR 32, **1**, 28-48 (2005)

37. C. Cooper, J. Fletcher, S. Wanhill, D. Gilbert, and R. Shepherd. Pearson Edu (1998)

6

Gender Differences in Perceived Importance and Performance of Penang Island Attributes

Shida Irwana Omar[1], Gelareh Abooali[2], Badaruddin Mohamed[3], Diana Mohamad[4]

[1,3,4]Sustainable Tourism Research Cluster, Universiti Sains Malaysia, 11800, Penang, Malaysia
[2,3]School of Housing, Building and Planning, Universiti Sains Malaysia, 11800, Penang, Malaysia

Abstract. This paper examines the gender differences in perceived importance and performance of Penang Island attributes. The data was drawn from questionnaire survey of 801 international tourists who visited the island between August and November 2012. Previous studies related to gender differences in Malaysian destinations are found scarce and neglected, thus this paper aims to bridge this knowledge gap. The needs to study gender differences are related to the suggestions that men and women engage in different leisure activities, possess different travel motivations and perceive differently when embarking for holiday. The study found a number of gender similarities and differences between the men and women tourists, in terms of their travel style and perceptions of importance and performance of destination attributes. These results indicate that gender may not be the only influence on behaviour and perceptions, and those men and women should not be regarded as homogenous groups.

1 Introduction

The way to which the individuals identify with masculine and feminine identity is believed to have an impact on consumer behaviour. This topic has received attentions from consumer researchers for nearly more than 40 years yet it requires more studies [1]. Gender was acknowledged as a potentially functional variable for market segmentation as it meets [2] criteria for segmentation. The segments of male and female are substantial adequate and worthy to develop marketing strategies for, comparatively easy to measure and uncomplicated to access. However, Bem [3] and Spence [4] have introduced two fundamental gender identity theories to explain the effect of gender on consumption behaviour. The Bem's gender schema theory explains that individual behaviour, attitudes and traits are consistent with their gender identity. While Spence's theory considered gender identity as a predictive factor when gender related traits are likely to have impact. Both of these theories emphasized that gender is significantly linked to different consumer variables such as leisure activities and preferences as well as shopping behaviour. As claimed by Deem [5], girls are tended to spend a considerable proportion of their leisure activity for dancing, shopping and visiting relatives, compared to boys. Therefore, the understanding on the relationship between gender and tourist behaviour is important to the tourism industry. Although it is commonly believed that in modern times, the differences between the travel patterns of men and women are much less pronounced than before, gender differences related to travel and tourism still remain substantive [6].

In the context of tourism industry, the failure to understand and implement gender perspective can lead the service providers into a gender-blind market and dissatisfaction [7]. Gender differences in everyday leisure behaviour environment have received more attention compare to tourism context, for instance, participation in leisure activities [8], tourists travel pattern [9], travel preferences and experiences [9-10], travel motivation [11], and travel decision making processes [12]. Kinnaird and Hall [13] touches on the tourism development perspective focusing on the gender perspective where it is learned that tourism processes were constructed from gendered societies, ordered by gender relations. Further, gender relations over time inform, and are informed by the interconnected economic, politic, social, cultural and environmental dimensions of all societies engaged in tourism development. Issues of power, control and equalities were then articulated through race, class and gender relation in the tourism practices.

Differences in the gender behaviour may be related to the socio-cultural norms [14], the social-power relations [15] and values associated with the places in which they live. Tourists' perceptions are influenced by the comparisons that they make with facilities, attractions, and service standards that they have encountered elsewhere [16]. Leontidou and Kinnaird [17] mentioned that boundaries between work and leisure, host and guest, and women and men shift in response to the impacts of tourism. Gibson and Yiannakis [18] discussed the concept of tourism and leisure motivation in understanding tourist behaviour and it has been widely studied since the 1970s. McGehee et al. [19] found that women were more likely to be motivated by culture, opportunities for family bonding and prestige, while men placed more importance on sports and adventure when engaging in the pleasure travel experience. While men seek action and adventure which taking risks, women are more likely searching for cultural and educational experiences, with security and safety as a priority [20]. Freysinger [21] suggested meaning of leisure itself differ between men and women in midlife. Mattila et al. [22] investigated the influence of gender and religion on potential health-risk behaviour and on destination-related expectations of college students on spring break vacation. Sirakaya and Sonmez [22] found that females were depicted in such 'traditional stereotypical' poses as subordinate, submissive and dependent disproportionately more often than males.

To date, researches and discussions in gender differences in tourism context are still lacking [23]. Indeed, gender related studies in the setting of Malaysian destinations were also negligence. In light of these considerations, this study attempts to provide some gendered insights into tourist's travel purpose to Penang Island. In particular, the study intends to examine the gender differences in perceived importance and performance of destination attributes among international tourists.

2 Methodology

Targeting the international tourists with minimum age of 18 who visited the Penang Island between August-November 2012, this paper has managed to gather information from 801 international tourists by means of questionnaire survey (443 male, 358 women), of which, accounted for 80.1% response rate. The respondents were approached at several tourist spots throughout the island as well as at the gateways namely the airport, bus terminal, ferry jetty and cruise pier. The survey instrument went through content validity by a panel consisting of tourism stakeholders such as hotel managers, travel agents, airline officials, airport staff and tourist attraction representatives. The instrument was then prepared in five languages included English, Malay, Mandarin, Arabic and Japanese. The respondents were asked to provide information on the purpose of trip taken, duration of stay, mode of travel, source of information, perceived image of Penang and travel arrangement. In addition, the respondents were required to rate 12 attributes of destination importance and 12 attributes of destination performance, based on a 5-point Likert scale. Simple frequencies, cross tabulation analysis and chi-square test were computed on the respondents' demographic, travelling characteristic and expenditure pattern. The significance level used for chi-square test was 0.05%. In the second stage, the reliability test was performed on each 12 attributes of destination importance and performance, to test the stability of variables. The Cronbach's Alpha for 12 attributes of destination importance for male group was 0.872 and 0.877 for female group. While the reliability value for 12 attributes of performance for male group was 0.885 and 0.872 for female group. All items which indicated strong homogeneity of the items, appeared to be worthy of retention. In the third stage, the importance-performance analysis

(IPA) was applied to determine how the international tourists (both male and female groups) rate the importance and performance of Penang attributes. In addition to IPA, a paired sample *t*-test was performed to determine whether any significant difference existed between the perceived importance and performance attributes of Penang Island from male and female tourists' point of view. While, an independent sample t-test was performed to identify the significant difference on perceived importance and performance of Penang's destination attributes between male and female.

3 Findings

3.1 Demographics of the Segments

The findings indicate that majority of tourists were from ASEAN region (20.4% male, 28.1% female). The average age of male travellers was 35 years old and female travellers was 32 years old indicating the dominant of young travellers in both groups. In terms of marital status, 59.0% male travellers were married while female travellers record a near balance percentage. Table 1 shows that more than 50% of female respondents reported a monthly income of more than RM5,000 and only 37.5% of male travellers recorded monthly income more than that ($X2 = 16.5$, p =.002). In terms of educational level 49.8% male travels had higher degree and 47.3% of female travellers hold a tertiary education. No significant difference was detected in terms of educational level between female and male respondents ($X2 = 6.79$, p =.147). This is while a significant difference was reported in terms of occupation ($X2 = 57.21$, p < .001). Male travellers were mostly professionals (44.1%) compare to female travellers. The result shows that female travellers record higher degree of unemployment compare to male travellers (36.5%).

Table 1. A Comparison of Education and Career Attainment of Male and Female International Tourists

Demographic Profile	Gender	
	Male (N=443)	Female (N=358)
Education attainment		
Higher degree	49.8%	38.9%
Tertiary education	41.9%	47.3%
Secondary education	6.3%	12.7%
Primary education	1.4%	0.6%
No formal education	0.7%	0.6%
	$X^2 = 16.5, p = .002$	
Monthly income (equivalent to RM)		
< RM5,000	37.5%	50.3%
RM5,001 – RM10,000	25.5%	20.3%
RM10,001 – RM50,000	32.2%	25.2%
RM50,001 – RM100,000	1.9%	2.8%
> RM100,001	2.9%	1.4%
Average	RM15,382.36	RM12,335.17
Maximum	RM222,380.00	RM306,250.00
	$X^2 = 6.79, p = .147$	
Occupation		
Legislators, senior officials & managers	10.4%	5.5%
Professionals	44.1%	23.5%
Technicians & associate professionals	16.0%	22.5%
Clerical workers	2.8%	5.1%
Service workers & shop sales workers	3.7%	6.1%
Craft & related trades workers	2.0%	0.0%
Skilled agricultural & fishery workers	0.8%	0.0%
Plant & machine-operators & assemblers	0.6%	0.7%
Unemployed (e.g. retiree, homemaker, student)	19.7%	36.5%
	$X^2 = 57.21, p < .001$	

3.2 Purpose of Trips Taken

In general, a significant difference was detected between male and female travellers (Table 2). Interestingly, despite the similar visitation trend for both genders (leisure, recreation and holidays), male travellers record higher number for business and professional purposes. Of importance, 0.7% of male travellers travelled to Penang with the purpose of religion/pilgrimages but none of female travellers travelled with the same reason.

Table 2. A Comparison of Trip Purposes of Male and Female International Tourists

Purpose of visit	Gender	
	Male (N=443)	Female (N=358)
Leisure/recreation/holidays	50.1%	55.0%
Business/professional	14.0%	5.0%
Visit friends/relatives (VFR)	12.9%	12.6%
Education/study/teaching	9.9%	10.9%
Honeymoon	3.8%	3.6%
Health treatment	2.9%	5.0%
Convention/conference/trade show	2.3%	2.2%
Incentive travel	1.4%	1.4%
Government affairs/official mission	1.1%	0.6%
Shopping	0.7%	2.2%
Religion/pilgrimages	0.7%	0.0%
Sporting tournament/event	0.2%	1.1%
	$X^2 = 26.70, p = .005$	

3.3 Image of Penang as Perceived by the Segments

Penang cuisine (20.7%), world heritage site (20.8%), sandy beach (19.9%), and multicultural society (17.8%) were associated to the image of Penang as perceived by female travellers. Same attributes shaped the image of Penang for male travellers as well indicating that their perception is not different.

Table 3. A Comparison of Penang Images as Perceived by Male and Female International Tourists

Image of Penang	Gender	
	Male (N=443)	Female (N=358)
Local cuisine	20.1%	20.7%
Sandy beach	19.9%	19.9%
World heritage site	19.7%	20.8%
Multicultural society	18.0%	17.8%
Shopping paradise	10.3%	9.4%
International events	4.6%	3.9%
Health services	4.6%	4.2%
Folkdance/cultural performance	2.3%	2.7%
Others (education centre, national park & business)	0.6%	0.6%

3.4 Importance-Performance Analysis

For the international male travellers, the mean importance for the plotted data was 3.72 and the mean performance rating was 3.65. "Safety and security" and "image of destination" scored high as most important attributes of Penang perceived by international male travellers. On the other hand, for the international male travellers, the mean importance for the plotted data was 3.82 and the mean performance rating was 3.68. In line with international male tourists, "safety and security" was the most importance attributes with high level of performance. This is followed by "image of destination" which scored high in both importance and performance (Table 4).

Table 4. Mean Ratings of Importance and Performance of Destination Attributes

Attribute	Importance (I)				Performance (P)				Difference (MP – MI)	
	Mean (M)		Std. Dev.		Mean (M)		Std. Dev.			
	Male	Female	Male	Female	Male	Female	Male	Female	Male	Female
(1) Image of destination	3.90	3.94	0.948	0.935	3.87	3.88	0.793	0.776	-0.03	-0.06
(2) Variety of tourism attractions	3.84	3.91	0.961	0.927	3.76	3.74	0.839	0.859	-0.08	-0.17
(3) Cultural/ historical uniqueness	3.67	3.75	1.059	1.014	3.76	3.71	0.887	0.970	0.09	-0.04
(4) Value for money	3.79	3.85	0.992	0.944	3.72	3.77	0.840	0.844	-0.07	-0.08
(5) Safety and security	4.01	4.10	0.958	0.955	3.88	3.88	0.847	0.796	-0.13	-0.22
(6) Accessibility to the destination	3.83	3.95	0.961	0.902	3.65	3.76	0.855	0.832	-0.18	-0.19
(7) Friendliness of the people	3.77	3.77	1.013	0.977	3.78	3.87	0.966	0.993	0.01	0.10
(8) Availability of information	3.62	3.73	0.968	0.911	3.51	3.63	0.913	0.884	-0.11	-0.10
(9) Ease of communication	3.39	3.55	1.101	1.042	3.57	3.65	0.974	0.944	0.18	0.10
(10) Cleanliness of destination	3.62	3.75	1.010	0.983	3.42	3.32	0.986	1.012	-0.20	-0.43
(11) Accommo-dation services	3.69	3.84	1.015	0.952	3.63	3.66	0.921	0.890	-0.06	-0.18
(12) Local transport services	3.54	3.68	1.070	1.047	3.27	3.33	1.060	0.987	-0.27	-0.35
Total	44.67	45.82	-	-	43.82	44.20	-		-	-1.62
Central line	**3.72**	**3.82**	-	-	**3.65**	**3.68**	-		-	-

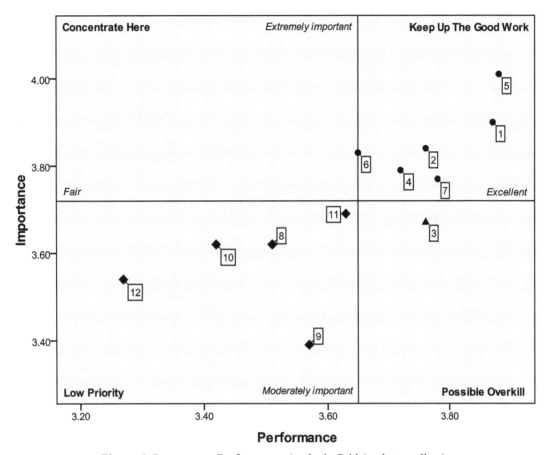

Figure 1. Importance-Performance Analysis Grid (male travellers).

From Figure 1, none of the items were identified in the Concentrate Here quadrant. The "image of destination", "variety of tourism attractions", "value for money", "safety and security", "accessibility to the destination" and "friendliness of the people" were plotted in the Keep Up the Good Work quadrant. The "availability of information", "ease of communication", "cleanliness of destination", "accommodation services" and "local transport services" fall into the Low Priority quadrant. Furthermore "cultural/historical uniqueness" was plotted in Possible Overkill quadrant.

Figure 2 illustrates the results of the Importance-Performance Analysis grid for the sample group of international female tourists. As presented in the following figure, "image of destination", "variety of tourism attractions", "value for money", "safety and security "and "accessibility to the destination", were all classified in the Keep Up the Good Work quadrant. "Friendliness of the people" and "cultural/historical uniqueness" were plotted in the Possible Overkill quadrant and "availability of information", "ease of communication", "cleanliness of destination", and "local transport services" fall into the Low Priority quadrant. "Accommodation services" was considered to fall into Concentrate here quadrant.

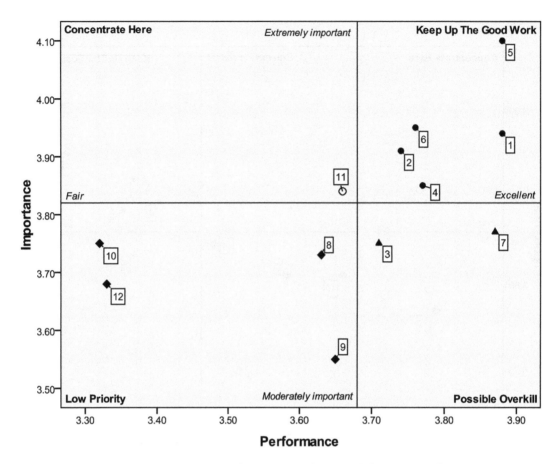

Figure 2. Importance-Performance Analysis Grid (female travellers)

To assess significant differences between male travellers' perceived importance and performance of Penang's attributes, a paired sample t-test was conducted. The results revealed that safety and security (t = 2.591), accessibility to the destination (t = 3.304), availability of information (t = 2.071), ease of communication (t = -2.897), cleanliness of destination (t = 3.211) and local transport services (t = 4.201) were found to be statistically significant, with $p < 0.05$. Another paired sample t-test found that variety of tourism attractions (t =3.205), safety and security (t =3.802), cleanliness of destination (t =6.471), accommodation services (t =3.225) and local transport services (t =5.954) were statistically significant ($p < 0.001$) between female traveller's perceived importance and performance of Penang's attributes. In addition, an independent sample t-test was performed to identify the significant difference on perceived importance of destination attributes between male and female travellers. The results revealed that ease of communication (t = -2.119) and accommodation services (t = -2.155) were found to be statistically significant ($p < 0.005$). Nevertheless, there found to be no statistically significant difference on perceived performance of Penang's attributes between male and female.

4 Discussions and Conclusion

Similarly to Collins and Tisdell [6] in relation to purpose of visit, this paper observes male travellers present a higher result for business while at the same time, record identical result with female travellers for leisure. As genders are lowly depending on tour package, appropriate information centres and other source of information on site are indeed imperative. In cases of perceived image, both genders associated Penang Island with cuisine, sandy beach, and multicultural society; with female travellers strongly interlink these images with world heritage site, compared to male travellers. Mceczkowski [19] argues that this happens as women are more motivated by cultural attributes of the destination. Despite the different requirements regarding some of the destination attributes (see also [23-24]), both genders agreed on selecting "image of destination", "variety of tourism attractions", "value for money", "safety and security "and "accessibility to the destination", as the most important attributes that at the same time performed well and satisfied tourists. Having said this, the Penang Island marketers are advised to further enhance these attributes. Although "cultural/historical uniqueness" was reported with over focused attribute by both groups while "friendliness of people" was grouped into overkilled quadrant by female travellers, these factors should not be neglected by the tourism marketers. Female travellers selected "accommodation services" to put under more concentration as the availability of safe, comfortable and affordable accommodation aspects are of their concerns [25]. Within this paper knowledge, these findings could assist Penang managers and marketers to prioritize the allocation consistent with their customer preference and priority. However, applying IPA coupled with other variables such as region, age or education level could be other practices for the further study. Inspecting the perception of different market segment towards the quality of destinations attributes can assist marketers to tackle the exact preferences of each group.

5 Acknowledgements

The authors would like to extend their appreciation to the following institutions that made this study and paper possible:

- Penang Global Tourism for granting the research grant called Penang International Travelers Survey 2012 (Grant No. U527); and
- Universiti Sains Malaysia for granting the Research University Grant called Tourism Capacity and Impact Studies (Grant No. 1001/PTS/8660011).

References

1. K.M. Palan, Gender identity in consumer behavior research: a literature review and research agenda, Academy of Marketing Science Review, **10**, 1-31 (2001)
2. J.R. Rossiter, Market segmentation: a review and proposed resolution, Australian Marketing Researcher, **11**, 1, 36-58 (1987)
3. S.L. Bem, *Gender schema theory: a cognitive account of sex typing*, Psychological Review, **88**, 4, 354-364 (1981)
4. J.T. Spence, Masculinity, feminity, and gender-related traits: a conceptual analysis and critique of current research, Progress in experimental personality research, **13**, 1-97 (1984)
5. R. Deem, All work and no play?: a study of women and leisure, Milton Keynes: Open University Press (1986)
6. D. Collins, & C. Tisdell, Gender and differences in travel life cycles, Journal of Travel Research, **41**, 2, 133-143 (2002)
7. S. Westwood, A. Pritchard, & N.J Morgan, Gender-blind marketing: businesswomen's perceptions of airline services, Tourism Management, **21**, 4, 353-362 (2000)
8. N. Carr, A study of gender differences: young tourist behaviour in a UK coastal resort, Tourism Management, **20**, 2, 223-228 (1999)
9. J. Firestone, &B.A Shelton, A comparison of women's and men's leisure time: subtle effects of the double day, Leisure Sciences, **16**, 1, 45-60 (1994)
10. M.J. Harvey, & C.C. Harris, Gender and community tourism dependence level, Annals of Tourism Research, **22**, 2, 349-366 (1995)
11. F. Meng, & M. Uysal, Effects of gender differences on perceptions of destination attributes, motivations, and travel values: an examination of a nature-based resort destination, Journal of Sustainable Tourism, **16**, 4, 445-466 (2008)

12. Z. Mottiar, & D. Quinn, Couple dynamics in household tourism decision making: women as the gatekeepers? Journal of Vacation Marketing, **10**, 2, 149-160 (2004)

13. V. Kinnaird, & D. Hall, Conclusion: the way forward in Kinnaird, V. & Hall, D., Tourism: a gender analysis, Chichester: Wiley (1994)

14. E. Pawson, & G. Banks, Rape and fear in New Zealand City, Area, **25**, 1, 55-63 (1993)

15. A. Caballe, *Farm tourism in Spain: a gender perspective,* GeoJournal, **48**, 3, 245-252 (1999)

16. E. Laws, Tourist destination management: issues, analysis and policies, New York: Routledge (1995)

17. L. Leontidou, & V. Kinnaird, Gender dimensions of tourism in Greece: employment, subculturals and restructuring, in Kinnaird, V. & Hall, D., Tourism: a gender analysis,(1994)

18. H. Gibson, & A. Yiannakis, Tourist roles: needs and the lifecourse, Annals of Tourism . Research, **29**, 2, 358-383 (2002)

19. Z. Mceczkowski, World trends in tourism and recreation, New York: Peter Lang. (1990)

20. V.J. Freysinger, The dialectics of leisure and development for women and men in mid-life: an interpretive study, Journal of Leisure Research, **27**, 61-84 (1995)

21. A. Mattila, Y. Apostolopoulos, S. Sonmez, L. Yu, & V. Sasidharan, The impact of gender and religion on college students' spring break behaviour, Journal of Travel Research, **40**, 193-200 (2001)

22. E. Sirakaya, & S. Sonmez, Gender images in state tourism brochures: an overlooked area in socially responsible tourism marketing, Journal of Travel Research, **38**, 4, 353-362 (2000)

23. N.G. McGehee, L. Loker-Murphy, & M. Uysal, The Australian international pleasure travel market: motivations from a gendered perspective, Journal of Tourism Studies, **7**, 1, 45-57 (1996)

24. N. Carr, *An exploratory study of gendered differences in young tourists perception of danger within London*, Tourism Management, **22**, 5, 565-570 (2001)

25. J.S.C. Hao, & C.O.S. Har, *A study of preferences of business female travelers on the selection of accommodation.* Paper presented at the 5th Asia Euro Conference 2014, 19-21 May 2014, Selangor, Malaysia.

7

Transformation to Eco-Agri Tourism: The Case of Casile, Cabuyao City, Laguna, Philippines

Troy P. Tuzon[1], Lira Jane A. Hilao[2], Irish Renerie D. Marana[3], Kevin N. Villalobos[4], Enrico Garcia[5], Merlita C. Medallon[6]

[1,4]Faculty of the College of International Tourism and Hospitality Management, Lyceum of the Philippines University – Laguna, Calamba City, Laguna, Philippines
[2,3]Students of the College of International Tourism and Hospitality Management, Lyceum of the Philippines University – Laguna, Calamba City, Laguna, Philippines
[5]Faculty of the College of Arts and Sciences, Lyceum of the Philippines University – Laguna, Calamba City, Laguna, Philippines
[6]Research Director, Lyceum of the Philippines University – Laguna, Calamba City, Laguna, Philippines

Abstract. The study was conducted to determine the acceptability of the residents of Barangay Casile, Cabuyao, Laguna, Philippines in transforming their locality into an eco-agri tourism site. A total of 241 residents participated in the data collection using a survey questionnaire and interviews. Barangay Casile is an agricultural area and is also noted for its natural heritage such as the Matang Tubig River and Falls and the Marcos Twin Tower. Because of this, the local government unit of Cabuyao City plans to develop the area as a nature- based tourism destination specifically as an eco-agri tourism site. The survey revealed that the respondents agreed on the proposition of transforming their area into agri-tourism site. Cultural acceptability ranks the highest which means that the locals are open on the possible effects on their culture that the development could bring them. Economic and social acceptability were also ranked high because of the income they could get from the influx of tourists. Environmental acceptability is the least agreeable because most of the respondents were environment sensitive and are concerned with the changes to the natural façade of their area. It can be concluded that agri-tourism development involving local residents provides control over the development and management of the project.

1 Introduction

Eco-agri tourism is a combination of 'Ecotourism' and 'Agri-tourism'. This type of tourism aims to sustain the culture and nature of the place while promoting agriculture as the tourism attraction. Both ecotourism and agri-tourism were considered as Nature- based Tourism because it both depends directly to nature. However, eco-agri tourism mainly focus on sustainable yet community-based tourism, which is the current trend within the tourism industry nowadays. This type of tourism requires the participation of the local community as the host and as attraction itself.

Nature-based tourism is the type of tourism that relies on experiences directly related to natural attractions. It directly depends on nature and includes ecotourism, adventure tourism, extractive tourism; farming or agri-tourism, wildlife tourism and nature retreats. Nature-based tourism is the trend because tourists are becoming more environment- sensitive. Nature-based tourism can indirectly promote conservation. Natural sites include topography, water, wildlife, protected natual areas, climate and vegetation and are pull factors of ecotourism [1].

The United Nations International Year of Ecotourism (IYE) of 2002 marked the rise of ecotourism as a new market opportunity advocating a form of sustainable development in rural developing world [2]. The main purpose of the declaration was to set preliminary agenda for the development of ecotoursim activities in the context of sustainable development.

In the Philippines, there are a lot of natural resources that are identified as tourist attractions. There are still a lot that could still be transformed into a nature-based tourism site. Barangay Casile is one of them. Located in the Cabuyao City, a town south of Manila, the community has promising resources that could be considered for tourist attraction. The area is known for its agricultural products and its natural heritage, the Matang Tubig River and Falls. It is also the site of the Marcos Twin Mansion. It is also characterized with highlands and cool breeze with average daily temperature of around 22° to 24°C [3]. It is strategically located and is accessible via land travel. Because of these, the local government of embarked in developing the areas as a nature-based tourism destination. However, there is a need need to integrate the public and stakeholder input in environmental decision-making.

The residents of Barangay Casile prefers to have community based tourism rather than commercial based tourism, according to the report of the local government unit. The residents want to stay as rural as they are to maintain their local lifestyle and culture. With this scenario, the study was conducted to determine the acceptability of the residents to transform their locality into an agri-tourism site. By getting their responses, the local government planners may have empirical data to show that the program has the approval of the local people.

1.1 Importance of the local people

According to Philippine Council for Agriculture, Forestry and Natural Resources Research and Development (PCARRD), there are three reasons why locals are important to be considered in monitoring and evaluating of an eco-tourism project [4]. First, local people make excellent information gatherers and possess a great deal of local knowledge. Second, local participation helps establish a stronger link between the planning and management of ecotourism and its beneficiaries or local stakeholders. Lastly, involving local people in the monitoring and evaluation process motivates them to plan and manage activities in a sustainable manner. Another study stated that tourists view indigenous cultures and local communities as products of the tourism experience that exist to be consumed [5].

Majority of the residents (65.6%) of Casile have been residing in the area for 13 or more years. Most of them are earning Php3,000 and below (41.9%) from farming (30.3%). Most of the residents are unemployed (26.1%). Those who had reached the elementary level (17.6%) would most likely belong to the aforementioned groups. For those who had attained at least seconday school (50.2%), they could get work in factories (12.0%). Given this demographic profile, opening new avenues for earning is welcome by the residents. Opportunities for new income generating activities will not be declined. Benefits can be gained by the residents if and when the area is open for tourists. On the other hand, the area and its residents may be vulnerable to some risks and changes.

The local government should be able to weigh the benefits and risks of the transformation plan. The local residents are directly affected by any of the good or bad results it may bring. Getting the insights of the local residents is deemed necessary. This will provide a sense of ownership to whatever decisions may be arrived at. The sustainability of the site will depend on how the community handled it. The attitude of the residents towards the development is parallel to the satisfaction level of the tourists. The locals are the host, they are one of the stake holders of tourism development and their participation is very important for this type of program.

1.2 Opportunities for eco-agri tourism development

Ecotourism development poses both opportunities and threats to the natural and social environments. If properly planned and implemented, ecotourism can easily result in positive impacts and create opportunities. Otherwise, it may threaten the natural resources and the local society as well. This is the same thing with eco-agri tourism development, if everything is properly managed and controlled, negative impacts would be lessened and would produce favorable opportunities [6].

Agritourism is a form of tourism where tourists experience traditional rural hospitality, nature and cultural experinces while helping the local community maintain their agricultural viability and diversify economically [7]. The development of agritourism varies in particular places. Considered as a new form of tourism it provides a supplementary commercial activity on local farms. In other countries, like in Indonesia, rural toursim developed in the plantation areas of Sumatra and Java. In Korea, farm tourism was developed through cooperative actions by households. In Malaysia, government funding supports agritourism centers for recreation and education [8]. In New Zealand, short stay volunteering on organic farms result in improved care and concern for the natural environment, support for organic movement and self-development among visitors [9].

Some of the positive impacts and opportunities offered by ecotourism according to Philippine Council for Agriculture, Forestry and Natural Resources Research and Development (PCARRD) are revenue generation, employment opportunities, stronger economy, environmental education, pride and appreciation.

Revenue comes from entrance or visitor use fees, which are charged directly to visitors or tourists for accessing and performing specific activities or for using special equipment in an ecotourism site. Creation of job opportunities is, more often than not, the biggest gain from operating tourism or an ecotourism project [10]. There will be hiring for guides, guards, office staff, or managers for tourism - related activities increase. More jobs means stronger economy. Ecotourism helps boost economics at the local, regional, and national levels. Ecotourism offers several ways in promoting environmental education. An example is during an exciting nature hike for instance, visitors are eager to learn about the local habitats. The interest, attention, and appreciation shown by visitors and tourists for local resources and cultural practices, is a manifestation of increased awareness and appreciation of local heritage and natural wealth [6].

With numbers of opportunities from eco-agri tourism, there are also lots of threats because the opportunities once mismanaged will be problems. Some of them are environmental degradation, economic instability, crowding and excessive development.

Environmental degradation is a problem most commonly associated with tourism because visitors may destroy the very resources they come to see [6]. The economic instability is also a problem because ecotourism can be an unstable source of income. Many factors are completely outside the control of local communities yet it affects levels of visitation and tourist demand. Tourists may start to compete with residents for space and is the start of crowding. Although development is a positive consideration, an excessof it may pose a major problem when a location becomes a popular tourist destination. Local businesses must be created through lodging, restaurants, and other services to cater to visitors' needs. With such, other environmental, cultural and social issues may prevail.

1.3 Theoretical framework

This study is anchored on two theories, Tourism Development Theory and Social Exchange Theory. The Tourism Development Theory shows the importance of understanding the local resident's reaction towards the tourism development. It states that the factor that may influence their reactions is essential in achieving a host community support for tourism development. The resident's support is tied to economic, social, cultural and environmental consequences. The principle of the study states that total tourism impact has four impact factors, and each impact factor influences the perception of other impact factors and the perceived total impact in varying degrees and different directions [10].

Social Exchange Theory [11] proclaims that residents are likely to participate in an exchange with tourists if they believe that they would likely gain benefits without incurring unacceptable costs. If residents perceive that the positive impacts of tourism development will be greater than the negative impacts, they are inclined to be involved in the exchange and, therefore, endorse future tourism development.

2 Method

A descriptive research design was used in this study. Data were gathered from 241 local residents using a researcher-developed questionnaire. The questionnaire was validated by experts prior to its administration. The questionnaire is composed of two parts. The first part gathered data on the demographic profile of the residents which is responded to using a provided checklist. The second part consists of statements that were responded to using a 5-point Likert scale. Data elicited in this part shows the level of acceptability of the residents on the transformation of Barangay Casile into an agri-tourism site in the environmental, cultural, social and economic aspects. The survey questionnaires were administered by the researchers. Guided data collection and interviews with key informants was done using an interview guide. The interviewees included some local officials and residents who have lived in the locality for more than ten years. The interviews further strengthen the responses provided in the questionnaire.

3 Results and discussion

3.1 Level of acceptance in terms of environmental, economic, cultural and social aspect

The survey shows that 57% of the local residents are open to new environmental projects that will be initiated in their barangay. There will be increasing support from the government for the local projects that will be established in the locality. With these there will be more assistance and benefits that the residents will be able to receive. The residents understand that there will be few changes in their surroundings but they cannot approve of the instance of letting the wildlife in Casile get disturbed. About 34% of the respondents believe that if there will be a possible increase in waste generation, it would do no good in their place.

This is supported by the statement of one of the caretakers, who said that increase support from the government would be a good idea but they could not accept the possible consequence of ruining their environment. In another interview, it was stated that minimal changes to the environment would be tolerable but not the things that could be detrimental to their natural resources.

The result shows that on the environmental aspect, acceptability is low implying that the respondents don't want their environment to be altered for some reasons. This is in accordance to the statement of one respondent who stated that ''whatever happens they want to preserve the maidenhood of their barangay''. They are very sensitive when it comes to the environment because a lot of residents of Casile depend on its agriculture as a source of livelihood.

The foregoing concerns had earlier been reported that exploitation of the natural resources had strong negative impacts on the ecological systems and sustainability of the planning of tourism market [12]. Another reported that although local residents agree that tourism has negative impacts and there was a great need to protect rural areas, they preferred to develop the natural attractions first to attract many more tourists and use the financial returns from tourism to protect the natural resources [13]. It was likewise reiterated that even if ecotourism represents one of the more eco-friendlh alternatives for the economic use of natural resources, poor ecotourism management may degrade the natural resources [14].

On the economic aspect, the local residents want to have more opportunities to gain income. About 76% of the residents agree that opening the locality into a tourism site would provide an increase in opportunities for employment. It would also strengthen the local income from tourism according to 71% of the residents. It was also agreed that there could be changes in the current type of business or occupation that they have. However, 34% of the respondents claimed that it could also result to increasing price of commodities.

One of the interviewees supported the result of the survey saying that more job opportunities for the locals would bring in more income. It was also mentioned that they are willing to have a change of career if it would lead to having an increase in income. The residents are open to having new jobs aside from farming which will bring additional income to them. On the other hand, another resident suggested that for those who already have jobs, they should continue on what they have started. The result for increasing price of commodities can be compensated with the ability of the residents to have more income and be able to pay for them. Concerns about future job security is compensated by more immediate monetary interests such as getting tips from tourists which eventually may play a role in building environmental appreciation. Tips represent an important supplement to regualr wages and daily bonuses which can account for up to 40% of a guide's total monthly earnings [15]. In another report, it was reiterated that a key feature of community based agri-tourism is the creation of rewarding, sustainable and relatively well-paid employment [16].

Results of the study concur with the statement that economic benefits are welcome as long as there is ethical business practice, adherence to highest labor standards and development and maintenance of local community infrastructure [17]. The welfare of the residents should be given priority. Ecotourism standards should be generated that stipulate benefits to local communities [18].

On the other hand, since most of the residents are farmers, there is acceptability in the economic aspect. The respondents are open to having new jobs aside from farming which will bring additional income to them. By introducing an immediate and potentially lucrative source of revenue, the growth of agri-tourism throughout the developing world has acted as an incentive for communities to protect and preserve natural areas [19].

Socially, 74% of the residents accept the fact that their barangay will be more popular if the development will be pursued. This will correspond to increase in security and attention from the government (71%). The residents also accept the fact that their population may possibly increase (51%) but likewise believe that the increase in noise (39%) that their barangay will experience may still be tolerable. This is supported by a resident who stated that it is acceptable for their barangay to be known and to be visited by lots of tourists. There is enthusiasm to welcome visitors who enhanced their sense of pride in the region. However, the thought of having an increase in noise shouldn't happen because the locals are used of having a peaceful place. Foucat [20] found the protection of natural sites as bery important for the development of social aspects such as community cohesion, organization and improvement in the condition of local people's health. Communal rather than individual benefits will be inculcated when young foreign people stay in the locality.

Interviews with local residents revealed the significance of maintaining cultural values. One of the local officials mentioned that they are welcoming the idea of having different groups of people visiting their place to be able to present the local culture and be more appreciative of their own culture. Appreciation of their own culture is still aspired by72% of the residents. Opening the area to visitors is a venue to present to other people the local traditions and the way of life. However, the fact that there could be some alterations on their local traditions (58%) and way of living is not discounted. The residents (66%) accept the fact that their perception in life would change because they believe that it could also be helpful. An interviewee said that the possible influence of tourists is acceptable and that the local residents must not be affected by the sudden flow of tourists. It was earlier noted that progressive social and cultural change that stems from tourism has an effect on intergenerational, gender or ethnic conflicts in communities where the status quo is disrupted [21]. Adverse socio-cultural impacts associated with codes of conduct and local norms had to be given much attention. Problems are linked to retention of traditional norms and values to the degree of contact with visitors who bring with them a different values and behavior.

Agri-tourism development involving local residents provides control over the development and management of the project. It is known that a major proportion of the benefits will remain within the communities. Community development encourages conservation, environmental education and sustainable use of natureal resources [15]. Community based agr-tourism serve the economic, social, cultural and environmental intests of host communities. Empowerment is a process through which ''individuals, households, local groups, communities, regions and nations shape their own lives and the kind of society in which they live'' [22-23].

3.2 Demographic factors that affect the acceptability of transforming Casile into an agri-tourism site

The locals from the age bracket of late adolescence and early young adulthood were the most affected in terms of economic and social because they are the ones who are involved in employment and socialization.

The perception in terms of age can affect in different ways on how people will think and act [24]. They stated that age is also a factor that also affects individual's perception on how they think and act. It also stated that age has a significant relationship with knowledge, attitude and behavior of the respondents.

Gender have significant relationship with the level of acceptance only in terms of social aspect. The culture creates differences in gender since there are behavior, expectation, roles, representation and sometimes values and beliefs that are specific to men and women.

The result shows that married people are more affected by economic and social changes because they usually have families to work for. This is supported by the study [24] who stated that being married drives one to find a job that could support their family necessities.

Educational attainment doesn't have significant relationship with the environmental, social, cultural and economic acceptability because even the local residents who had higher education were not able to have a deeper understanding about eco-agri tourism. The levels of acceptability are slightly correlated and none of them was significant. The result is contradicted by the study [25] which states that the educational attainment of individuals influence their perception about public issues and also contradicted with the study that the educational attainment has a significant relationship with the perception of the respondents [26].

The same with educational attainment, the type of occupation doesn't influence the level of acceptance of the respondents. This is because the development would be beneficial to all kinds of occupation the residents have. The locals were usually farmers and unemployed and they foresee the development of Brgy. Casile as an eco-agri tourism destination would be a big help for them. Environmental, economic, social and cultural acceptability were only slightly correlated and none of them were significant.

The result shows that monthly income does not have significant relationship in terms of environmental, economic, social and cultural aspects. Most of the respondents were earning Php 3000 and below and they are willing to change their current occupation or business for them to have a much better source of income.

Most of the respondents have been living in Brgy. Casile for at least 13 years. Their residency affects their perception in terms of economic and social aspect because of a possible change in source of income and change in the social environment because of the possible influx of tourists. Local residents of Casile were used to having a very peaceful and quiet place.

4 Conclusion

The respondents rated all the aspects of acceptability as agreeable but cultural acceptability rates as the highest and environmental acceptability as the lowest. The researchers concluded that environmental acceptability is the least agreeable because most of the respondents are environment sensitive and are concerned with nature. However, cultural acceptability ranks the highest which shows that the local residents are open to the possible effects on their culture that the development could bring them. Economic and social acceptability were also ranked high because of income considerations which is their primary need and if more tourists will come they will have more income. The inputs provided by the residents in this study is a guide to the local government planners on tourism development. Careful evaluation of the advantages and disadvantages brought it by ecotourism development should be done. The voice of the residents should be heard in fora and consultative meetings designed for the purpose. Although benefits can be enumerated, it should be considered that it takes a long journey before these can be achieved. The price of the dreamed economic advantage has to be paid with environmental and cultural pay-offs. A more in-depth probing on the issue of transforming Barangay Casile into an eco-agri tourism site should be done.

References

1. D. Weaver, and L. Lawton, *Tourism Management*. John Wiley & Sons, Australia.(2002)

2. J. Butcher, *The United Nations International Year of Ecotourism: a critical analysis of development implications.* Progress in Dev. Studies 6, **2**, 146–156 (2006)

3. Temperature of Cabuyao City. Retrieved March 23, 2013 from http://www.accuweather.com/en/ph/cabuyao-city/262695/weather-forecast/262695

4. PCARRD. Planning and Developing Community- based Ecotourism Projects in the Philippines. (2010).

5. S.Wearing, & J.Neil, Ecotourism: Impacts, Potentials and Possibilities? (2009).

6. A. Drumm, & A. Moore, Ecotourism Development: A Manual for Conservation Planners and Manager. (2005).

7. G. Veeck, D. Che & A. Veeck, *America's changing farmscape: A study of Agricultural Tourism in Michigan.* The Professional Geographer, **58**, 3, 235–248 (2006).

8. H. Choo & T. Jamal, *Tourism on organic farms in South Korea: a new form of ecotourism?* J. Sustainable Tourism. **17**, 4, 431–454 (2009).

9. A.J. McIntosh, & B. Bonnemann, S.Willing, *Workers on Organic Farms (WWOOF): The alternative farm stay experience?* J. Sustainable Tourism, **14**, 1, 82–99 (2006).

10. Y.Yoon, D.Gursoy, , & J.Chen, *Validating a tourism development theory with structural equation modeling.* Tourism Mgt. **22**, 4, 363-372. (2006)

11. J.H. Turner, *Handbook of sociological theory.* Kluwer Academic/Plenum Publishers, New York.(2002)

12. P. Chufamanee & J. Lønholdt, *Application of integrated environmental management through the preparation of an environmental action programme: Case study from the Songkhla Lake Basin in southern Thailand Lakes and Reservoirs.* Research and Management. **6**, 4, 323 (2001)

13. H. Goodwin & D. Roe, *Tourism, Livelihoods and Protected Areas: Opportunities for Fair-trade Tourism in and Around National Parks.* International Journal of Tourism Research. Res. **3**, 377-391 (2001)

14. W.J. Li, *Environmental management indicators for ecotourism in China's nature reserves:A case study in Tianmushan Nature Reserve.* Tourism Management. 004,25, 5, 559-564. (2003).

15. N. Kontogeorgopoulos, *Community-Based Ecotourism in Phuket and Ao Phangnga, Thaiiand: Partial Victories and Bittersweet Remedies.* J. Sustainable Tourism. 13, 1 (2005)

16. R. Scheyvens, *Promoting women's empowerment through involvement in ecotourism: Experiences from the Third World,* J. Sustainable Tourism **8**, 3,232-^9 (2000)

17. M. Honey, (ed.) *Ecotourism and Certification..* Washington, DC: Island (2002).

18. L.K. Medina, *Ecotourism and Certification: Confronting the Principles and Pragmatics of Socially Responsible Tourism.* J. Sustainable Tourism. **13**, 3 (2005)

19. J. Yamagiwa, *Bushmeat poaching and the conservation crisis in Kahuzi-Biega National Park, Democratic Republic of the Congo.* J. Sustainable Forestry **16**, 3-1, 115-35 (2003).

20. V.S.A. Foucat. Community-based ecotourism management moving towards sustainability, in Ventanilla, Oaxaca, Mexico.Ocean & Coastal Management, **45**, 8, 511-529. (2002).

21. C. Fabricius, *Towards strengthening collaborative ecosystem management: Lessons from environmental conflict and political change in southern Africa.* Journal of Tiic Royai

Society of New Zealand **31**, 4, 831 (2001).

22.   R. Scheyvens, *Tourism for Development: Empowering Communities*. Harlow: Prentice Hall. (2002).

23.   D. Timothy, *Tourism and community development issues*. In R. Sharpley and D. Telfer (eds) Tourism and Development: Concepts and Issues. Clevedon: Channel View, 149-64 (2002).

24.   N.Alcasid, R.Barrera, & C.Marfic, *The Perception of Guests Olympic Point Island Resort in Tingloy, Batangas towards the Effectiveness of Advertising Tools for Local Beaches*. Lyceum of the Philippines- Laguna. (2011).

25.   M. King & A. Mendoza, *Effects of RTV exposure to the culture of Mangyans in Safa, Sabang, Panimalayan, Oriental Mindoro*. Lyceum of the Philippines Laguna. (2012).

26.   A. Delos Santos, S.J. Alcalde & A.F. Marasigan, *The Perceived Effects of Indigenous Tourism in The Lives of Selected Aetas in Pastolan Village, Hermosa Bataan, Subic Bay Philippines*. Lyceum of the Philippines- Laguna. (2013).

8

Comparing Destination Image and Loyalty between First-time and Repeat-visit Tourists

M. Mohamad[1] , N. I. Ab Ghani[2]

[1,2]Faculty of Business Management and Accountancy, Universiti Sultan Zainal Abidin, Kuala Terengganu, Malaysia

Abstract. The objective of this study was to investigate the difference between destination image and loyalty among first-time and repeat-visit tourists. The study was undertaken to examine aspects of underlying factors of destination image that influenced tourists' willingness to recommend Malaysia to their friends and relatives as well as spread positive word-of-mouth to others. In addition, it was to ascertain the relationship between destination image and loyalty among first-time and repeat-visit tourists. The data was collected at Kuala Lumpur International Airport at the departure hall using self-administered questionnaires. 248 usable questionnaires were returned and analysed. The findings of the study revealed that both groups of tourists perceived Malaysia as providing a nature-based destination. The study also empirically proved that both first-time and repeat-visit tourists were willing to disseminate positive word-of-mouth and recommend Malaysia to their friends and relatives as a vacation destination to visit. However, there was a significant difference in destination loyalty between first-visit and repeat-visit tourists.

1 Introduction

Nowadays, the leading and single largest industry in the world is tourism and the importance of the industry is reflected through its economic contribution to the nation [1]. The industry promotes economic growth especially through income generation, employment opportunities and foreign-exchange earnings. Parallel to the global development in the sector, the tourism industry is also one of the important sectors that generates Malaysia's economic growth [2]. In 2012, it became the second major foreign-earning sector [3] next to manufacturing. Recognising the great economic potentials in the tourism industry, it was identified as one of the National Key Economic Areas in the Malaysia Government Transformation Programme (GTP) to achieve the country's Vision 2020: to become an advanced nation by year 2020 [4].

The 2013 Travel & Tourism Competitiveness Index (TTCI) revealed that, among the ASEAN countries, Malaysia ranked second after Singapore, followed by Thailand, Indonesia, Brunei, Vietnam, the Philippines and Cambodia. However, in the tourism world ranking, Switzerland, Germany and Austria lead the world in terms of travel and tourism competitiveness, with Spain, the United Kingdom, the United States, France, Canada, Sweden and Singapore achieving the first top 10 countries visited by tourists.

In the list, Malaysia was ranked 34th and it aspires to be within the top ten countries of the world in terms of global tourism receipts by 2015 [5] by focusing on the country's wealth of natural beauty and cultural heritage as reflected in the slogan "Malaysia, Truly Asia" that captures and defines the country's unique cultural diversity, festivals, traditions and customs, offering myriad experiences [6]. This image of Malaysia as a choice travel destination was disseminated through the promotional activies by the Malaysia Tourism Promotion Board (Tourism Malaysia).

This initiative was undertaken to influence them to visit and make returning visits to Malaysia. However, it was reported that between 2010 and 2012, the majority of the international tourists indicated that the trip to Malaysia was their first trip [7, 8]. This data indicated that efforts have to be stepped-up to encourage returning tourists to Malaysia. Morerover, as highlighted by the World Travel and Tourism Council [9] and Mintel [10], the main problem of the tourism industry in Malaysia is image. The theme of "Malaysia Truly Asia" focusing on promoting the country's image of a multi-racial and cultural society seems to not have had much influence on tourists to make return visits to Malaysia [11].

The above developments in Malaysia's travel and tourism industry denoted that a study on destination loyalty is crucial to uncover insights concerning retaining loyal tourists. The importance of securing loyal tourists is indeed enormous as loyal tourists are more likely to spread positive word-of-mouth based on their travel experiences of a destination and it can reduce marketing costs [12]. Moreover, Schiffman and Kanuk [13] claimed that it is more expensive to win new customers compared to keeping existing customers. Studies have shown that small reductions in customer defection can generate significant increase in profits as (1) loyal tourists pay less attention to competitors' destinations and are less price sensitive; (2) loyal tourists repeat visit; (3) servicing existing customers who are familiar with the destination is cheaper; and (4) loyal tourists spread positive word-of-mouth.

According to Haque and Highe [14], a loyal tourist will help to generate more revenue and it is considered an outcome of a successful tourism destination. Against this background, ascertaining the effect of destination image on destination loyalty is eminent to be carried out since such a study could provide insightful information pertaining to aspects that would inspire existing and potential tourists' selecting Malaysia as a holiday destination [15, 16]. According to Byeong and Nunkoo [17] and Li [18], destination image has positive impact on destination loyalty. Since the first-time tourists have limited knowledge about a destination compared to repeat-visit tourists, it is essential to segment them into two different groups to better understand their behaviours so that appropriate promotional strategies can be designed meeting their different requirements. Thus, the main aim of the study was to meet the following objectives:

1. To determine the underlying factors measuring destination image of first-time and repeat-visit tourists.

2. To determine the effect of destination image on destination loyalty for the first-time and repeat-visit tourists.

2 Literature Review

Destination loyalty is defined as the whole feelings and attitudes that encourage tourists to revisit a particular destination [19]. A study on destination loyalty was highlighted as one of the most critical subjects in tourism researches [20]. Creating a strong, consistent, different and noticable image that generates positive ideas for a destination [21] would develop a destination loyalty. Destination loyalty can be measured through three dimensions: behavioural approach, attitudinal approach and composite approach. Behavioural approach is measured by identifying the number of repeat-visit tourists [22] or respondents' intention to revisit [23] Attitudinal approach is measured through recommendation of the destination to others, positive word-of-mouth and assurance to a preferred destination [24].

Composite approach is a combination of behavioural and attitudinal approach that is used to describe wholly the idea of customer loyalty [22, 24]. This study applied a composite approach to measure destination loyalty by examining tourists' intention to revisit, recommendation of the destination and disimination of positive word-of-mouth to others.

Destination image is defined as the sum of beliefs, attitudes and impressions that individuals or groups hold towards tourist destinations or aspects of destination [25]. According to Pavlovic and Belullo [15], destination image has been studied for more than 30 years by other researchers as it is accepted as an important element of destination management [26, 21]. There are two major approaches in measuring destination image: three-dimensional continuum approach and three-component approach [27].

The three-dimensional continuum approach of image is referred to as attribute-holistic, functional-psychological and common-unique proposed by Echtner and Ritchie [28]. Attribute-holistic line reacted to the fact that destination image should include the perceptions of individual attributes such as accommodation facilities, friendliness of the people and climate, etc plus holistic impression such as mental picture or the imagery of the destination. Along the functional-psychological continuum, functional characteristics are more concerned with tangible aspects of the destination because they are directly observable or measurable, while psychological characteristics are intangible aspects because they are more difficult to measure or observe.

Common-unique continuum catered for the inspiration of individuals form perceptions based on common characteristics to those based on unique features or aura. The second approach of measuring destination image is a three-component approach which comprised cognitive, affective and conative components [29]. Cognitive component refers to the belief and knowledge about a destination's attributes. Affective component refers to the attachment or feeling towards a destination. Conative component of destination image refers to the onsite behaviour expressed by tourists developed from cognitive and affective images [27].

This study adopted a functional-psychological measurement of destination image, one of the dimensions mentioned in Echtner and Ritchie [28]. This is because it focused on particular destination attributes [30], it is simple to code, results are easy to analyse using sophisticated statistical techniques and easy to administer [31]. A recent study by Jamaludin, Johari, Kayat and Yusof [32] found that destination image has direct positive relationship with destination loyalty. Similarly, Mohamad, Rusdi and Mokhlis [33] suggested that favourable destination image will encourage foreign tourists to spread positive recommendations (attitudinal) as well as intention to repeat visitisation in the future (Behaviour).

3 Research Methodology

3.1 Target Population and Questionnaire Design

The target population in this study refers to the European tourists that visited Malaysia for a holiday, business trip, conference, visiting friends or relatives for at least one day but less than one year [34]. The purpose of choosing European tourists is based on two indicators proposed by the Kuala Lumpur structure plan 2020, namely tourist arrival and average length of stay. These indicators were used to evaluate tourism performance. Base on these indicators, it seemed that Europeans scored the highest range of tourists arrivals and average length of stay compared to other regions: America, Oceania, Asia, and Africa.

The items to measure destination image and destination loyalty were identified from the previous literature. The survey instruments consists of three sections. Section A contains 31 items to measure destination image. These items were adapted from the work of Echtner and Ritchie [35] using a 7-point Likert scale ranging from 1 as highly disagree to 7 as highly agree. Section B contains 5 questions on destination loyalty which were adapted from the work of Zeithmal, Berry and

Parasuraman [36] using a 7-point Likert scale from 1 as "not at all likely" to 7 as "extremely likely". The last section of the questionnare was designed to gather information about the tourists including country of residence, gender, age, marital status and purpose of visit. A content validity was conducted to ensure how well the dimensions and elements of the concept have been explained [37]. In this case, two academicians were involved in reviewing the questionnaire.

A pilot study with respondents (n = 100) that had a similar background with the actual respondents was carried out at the Kuala Lumpur International Airport (KLIA) in order to improve the quality and efficiency of collecting data. Exploratory Factor Analysis (EFA) was performed after conducting the pilot test to reduce and summarise items of destination image and destination loyalty. In addtion, EFA was conducted to identify the underlying factors representing the constructs in the study. Moreover, the pilot study was conducted to test the reliability and validity of the research instruments prior to the actual collecting of data.

3.2 Data Collection

Data collection for the actual study was carried out at the Kuala Lumpur International Airport (KLIA). A self-administered questionnaires was distributed to the respondents at the departure hall. The respondents completed the survey at his or her own pace which normally took not more than 20 minutes to complete. Enumerators would than collect the completed questionnaires from the respondents. A total of 1000 questionnaires were distributed at the pre-identified departure halls to all eligible respondents and 820 completed questionnaires were returned.

Two stages of sampling method were used. A systematic sampling method was used where, after a random starting point, every 5th intercepted respondent was included in the study. 820 respondents answered the questionnaire completely. After conducting the systematic sampling method, simple random sampling was choosen to select the study sample. The purpose of choosing simple random sampling is because it can reduce the potential human bias in the selection of cases to be included in the sample [38].

Hence, Statistical Package for Social Science (SPSS) software was used to select the respondents by "Random Sample of Cases". A sampling frame was created based on the 820 returned questionnaires because accurate data for the size of the target population for this study was not available [39]. A simple random-sampling technique using Statistical Package for Social Science (SPSS) software was used to select the respondents by "Random Sample of Cases". Based on the created sampling frame, a total of 420 respondents were selected as the sample size for the study representing approximately 50 percent of the population.

However, after conducting a data-cleaning process through deleting missing items and outliers, only 248 respondents with 143 respondents representing first-time tourists and 105 representing repeat tourists were used which was sufficient to provide statistical power for data analysis. It can be supported by Burn and Bush [39] that the recommended sample size using confidence interval method with p (estimates percent in the population = 50%, q (100 – p) = 50%, and e (acceptable sample error expressed as a percent) between ±5% and ±10% at 95% level of confidence, whereby the calculated sample size (n) is between 96 and 384. Therefore, the usable sample size of 248 met the sample-size requirements of Burn and Bush [39].

3.3 Data Analysis

Discriptive analysis such as means and frequencies were applied to examine the respondents' demographic profile. Confirmatory Factor Analysis (CFA) was applied in this study to confirm the measurement model derived by EFA [40]. After conducting Confirmatory Factor Analysis (CFA), assessment for reliability and validity were applied to evaluate the quality of the measurement process [41]. Reliability was assessed using two criteria, namely internal reliability and construct reliability. Internal reliability was used to ensure that the research instruments were from free random error or without bias using Cronbach' Alpha or coefficient alpha to test the scale of destination images and destination loyalty respectively [42]. Hair et al. [40] recommended that the value for alpha coefficient greater and equal to 0.7 is generally considered to be the acceptable lower limit of reliability. Structural Equation Modelling (SEM) was applied to the data set to test the causal relationship between destination image and destination loyalty simultaneously.

Construct Reliability (CR) was used with SEM model to measure reliability and internal consistency of the measured variables [40]. A value of 0.6 or higher is acceptable to achieve construct reliability [43]. Construct validity was performed to measure the extent to which a set of items actually reflect the thoeretical latent construct. Validity of the construct were assessed using convergent validity and discriminant validity. Convergent validity is achieved by checking the Average Variance Extracted (AVE). An AVE of 0.5 or higher is a good rule of thumb suggesting adequate convergence [40]. Discriminant validity can be fulfilled by looking at the square root values of AVE constructs and comparing them with the correlation estimates between two constructs [40]. Validity is achieved when the square root of AVE is higher than the values of correlations between constructs.

4 Findings

4.1 Demographic's Profile

Most of the European tourists visiting Malaysia for the first-time were from the Western European region (50.3%), namely countries of the Netherlands, Germany, France, Switzerland, Belgium, Austria and Holland. Majorities of repeat-visit tourists were from the Northern European region (54.3%), namely countries of the United Kingdom, Sweden, Ireland, Scotland, Norway and Finland. Both groups of tourists were dominated by male tourists with 59.4% for the first-time tourists and 64.8% for the repeat tourists.

Majority of the first-time and repeat-visit tourists visiting Malaysia were single or living with their partner which comprised 71% and 75% respectively. Most of the first-time tourists represent younger age group (82%) compared to repeat-visit tourists (53%). The purpose of visiting Malaysia for both groups was for holidaying.

4.2 Assessment of Normality, Reliability and Validity

The normality test was conducted by looking at the skewness and value of mutivariate kurtosis. The suggested value for skewness ranged between ± 3.00 and kurtosis less than 8.00 [44] although some would suggest that the absolute value of skewness shoud be ± 1.00. However, the use of SEM using the Maximum Likelihood Estimator (MLE) is fairly robust to skewness greater than ± 1.00 if the sample size is large and a sample size greater than 200 is considered large. The value of mutivariate kurtosis should be less than 50.0 [45]. In this study, the values of skewness and kurtosis for both first-time and repeat-visit tourists are less than the recommended cut-off points. In addition, multivariate kurtosis for both first-time and repeat-visit tourists are less than 50.

Thus, these values indicated that there is no univariate non-normality affiliated with the data. Reliability and validity tests were performed on both first-time and repeat-visit tourists measurements of destination image and loyalty. Table 1 and Table 2 illustrate the outputs from the tests measuring destination image and loyalty respectively. The analyses indicated that the factor loadings of the items measuring destination image and loyalty for both first-time and repeat-visit tourists achieved unidimensionality, with all the factor loadings being equal to or more than 0.6. In addition, the results of these tests indicated that the Cronbach's alpha coefficient value (α) met the required cut-off point and the analysis revealed that all items were free from random errors.

Meanwhile, the values of Average Variance Extracted (AVE) and Composite Reliability (CR) also achieved the required levels which are above 0.5 and 0.7 respectively. Results in Table 1 and Table 2 suggested that all items measuring destination image and loyalty respectively for both first-time and repeat-visit tourists fulfilled the requirements of reliability and convergent validity. Table 3 and Table 4 present the discriminant validity index summary for both first-time and repeat-visit tourist. The results indicated that the diagonal values (the square roof of AVE) are higher than the correlations between the respective constructs suggesting that the discriminant validity for the constructs is achieved.

4.3 Structural Models Goodness-of-fit

Confirmatory Factor Analysis (CFA) was used to confirm the measurement model after conducting Exploratory Factor Analysis (EFA). The result from EFA would provide the underlying factors that best represent the data together with their respective measuring items. Following EFA, CFA was carried out to test the goodness-of-fit of the variables measuring the studied constructs. Any measuring items that obtained factor loadings of less than 0.6 and squared multiple correlations (R^2) of less than 0.4 should be dropped from the analysis [45] as supported by the literature. Figure 1 and Figure 2 illustrates the structural model that depicts the relationship between destination image and destination loyalty for the first-time and repeat-visit tourists visiting Malaysia respectively. Several indexes were used to test the structural model goodness-of-fit as indicated below. The results of the tests proved that these models achieved fitness indexes at the acceptable level of goodness-of-fit as illustrated in Figure 1 and Figure 2.

Table 1. Reliability and convergent validity of destination image for first-time and repeat-visit tourists

Items	First-time Tourist				Repeat-visit Tourist			
	Loading	α	AVE	CR	Loading	α	AVE	CR
Safe and Clean (F1)		0.70	0.54	0.70	na	na	na	na
There is a lot of crime in Malaysia (D30)*	0.61	na	na	na	na	na	na	na
In general, Malaysia is a safe place to visit (D65)	0.85	na	na	na	na	na	na	na
Natural and adventurous (F2)		0.75	0.53	0.77	na	0.89	0.5	0.8
Malaysia offers the chance to see wildlife (D38)	**0.83**	**na**	**na**	**na**	**0.80**	**na**	**na**	**na**
Malaysia offers a lot in terms of scenic beauty (D46)	**0.74**	**na**	**na**	**na**	**0.79**	**na**	**na**	**na**
A holiday in Malaysia is a real adventure (D20)	**0.60**	**na**	**na**	**na**	**0.74**	**na**	**na**	**na**
Malaysia is a restful and relaxing place to visit (D32)	na	na	na	na	0.70	na	na	na
Malaysia has nice beaches for swimming (D42)	na	na	na	na	0.70	na	na	na
Good facilities for sports and recreational activities are available (D49)	na	na	na	na	0.64	na	na	na
There are many places of interest to visit in Malaysia (D61)	na	na	na	na	0.73	na	na	na

Note: na = not applicable

Table 2. Reliability and convergent validity of destination loyalty for first-time and repeat-visit tourists

Items	First-time tourist				Repeat-visit tourist			
	Loading	α	AVE	CR	Loading	α	AVE	CR
Loyalty:		0.85	0.69	0.90		0.91	0.75	0.92
Will suggest Malaysia to friends and relatives as a vacation destination to visit (L2)	1.00	na	na	na	0.97	na	na	na
Will encourage friends and relatives to visit Malaysia (L3)	.919	na	na	na	0.95	na	na	na
Will say positive things about Malaysia to other people (L1)	.808	na	na	na	0.78	na	na	na
Will consider Malaysia as a vacation choice to visit in the future (L4)	.521	na	na	na	0.73	na	na	na

Note: na = not applicable

Table 3. Discriminant Validity Index Summary First-Time Tourists

Constructs	Factor	Safe and Clean (FI)	Natural Attractions (F2)	Loyalty
Destination Image	Safe and Clean (F1)	**0.73**		
	Natural Attractions (F2)	0.43	**0.73**	
Loyalty	na	0.46	0.55	**0.83**

Note: na = not applicable

Table 4. Discriminant Validity Index Summary Repeat-Visit Tourist

Constructs	Destination Image	Loyalty
Destination Image	**0.71**	-
Loyalty	0.68	**0.87**

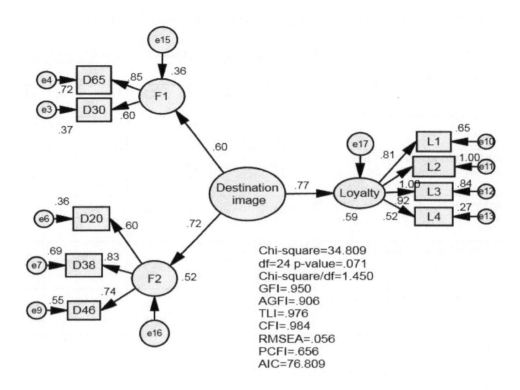

Figure 1. Structural model of destination image and destination loyalty for first-time tourist

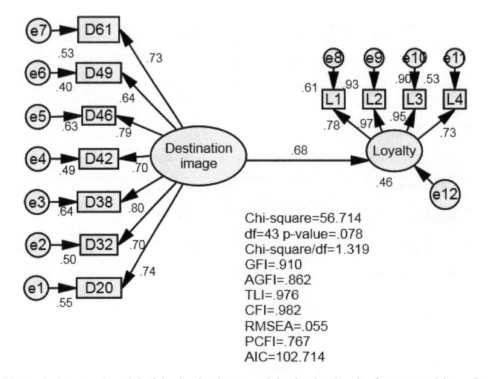

Figure 2. Structural model of destination image and destination loyalty for repeat-visit tourist

4.4 The Causal Effect of Destination Image on Destination Loyalty

The findings in Figure 1 indicated that the five items are grouped into two underlying factors measuring destination image for the first-time tourists. These factors are labelled as "Safe and Clean" and "Natural Attractions". On the other hand, the findings in Figure 2 suggested that destination image for repeat-visit tourists was manifested by seven items. Loyalty construct for both groups of tourists were manifested by four items as depicted in Table 2. The results in Table 1 also specified that destination image had a causal effect on destination loyalty for both groups of tourists as indicated by the significant p-values (0.001) for both groups of tourists. An earlier study by Mohamad and Ab Ghani [46] suggested that there were six underlying factors that measured first-visit tourists' destination image namely "safe and clean", "natural attractions", "tourists activities', "political stability", "beaches" and "price". Interestingly, this study proposed that only two factors which are identified as "safe and clean" and "natural attractions" had causal effects on destination loyalty among first-visit tourists. Remarkably, three items grouped in "natural attractions" for the first-time tourists also appeared in the repeat-visit measurement of destination image. These items are marked bold in Table 1, Table 5 and Table 6. Thus, the study suggested that both first-visit and repeat tourists agreed that Malaysia, as a travel destination, offers natural attractions in terms of natural scenic beauty and the chance to see wildlife which make visiting Malaysia an adventurous holiday.

In addition, the findings of the study also proposed that there are four items that measure destination loyalty for both groups of tourist. Both groups would suggest and encourage friends and relatives to visit Malaysia as a vacation destination. Moreover, they would consider Malaysia as a vacation choice to visit in the future and disseminate positive word-of-mouth about Malaysia to other people. However, the result of the independent t-test revealed that the two groups of the respondents differ significantly (t =2.25, p < 0.004) in destination loyalty. The null hypothesis that there is no difference of means between the two groups is rejected. The result indicated that, repeat-visit tourists have a higher level of loyalty (mean = 6.20) compared to the first-time tourists (mean = 5.96) on a scale of 1 to 7.

Table 5. The unstandardized regression weight for the first-time tourist

Construct	Path	Construct	Estimate	S.E.	C.R.	P
Loyalty	<---	Destination image	0.962	.233	4.123	***
Safe and Clean (F1)	<---	Destination image	0.780	.180	4.331	***
Natural and Adventurous (F2)	<---	Destination image	1.000			

Table 6. The unstandardized regression weight for the repeat-visit tourist

Construct	Path	Construct	Estimate	S.E.	C.R.	P
Loyalty	<---	Destination image	0.716	0.103	6.961	***
Malaysia offers the chance to see wildlife (D38)	<---	Destination image	1.000			

5 Discussions and Conclusion

This study proposed that the image of nature-based tourism should become the major selling point of Malaysia as a travel destination as opposed to cultural diversity as is being promoted and emphasised in the promotional campaign under the tag line "Malaysia Truly Asia". Empirical evidence from this study suggested that both first-time and repeat-visit tourists believed and formed impressions that Malaysia offers nature-based tourism. The natural scenic beauty with the chance to see wildlife accompanied by a host of adventurous activites, in turn influenced tourist destination loyalty. These unique aspects of destination image perceived by the tourists reflected their demand for ecotourism products. Therefore, it is strongly advised to Tourism Malaysia to focus on developing and enhancing the potentials of ecotourism sector. Ecotourism is regarded as travelling to relatively undisturbed natural areas that have low visitor impact [47]. According to the International Ecotourism Society (TIES), the ecotourism participants require a variety of activities, which include land and water-based activities, however the most popular of them are wildlife watching, visiting protected areas and hiking [48]. Efforts should be undertaken to ensure that tourism developments in Malaysia would comply to meeting the requirements of ecotourism that usually conveys a great concern on an environmentally friendly, relatively undisturbed natural areas and promotes conservations whilst providing beneficial social economic activities to the local pupulations. The importance of ecotourism seems to be increasingly recognised as having great potentials to attract tourists, especially foreign tourists, to Malaysia based on recent intiatives undertaken by Toursim Malaysia to introduce and promote ecotourism products. The variety of products includes tropical forests, mountain and hills, lakes, caves and the many species of flora and fauna [47]. However, there are other aspect of destination image that should be highlighted in the promotional activities, especially among first-time tourists such as safety. Recent incidents of kidnapping and terrorist threats on the eastern coast of Sabah and the islands close to the southern Philippines, and incidents of Malaysia airlines disasters probably would affect Malaysia's destination image in term of safety. Adequate measures should be undertaken to assure potential tourists that visiting Malaysia is relatively safe compared to the other ASEAN countries, and these incidences were isolated cases. Though, this is not an issue of great concern to the repeat-visit tourists since they had better knowledge about Malaysia compared to the first-visit tourists based on their past travel experiences. Their returning trips to Malaysia are not only because of the many interesting places to visit with good facilities for sports and recreational activities, but also because of the nature-based activities that would occupy them with a lot of adventurous holiday activities. These are the critical aspects that Tourism Malaysia should focus on in the efforts to sustain the development in the Malaysia tourism industry in the future. This is crucial to ensure that Malaysia remains competitive and offers travel experiences fulfilling the requirements of the global tourism industry that demands quality travel experiences.

References

1. Md. Anowar Hossain Bhuiyan, C. Siwar, S. Mohamad Ismail, Tourism development in Malaysia from the perspective of development plans, Asian Soc. Sci. **9**, 9, 11-18 (2013)
2. M. Khairul Hisyam Hassan, S. Tarang Jenggie, The economic impacts of tourism sector on Malaysian economy, BIMP-EAGA Conference, Kota Kinabalu, 2012
3. Tourism Malaysia, Malaysia tourists profile 2012 by selected markets, Malaysia, Tourism Malaysia, Ministry of Tourism (2012)
4. Performance Management and Delivery Unit (PEMANDU), Prime Minister's Department Government transformation program – the roadmap, Kuala Lumpur, Percetakan Nasional Malaysia Berhad (2010)
5. Tenth Malaysia Plan 2011 – 2015, Kuala Lumpur, Percetakan National Malaysia Berhad (2010)
6. Tourism Malaysia, http://corporate.tourism.gov.my/trade.asp?page=malaysia_truly&subpage =history (2014).

7. Tourism Malaysia, Malaysia tourists' profile 2010 by selected markets, Malaysia, Tourism Malaysia, Ministry of Tourism, (2010)
8. Tourism Malaysia, Malaysia tourists' profile 2011 by selected markets, Malaysia, Tourism Malaysia, Ministry of Tourism, (2011)
9. WTTC, Malaysia: the impact of travel and tourism on jobs and economy, http://www.wttc.org/bin/pdf/original_pdf_file/malaysia2002.pdf. (2002)
10. Mintell, London, Mintell International Group Ltd. (2011)
11. A. Kadir Lebai Din, Malaysia as an imagined destination the selling points, Universiti Utara Malaysia Press, Sintok (2010)
12. M. Yue, Destination image building & its influence on destination preference & loyalty of Chinese tourists to Australia, PhD Dissertation, Polytechnic University Hong Kong (2008)
13. L. G. Schiffman, L. L. Kanuk, *Consumer behaviour*, New Jersey, Pearson Prentice Hall (2007)
14. A. Haque, A. Highe Khan, Factors influencing of tourist loyalty: A study on tourist destinations in Malaysia. In Conference: proceedings of 3rd Asia-Pacific business research conference, Kuala Lumpur, Malaysia, 25 – 26 February 2013, pp. 1-16 (2013)
15. D. Krizman Pavlovic, A. Belullo, Internet – an agent of tourism destination image formation: Content and correspondence analysis of Istria travel related websites, from http://bib.irb.hr/datoteka/323634.Krizman-Pavlovic_Belullo.pdf. (2011)
16. J. Gill Choi, T, Tkachenko, S. Sil, On the destination image of Korea by Russian tourists. Tourism Manage. 1-2 (2010)
17. D. Byeong Park, R. Nunkoo, Relationship between destination image and loyalty: developing cooperative branding for rural destinations. In Conference: 3rd international conference on international trade and investment, University of Mauritius, 4 – 6 September 2013
18. H. Li, Analysis of formation mechanism of revisit intention: data from East China. In Conference: International conference on global economy, commerce and service science, Phuket, Thailand, 11 -12 January 2014, pp. 246-252 (2014)
19. C. Hsu, L. Killion, G. Brown, M. J. Gross, S. Huang, Tourism marketing: an Asia - Pacific perspective, Milton, Qld: John Wiley & Sons Australia, Ltd. (2008)
20. A. Puad Mat Som, S. Fatemeh Mostafavi Shirazi, A. Marzuki, J. Jusoh, A critical analysis of tourist satisfaction and destination loyalty, J. Global Manage., **2**, 1, 178-183 (2011)
21. A. Ramazan, K. Sule, A destination image as a type of image and measuring destination image in tourism: Amasra case. Eur. J. Soc. Sci., **20**, 3, 478-488 (2011)
22. P. Mechinda, S. Serirat, N. Gulid, An examination of tourists' attitudinal and behavioral loyalty: comparison between domestic and international tourists, J. Vac. Mktg., **15**, 2, 129-148 (2009)
23. S. Campro Martinez, J. B. Garau Vadell, M. Pilar Martinez Ruiz, Factors influencing repeat visits to a destination: The influence of group composition, Tourism Manage., **31**, 862-870 (2010)
24. P. Rauyruean, K. E. Miller, Relationship quality as a predictor of B2B customer loyalty, J. Bus. Res. **60**, 21-31 (2007)
25. D. Weaver, L. Lawton, Tourism management, Australia: J. Wiley (2010)
26. A. D. A. Tasci, D. F. Holecek, Assessment of image change over time: The case of Michigan , J. Vac. Mktg. **13**, 4, 359-369 (2007)
27. H. Zhang, X. Fu, L. A. Cai, L. Lu, Destination image and tourist loyalty: a meta-analysis, Tourism Manage. **40**, 213-223 (2014)
28. C. M. Echtner, J.R. Brent Ritchie, The meaning and measurement of destination image, J. Tourism S., **14**, 1, 37-48 (2003)
29. S. Baloglu, K. W. McCleary, A model of destination image formation, Ann. Tourism Res., **26**, 1, 868-897 (1999)
30. S. Stepehenkova, A. M. Morrison, Russia's destination image among American pleasure travellers: Revisiting Echtner and Ritchie, Tourism Manage., **29**, 548-560 (2008)

31. R. Abdul Rashid, H. Nizam Ismail. Critical analysis on destination image literature roles and purpose. In Conference: 2nd international conference on built environment in developing countries, ICBEDC 2008, Universiti Sains Malaysia, Penang, 3 – 4 December 2008, pp. 1812-1827 (2008)

32. M. Jamaludin, S. Johari, A. Aziz, K. Kayat, Yusof, A. Raheem Mohamad Yusof, Examining structural relationship between destination image, tourist satisfaction and destination loyalty, Int. J. Independent Res. S., **1**, 3, 89-96 (2012)

33. M. Mohamad, A. Rusdi Abdullah, S. Mokhlis. Tourists' evaluations of destination image and future behavioural intention: the case of Malaysia, J. Manage. Sustainability, **2**, 1, 181-189 (2012)

34. R. C. Mill, A. Morisson, *The tourism system*, Hempstead: Prentice Hall (1985)

35. C. M. Echtner, J.R. Brent Ritchie, The measurement of destination image: An empirical assessment, J. Travel Res. **31**, 4 (1993) 3-13 (1993)

36. V. A. Zeithaml, L. L. Berry, A. Parasuraman, The behavioral consequences of service quality J. Mktg. **2** (1996) 31-46.

37. U. Sekaran, Research methods for business, New York, John Wiley & Sons, Inc. (2000)

38. Leard Dissertation, Simple random sampling, http://dissertation.laerd.com/articles/simple-random-sampling-an-overview.php. (2012)

39. A. C. Burn, R. F. Bush, Marketing research: online research applications, New Jersey, Upper Saddle River (2010)

40. J. F. Hair jr, W. C. Black, B. J. Babin, R. E. Anderson, R. L. Tatham, *Multivariate data analysis*, New Jersey, Pearson Prentice Hall (2010)

41. T. Jitpaiboon, The roles of information systems intergration in the supply chain integration context – firm perspective, PhD Dissertation, University of Toledo (2005)

42. N. K. Malhotra, Marketing research: An applied orientation, New Delhi, Prentice-Hall (2007)

43. Z. Awang. A handbook on SEM for academicians and practitioners: the step by step practical guides for the beginners, Bandar Baru Bangi, MPWS Rich Resources (2014)

44. R. B. Kline, *Principle and Practice of Structural Equation Modeling*, New York, The Guilford Press (2005)

45. Z. Awang. A handbook on structural equation modeling using AMOS, Malaysia, Universiti Technologi MARA Press (2012)

46. M. Mohamad, N. Izzati Ab Ghani, Destination image differences between first-time and repeat-visit tourists: The Malaysian case J. App. Sci. **14**, 20, 2476-2486 (2014)

47. Tourism Malaysia. Tourism Malaysia Annual Report, Malaysia, Tourism Malaysia, Ministry of Tourism (2012)

48. The International Ecotourism Society, Ecotourism Reports, (2012)

9

An Influence of Outdoor Recreation Participants' Perceived Restorative Environment on Wellness Effect, Satisfaction and Loyalty

Jin-OK Kim[1], Jin-Eui Lee[2], Nam-Jo Kim[3]

[1,2,3]Division of Tourism, Hanyang University, 222 Wangsimni-ro, Seongdong-gu, Seoul 133-791, South Korea

Abstract. During recent years in Korea, the participants in outdoor recreation have significantly increased, and relevant industries have also shown a great growth. This phenomenon is to pursue outdoor recreation based on nature as a way of maintaining healthy lifestyle. This study aimed to explore how perceived restorative environment influences wellness, satisfaction, and loyalty by researching climbers in the National Park. The data were collected at four times only on weekends from 12th July to 20th July 2014 at the entrance of Mt. Dobong in Mt. Bukhand National Park in Seoul. Researchers selected every 5th visitors with systematic sampling. Out of 420 collected questionnaires, except from 20 questionnaires which include unanswered items, 400 questionnaires were used for empirical analysis. The result of the analysis by using SEM shows that perceived restorative environment has a critical influence on wellness, and this wellness also affects satisfaction and loyalty. This result of the research provides a useful insight into how policy makers and practitioners in the National Parks, urban parks and Ministry of Health and Welfare develop the places for outdoor recreation based on nature in order to pursue wellness as a way of the improvement of the public health.

1 Introduction

As outdoor recreation has been recently booming in Korea, the extraordinary growth in outdoor industry is perceived as an unprecedented phenomenon which cannot be found in any other places in the world. This attributes to the increase of leisure time due to 40 hours of working time per week, a raise of pay, and the growth of interests in health and wellbeing. The contemporary population who resides in urban areas tends to pursue wellness through outdoor recreation based on nature in order to relieve work-related stress and tensions due to the urban environment.

Wellness pursues not only physical health but also emotional, physical, intellectual, social, occupational, and spiritual wellness [1], and the ultimate aim of this wellness is balanced happiness of life [13]. The study on the relationship between nature-based activities and psychological health has been actively conducted worldwide to find the causes and effects resulted from outdoor reareation activities pursuing wellness. They are mainly the study on the effect on health restoration through experimental methods such as restoration experience based on restorative environment perception [6], the gap between nature environment and urban environment [12], the study that proves the effect through physical measurement as well as psychological measurement as a result of the development of science [11], the degree of satisfaction of wellness tourism [17]. In reality, though, there is lack of the research on the correlation between multi-dimensional wellness and perceived restorative environment on nature-based outdoor recreation which people in the contemporary world generally pursue in their daily lives.

2 Literature Review

Restorative environment is a main concept of Attention Restoration Theory and the environment that does not require directed attention but restore fatigue and energy [16]. The feature of restoration environment in attention restoration can be measured in four perspectives including 'being-away', 'fascination', 'coherence', and 'compatibility' [15]. Compatibility refers to the quality that environmental condition is equated to purposes and character the person requested. It should be easy to move from the place the direction that one prefers.

Wellness is not new one in public health and medical history but started as a way of expression to escape from a pain of disease for a holy purpose and the notion of wellness has a meaning of more than the absence of disease [9]. Since then, many scholars have defined the core notion of wellness not as simply absence of disease but as pursuit of more than that [5]. This wellness is a process of achieving wellbeing [7] and can be explained as an individual's positive health condition such as the quality of life and wellbeing in a multidimensional state [3]. Therefore, the purpose of wellness is health, physical training, the quality of life, the balance of happiness, tension-relief and stress-ease [13].

Many studies show that people tend to better recover in natural environment than green environment in urban environment [4].

Hypothesis 1: Perceived restorative environment will have a critical influence on mental wellness.
Hypothesis 2: Perceived restorative environment will have a critical influence on emotional wellness.
Hypothesis 3: Perceived restorative environment will have a critical influence on social wellness.

Customers' satisfaction is very important, and as satisfaction in tourism industry can determine a company's survival or failure, the perception on customers' satisfaction is always crucial [14]. In previous research, wellness was found to have a positive effect on satisfaction [17]. Therefore, this study has established the hypothesis that wellness pursuit in natural environments will affect satisfaction of nature-based outdoor recreation as follows:

Hypothesis 4: Mental wellness will have a beneficial effect on satisfaction.
Hypothesis 5: Emotional wellness will have a beneficial effect on satisfaction.
Hypothesis 6: Social wellness will have a beneficial effect on satisfaction.

Loyalty is the most important variable of marketing in business [2]. The loyalty and purchase intentions have been used reciprocally in marketing and tourism [18]. Therefore, based on previous research, this study has established the hypothesis to explore how much satisfaction of outdoor recreation for health can affect in natural perceived restorative environment of nature as follows:

Hypothesis 7: Satisfaction will have a beneficial influence on loyalty.

3 Method

3.1 Measurement

This study aimed to reveal how perceived restorative environment affects wellness effect and satisfaction behavior intentions. Therefore, perceived restorative environment is divided in five different elements of Berto's simple scale. Wellness effect was based on Huttler's six areas and previous studies, and Kim (2001) created five areas of Korean wellness life style scale (KWLESS) for Korean context.

3.2 Data Collection

The data were collected at four times only on weekends from 12th July 2014 to 20th July 2014 at the entrance of Mt. Dobong in Mt. Bukhand National Park in Seoul. The place of data collection included the subway station of Mt. Dobong and bus stops, where there was the most numbers of pedestrians staying because of transportation convenience. For the systematic sampling, the researchers selected every 5th visitors for the questionnaire among mountain climbers who got out of the exit. As there was the popular time of climbing, the rate of rejection of response was high. The number of questionnaires distributed was 1,125 and 420 questionnaires were collected among them. Based on this process, the rate of response is 37.33%. Out of 420 questionnaires collected, 20 questionnaires were deleted because they include unanswered items. Finally 400 questionnaires were used for empirical analysis.

3.3 Data Analysis

SPSS 18.0 was use for the data analysis of 400 questionnaires for frequency analysis, exploratory factor analysis, and reliability analysis. Also, in this study, the two-stage testing procedure was adopted by using AMOS 18.0.

4 Results

4.1 Characteristics of Respondents

The general characteristics of respondents are shown in Table 1. The rate of the gender of respondents is similar between male and female, 49.5 and 50.5%, respectively.

Table 1. Characteristics of Respondents

Characteristics		n	%	Characteristics		n	%
Gender	Male	198	49.5%	Marital Status	Single	149	37.3%
	Female	202	50.5%		Married	246	61.5%
					Other	5	1.3%
Education	High school or less	149	37.3%	Age	Below 19	56	14.0%
	Junior College	53	13.3%		19 ~ 29	56	14.0%
	University	183	45.8%		30 ~ 39	67	16.8%
	Graduate school	15	3.8%		40 ~ 49	84	21.0%
Occupation	Professional	49	12.3%		50 ~ 59	97	24.3%
	Business	50	12.5%		Over 60	40	10.0%
	Service	49	12.3%	Monthly Household Income (US$=1,000 Won)	Less than 1 million won	74	18.5%
	Clerical	54	13.5%		1-2.99 million won	126	31.5%
	Official	19	4.8%		3-4.99 million won	129	32.3%
	House wife	50	12.5%		5-6.99 million won	43	10.8%
	Student	89	22.3%		7-8.99 million won	18	4.5%
	Unemployed	19	4.8%		Over 9 million won	10	2.5%
	Others	21	5.3%				
Total		400	100%	Total		400	100%

4.2 Measurement Model

This study used Confirmatory factor analysis to analyze structural relationships, and structure model as the two-stage testing procedure [10].

Table 2. Goodness-of-fit Indices

Model	CMIN	DF	CMIN/DF (Normed x^2)	NFI	TLI	CFI	RMSEA
Measurement Model	466.011	211	2.209	.915	.942	.951	.055
Structural Model	526.785	218	2.416	.904	.932	.941	.060
Suggested value			<3	>0.9	>0.9	>0.9	<0.08

Note. NFI: Normed Fit Index, NNFI: Non-Normed Fit Index, CFI: Comparative Fit Index, RMSEA: Root Mean Square Error of Approximation.

4.3 Confirmatory Factor Analysis

Reliability analysis was adopted in order to test reliability of a measurement model of construct.

Table 3. Results of Confirmatory Factor Analysis

Factor	Observed Variable		Convergent Validity				α
			λ	C.R.	AVE	CR	
Perceived Environmental Restorativeness	This is a place away from everyday demands where I would be able to relax and think about what interests me. (being away)		.617		.532	.850	.806
	This place is fascinating; it is large enough for me to discover and be curious about things. (Fascination)		.713	11.815			
	That is a place where the activities and the items are ordered and organized. (Coherence)		.642	9.162			
	That is a place which is very large, with no restrictions to movements; it is a world of its own. (Scope)		.610	8.435			
	In this place, it is easy to find my way, move around, and do what I like. (Compativility)		.600	8.442			
Wellness	Spiritual	Mountain climbing enhances achievement.	.703		.801	.941	.897
		Mountain climbing enhances a motivation of life.	.879	16.624			
		Mountain climbing enhances the worth of life.	.870	16.050			
		Mountain climbing enhances self-confidence.	.874	16.113			
	Emotional	Mountain climbing provides mental comfort.	.817		.743	.896	.822
		Mountain climbing eases stress.	.854	18.226			
		Mountain climbing helps positive attitude.	.687	13.694			
	Social	Mountain climbing enhances a sense of altruism.	.652		.685	.866	.803

		λ	C.R.	AVE	CR	α
	Mountain climbing enhances respect of others.	.866	13.653			
	Mountain climbing improves social relationship.	.771	11.478			
Satisfaction	Mountain climbing satisfies my expectation	.707				
	I am satisfied with my decision to visit mountain climbing	.804	17.569	.719	.885	.870
	I feel very good with mountain climbing	.815	14.598			
	Overall, I am satisfied with the mountain climbing	.816	14.585			
Loyalty	I would like to visit mountain climbing next time	.758				
	I will recommend the mountain climbing to my friends and neighbors	.821	16.386			
	I will prioritize mountain climbing over other outdoor recreation when deciding whether to activity	.657	13.019	.704	.904	.924
	I will spread positive word-of-mouth about the festival	.816	16.268			

Note. λ: Factor loading, C.R.: Critical Ratio, AVE: Average Variance Extracted, CR: Construct Reliability, α: Cronbach's Alpha.

As shown in Table 4, discriminant validity and nomological validity were analyzed by correlations of confirmatory factor analysis. There are three kinds of method in order to test discriminant validity which shows the difference among latent variables [8]. The first way is that if average variance extracted between two factors is higher than coefficient of determination (r^2), which is square of each factor's correlation coefficient, it can be said that discriminant validity between two factors is achieved. The second way is a method of using standard error which $\phi \pm 2 \times S.E.$ is lower than 1. The last way is to identify discriminant validity through the difference of x^2 between unconstrained model and constrained model. In this study, the first method was used to test discriminant validity, and as in Table 4 discriminant validity was achieved since coefficient of determination (r^2), which is square of each factor's correlation coefficient, was generally lower than average variance extracted. However, as coefficient of correlation between satisfaction and loyalty was higher than average variance extracted, discriminant validity was verified by using the second method, standard error of correlation coefficient. Correlation coefficient of satisfaction and loyalty is $[.87 \pm 2 \times .025 = .92 \sim .82]$ by applying 0.865 and 0.025, which is the standard error between two latent variables, into $[\phi \pm 2 \times S.E.]$, and discriminant validity is achieved as it does not include 1.

Table 4. Measure Correlations, Squared Correlations

Constructs	PRS	SPW	EMW	SOW	SA	LO
PRS	**.532**					
SPW	.641*** (.410)	**.801**				
EMW	.622*** (.386)	.726*** (.527)	**.743**			
SOW	.521*** (.271)	.603*** (.363)	.532*** (.283)	**.685**		
SA	.583*** (.309)	.527*** (.277)	.555*** (.308)	.432*** (.186)	**.719**	
LO	.547*** (.299)	.563*** (.316)	.551*** (.303)	.498*** (.248)	.865*** (.748)	**.704**

Note. *p<.05, **<.01, ***p<.001, The number in the parentheses indicate R Squared(r^2), Diagonal Bold text is Average Variance Extracted (AVE)

4.4 Test of Hypotheses

Research model analysis in figure 1, perceived restorative environment is a high path coefficient and is found to have a crucial influence on mental, emotional and social effect of wellness. This great effect can be proven in the result of the study that mountain climbers perceive the environment of Mt. Bukhan National Park as the best environment in wellness-pursuit. Also, it has been found that mental, emotional and social effects of wellness have a positive influence on satisfaction, and emotional effect has the greatest influence on satisfaction. This shows that people are satisfied with health-pursuit through climbing in Mt. Bukhan National Park. It is found that satisfaction of outdoor recreation climbing has a great influence on loyalty. This result shows that urban residents pursue health in natural environments, and climbers who enjoy outdoor recreation regard perceived restorative environment of Mt. Bukhand National Park as a natural environment as the optimal place for health-pursuit.

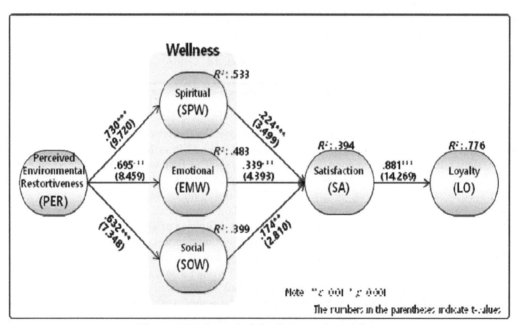

Figure 1. Estimates of the Structural Model.

5 Conclusion

The theoretical implication of this study is to explore the relationship between natural restorative environment perception and wellness with the participants in nature-based outdoor recreation based on the previous study that natural restorative environment perception has a crucial effect on restorative experience. Also, based on the result of research, the study can provide academic theoretical expansion and practical implication as follows. Perceived restorative environment in this study is found to have a great influence on spiritual, emotional and social wellness. This result means that climbers who were participated in outdoor recreation in a natural environment of National Parks have a positive perception on natural restorative environments, and therefore this perception affects wellness for health-pursuit. For the public health, in order to make people easily use nature-based National Parks, it needs to develop trails according to the features of National Parks, and build up parks of greener environment where people can enjoy nature in cities, because this can reduce stresses due to overwork and noise people in cities experience. Companies in high-floor buildings can make the roof of the building into gardens in order to ease stress due to overwork and consequently enhance efficiency in work by making natural environment.

Also, satisfaction is found to have a great effect on loyalty. This result shows that as people in the contemporary world who pursue wellness have a high degree of satisfaction through nature-based outdoor recreation, nature-based outdoor recreation needs to be conducted for actively pursuing wellness. In the time when the urban population has increased, the places where people can enjoy nature-based recreation should be built up around cities in order to ease various kinds of stress from urban life such as stress from urban environment and work-related stress. Through this effort, people can pursue wellness for a better life, and the government should prepare for the improvement of the cities' environment in a long term for the public health.

References

1. B. Hettler, *The six dimension of wellness model* (NWIN, 1976)
2. C. A. de Matos, J. L. Henrique, F. de Rosa, JSM, **27,** 526 (2013)
3. C. B. Corbin, R. P. Pangrazi, PCPFSRD (2001)
4. C. Song, H. Ikei, Y. Tsunetsugu, J. Lee, T. Kagawa, Y. Miyazaki, JGND, **3,** 1 (2013)
5. C. Voigt, J. Laing, MTTHC, 30 (2013)
6. C. Wolsko, K. Lindberg, EP, **5,** 80 (2013)
7. D. Gill, L. A. Bedini, LHW, 11 (2010)
8. F. J. Hair, W. C. Black, J. B. Babin, R. E. Anderson, *Multivariate Data Analysis* (Pearson Education, 2010)
9. H.. L. Dunn, JNMA, **49,** 255 (1957)
10. J. C. Anderson, D. W. Gerbing, PB, 103, 411 (1988)
11. L. Tyrväinen, A. Ojala, K. Korpela, T. Lanki, Y. Tsunetsugu, T. Kagawa, EP, **38,** 1 (2014)
12. M. P. White, S. Pahl, K. Ashbullby, S. Herbert, M. H. Depledge, JEP, **35,** 40 (2013)
13. M. Smith, L. Puczkó, *Health Tourism and Hospitality* (Routledge, 2014)
14. M. Uysal, J. A. Williams, *Current issues and development in hospitality and tourism satisfaction* (Routledge, 2013)
15. R. Berto, JEP, **25** (2005).
16. S. Kaplan, JEP, 1**5,** 169 (1995)
17. Y. Choi, J. Kim, C. K. Lee, B. Hickerson, APJTR, 1 (2014)
18. Y. S. Yoon, J. S. Lee, C. K. Lee, IJHM, **29,** 335 (2010)

10

Sustainable Tourism Related SMEs through Strategy Identification

Mastura Jaafar[1], Mana Khoshkam[2], Munira Mhd Rashid[3], Norziani Dahalan[4]

[1,2,3]School of Housing Building and Planning, Universiti Sains Malaysia, 11800 Penang, Malaysia
[4]School of Distance Education, Universiti Sains Malaysia, 11800 Penang, Malaysia

Abstract. It should be pointed out that expansion of tourism sector relies on micro, small and medium enterprises exist in various related region. This particular study was conducted in Lenggong Valley, Perak to assess the existing strategies in the attempt to develop sustainable tourism related SMEs. Potential businesses in the area were measured using four traditional SWOT inclusive strengths, weaknesses, opportunities, and threats. The results from observation reveal interesting findings in relation to internal and external factors evaluation of tourism related SMEs. Therefore, this study presents the strategies for development of sustainable tourism related SMEs in the Lenggong Valley, which serve the purpose of assessing the potential business of tourism related SMEs and entrepreneurs. In-depth inspection of tourism strategies are critically considered when creating public policy that benefits the area and the local community.

1 Introduction

In general, the augmentation of tourism industry is very much relies on micro, small and medium enterprises exist in various related sector. At present and in the near future, tourism industry has and will show a huge influence in Malaysia economic development. In favour for tourism to be beneficial in relations to economic development, poverty reduction, income generation and enhancing rural means of living, it should be related with the local economies activities for instance the agriculture and micro and small scale enterprises [1]. Tourism and entrepreneurial activities are complementing each other's, as the development of tourism depends on the SMEs while in the same way SMEs activities also require the help of tourism in way to grow and survive. This can be explained by the fact that tourism sector help to generate opportunities for the local community to start a business activity, while tourism sector depends on the SMEs activities to provide the tourist's needs and wants. Tourism is conservatively a small and medium- sized enterprises industry as in the point that majority of the tourist amenities are provided by the small and medium-sized businesses [2]. According to the WTO-OMT definition:

"Sustainable tourism development meets the needs of present tourists and host regions while protecting and enhancing opportunities for the future. It is envisaged as leading to management of all resources in such a way that economic, social and aesthetic needs can be fulfilled while maintaining cultural integrity, essential ecological processes, and biological diversity and life support systems."[3].

According to the National SME Development Council (NSDC) definitions, micro enterprise in services sectors, are the enterprise with full-time employees of less than 5 people, and having sales turnover less than MYR 200, 000 while a small enterprise are the enterprise with full-time employees of between 5 and 20, with the annual sales turnover of between MYR 200, 000 and less than MYR 1million. In rural areas, small-scale enterprises are normally dominating the economic scene. These enterprises reflect local resource capabilities [4];. Unlike urban tourism, rural tourism offers a market for small businesses and brings economic benefits to businesses and local development. The tourism empowerment to stimulate the development of small businesses and increases economic multipliers [5-6] enable tourism to be acknowledged as a development tool for reviving those declining traditional industries [7]. The existence of small and micro enterprise is always based on the strength of its rural areas with certain qualities symptomatic of its situation, such as natural beauty, quietness, and uniqueness[8]. Many small businesses in rural areas are established in respond to the demand for attractions in those areas [9]. Small enterprises are normally owned by families from the local community and often producing local agricultural products and cultural activities [10].

The data given by Lenggong Development Authority reported that based on 374 business premises registered, 70% of business activities include wholesale, retail trade and vehicles workshop, 16% are food and beverage service, 11% are personal services and other activities, 2% are storage of tobacco and latex (rubber-based) and 0.5% are the accommodation service [11]. Even this data does not capture the real small and micro enterprise in Lenggong; however it can be used to generally explain the profile of businesses in Lenggong Valley. The above data reflect the current situation of SMEs development in Lenggong Valley. It showed few conclusions:

1. The site has been recognised as a World Heritage Site (WHS) by the United Nations Educational, Scientific, and Cultural Organisation (UNESCO) on 30 June 2012; however the existing business does not grow in according to tourism development in Lenggong Valley.

2. Major economic sector in Lenggong Valley involve in agricultural related activity [12]. Based on survey on 500 local community, some of them already involve in small-scale business activity, however the exposure on opportunities on rural and tourism businesses have not been explored in Lenggong Valley. Thus, there is a very good business potential to be explored to address the need of the tourist.

3. The site is rich with heritage and non-heritage attraction that could be explored into archaeological and heritage tourism, eco-tourism, food, agro and culinary tourism. However, the use of local resources has not been fully utilized to reflect the uniqueness of the area.

4. Most of them are self employed and involved in business related to agricultural and fisheries. However their business cannot survive due to lack of capital and personal discouragement [12]. Sustainability of SMEs needs to be address to ensure the sustainability of the business particularly, Lenggong Valley in Malaysia.

Based on the above justifications, the purpose of this study is to evaluate existing strategies for the development of sustainable tourism related SMEs in the Lenggong Valley of Malaysia. An analysis was conducted to measure the potential business activities thorough variety of tourism related SMEs initiatives within their strengths, weaknesses, opportunities offered and potential negative threats, on the area and its entrepreneurs.

1.1 Lenggong Valley as Heritage Destination

Lenggong Valley is a popular site for its archaeological heritage and was recognised as a World Heritage Site (WHS) by the United Nations Educational, Scientific, and Cultural Organisation (UNESCO) on 30 June 2012 because of its rich archaeological heritage, showing evidence of human settlement during the Palaeolithic era and a meteorite hit Bukit Bunuh area for about 1.83 million years ago [13]. Other unique elements that contributed to the recognition of Lenggong Valley by UNESCO as a WHS include the presence of an undisturbed Palaeolithic stone tool workshop, the discovery of the australomelanesoid "Perak Man" in 1991, and a number of caves that show evidence of prehistoric burials.

Apart from the human civilization findings, Lenggong is also such an attractive place. The Valley is surrounded by the greenery of Titiwangsa Ranges and Bintang Ranges which made it as a habitat for many species of flora and fauna. Lenggong is also rich with nature attractions such as waterfalls cascade and caves. It has several beautiful waterfalls cascade such as Lata Randu and Lata Kekabu. Moreover, it is a place for almost 20 caves to be explored including the popular caves such as Gua Harimau, Gua Puteri, Gua Kajang, Gua Kelawar, Gua Teluk, Gua Asar.

Beside, Lenggong is also quite a well- known for its economic activities. The local community produces agro products such as "serunding", "dodol", preserved fishes, black paper spices, and run activities of farming cattle and goats in a small scale. It is also a home for the largest deer's far in Malaysia under the supervision of the federal government. Lenggong Valley is also recognized for its freshwater fish and fish preserved according to local tradition. These economic activities are supported by the local government by which Hulu Perak District Local Plan 2002-2015 had come out with the effort to develop a concept of 'one product one village'.

1.2 Tourism Related SMEs in Lenggong Valley

The tourism industry comprises a variety of businesses and ventures opportunities which relate to tourist experiences and activities. In general, the category of business activities in tourism into four that are food and accommodation services, retail and souvenir, travel agent, transport and sport, and others which represent other than as had been mentioned [14]. The three main potential tourism ventures identified by [15] are active recreation sites, sites of interest and accommodations. Sites of interest comprise activities such as heritage sites, arts and craft centres, zoos, small museums that usually provide education themes. Whereas active recreation sites offer active physical experiences, either through ''soft'' activities such as bicycle riding, nature walks and camping or ''challenging'' activities such as hiking, climbing and rappelling, mountain- biking and scuba. SMEs in tourism have becoming an important focus. This section will reveal internal and external factors of SMEs in Lenggong Valley.

1.2.1 Heritage attraction [16]

Archaeological tourism
Archaeological treasure
- Human skeletons (Perak Man) in Lenggong Museum
- Meteorite impact at Bukit Bunuh
. **Archaeological sites**

Heritage tourism
Historical attraction
- Cemeteries of popular people in ancient year such as, Makam Tok Lalang, Makam Tok Sendalu, Makam Tok Tan Lela Setia, Makam Tok Busu Sega
- Rumah Limas, an ancient house with the design of Johor's style
- Kubu Melayu, fortress was made during the war in the past years.
- Masjid Jamek Lenggong, an ancient mosque with the design of English style and resemble the castle in Kuala Kangsar.
- Masjid Abudiyah an ancient mosque with the design of Acheh's style

Eco tourism/agro tourism
Flora and fauna
- Malaysia's largest deer's farm
- 100 species of birds
- 20 species of fishes
- Diversity of flora and herbs

Ecotourism/Natural tourism
Natural Attraction
- Rainforest of Titiwangsa Ranges and Bintang Ranges
- Cascade waterfalls such as Lata Randu and Lata Kekabu and more.
- More than 20 caves such as Gua Harimau, Gua Puteri, Gua Kajang, Gua Kelawar, Gua Teluk, Gua Asar
- Lake Raban

1.2.2 Non- heritage attraction

Agro/food tourism
Activities of local community
- Local food such as dodol, serunding, black pepper spices
- Local traditional food such as Kekebe, Belotak and pekasam
- Food event
- Homestay activities
- Kayaking at Raban Lake

2 Methodology

The methodology of this study is based on the descriptive method and interpretation of tourism related SMEs activities in heritage and non-heritage areas in Lenggong Valley. A conceptual data collection was adapted to the SMEs activities using SWOT (strength, weakness, opportunity and threat) strategies; the SWOT outputs bring some relevant strategies in the study area. This analysis aims to identify the strengths and weaknesses of an area which is consider to the opportunities and threats in the specific sites such as the study area of this research. The result of the strategic planning method shows the strategic position and necessary actions in the rural areas with regard to the tourism related SMEs in Lenggong Valley with potential businesses opportunities which is reveal in the following statements (see Table 1).

Table 1. SWOT Matrix and Determination of Strategies

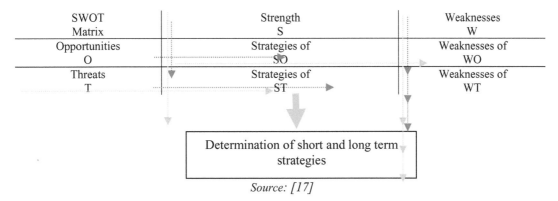

SWOT Matrix	Strength S	Weaknesses W
Opportunities O	Strategies of SO	Weaknesses of WO
Threats T	Strategies of ST	Weaknesses of WT

Determination of short and long term strategies

Source: [17]

There are four main approaches in the SWOT analysis which are applicable to the conditions of the study area. In line with our earlier observations these include:
1. ***Diversification strategy:*** proposes the use of inherent strengths to remove threats (ST).
2. ***Competitive strategy***: strengths and opportunities should be pointed out by this strategy for the creation of practical solutions (SO).
3. ***Defensive strategy:*** proposes to remove internal weaknesses and to avoid threats (WT).
4. ***Invasive strategy***: proposes to remove weaknesses and to use opportunities (WO)[18].

Therefore, the following statements are accurate about the strategies which are except the result of the SWOT analysis of the internal and external factors related to strategies which are evaluate the tourism related SMEs in Lenggong Valley.

3 Results and Discussion

To evaluate the objectives, strategies, and policies which are revealed in the internal and external factors in current analysis, the research has been explored the strengths, weakness, opportunities, and threats of tourism related SMEs in Lenggong Valley.

Table 2. Internal factors evaluation of tourism related SMEs in Lenggong Valley

Strengths	Weaknesses
1. Majority of the local population are self employed and easy to establish business 2. Small business offers ownership, independent decision making, small amount of capital, small risk and easy to manage. 3.Strong tie with family and friends to support business 4.Produce production in small volume which easy to innovate and is suitable for tourism sector such as craftsmanship/handy craft 5.Knowledge of producing traditional product from local resources	1. Lifestyle entrepreneur with lack of entrepreneurial skill and have non-economic goals. 2.Tied with their traditional culture such as involvement in agricultural and fisheries 3. Small size offers high tendency for discontinuity 4. Diseconomies of scale, limited capital, lack of means to growth 5. Limited opportunities, limited information, and limited staff 6.Limited knowledge in running business/IT 7.Limited support/motivation 8. Lack of resources especially fish in producing dried fish such as fish. 9.Lack of involvement in association

Table 3. External factors evaluation of tourism related SMEs in Lenggong Valley

Opportunities	Threats
1. Increasing of tourist due to UNESCO Archaeological site status 2. Many potential activities such as cultural, heritage, rural, education, food production business gained high recognition with export business to Brunei and Singapore. 3. Many supporting sectors especially series can be explored such as IT, transportation and accommodation 4. Many unique resources can be used as a source to process such as man power and raw material thus opportunity for product innovation is high 5. Many local agencies involves in preparing for the training and capital Amanah Iktiar, MARA and TEKUN. 6. Strong networking and back up-village community 7. Lenggong Valley is planned to be one of the targeted rural development area in Perak 8.Level of competition is low	1. Lack of accessibility to information and knowledge 2. Difficulties accessing financial resources/Lack of capital/ the amount of loan is small. 3. Lack of accessibility to investment (technology equipment and know-how) 4. Non-conformity of standardization 5.Lack of quality awareness and lack of mutual recognition schemes 6. Lack of opportunity recognition 7. Lack of monitoring on business sustainability

3.1 *TOWS Matrix*

TOWS Matrix (threat, opportunity, weakness and strength) illustrates how external opportunities and threats in front of an exacting situation can be coordinated with the internal strengths and weaknesses, to result in four sets of possible strategic alternatives [19]. Accordingly, the variation of the SWOT analysis and TOWS matrix is in Table 4.

Table 4. TOWS Matrix

Competitive strategies on the basis of strength points and opportunities (**SO**)	**Invasive** strategies on the basis of the strength points and opportunities (**WO**)
- Majority of the local population are self employed and easy to establish business to cater the increasing number of tourist due to UNESCO Archaeological site status (S1, O1) - Increase and establish business can supporting many other sectors or activities especially related to tourism such as IT, transportation and accommodation and provide work opportunities (S1, O2, O3) - Provide information and training from local agencies help to increase small business ownership, independent decision making, amount of capital and sustainability (S2, O4) - Increase number of small business ownership is one of the targeted rural development under New Economic Model and improve the level of competition which is low (S2, O5) - Existing knowledge embedded in local people and the avaibility of resources can be explored to produce Lenggong specific products for tourist (S5,O3,O6)	- There should be an initiative to inculcate business culture among the local community including increasing their involvement in association(W1,O4,O5) - The experts can train to product food business that can gained high recognition with export business to Brunei and Singapore (W1, W2,W3,W4,O4,O5) - Collective experience of a number of experts can make availability of manpower (W1, W2,W3,W4,O3,O4) - Local people should be involves for training and other activities such as as cultural, heritage, rural, education etc.(W5,O2,O3)
Diversification strategies on the basis of the strength points and threats (**ST**)	**Defensive** the strategies on the basis of the weak points and threats (**WT**)
- Point out special strong tie with family and friends to support business and sustainability(S3 , T4,T5) - State policies and guidelines should be drawn production in small volume which easy to innovate and is suitable for tourism sector (S4, T5) - Various local and federal agencies should support the development of small scale business to increase their business sustainability (S2,T1,T2,T3,T4,T5)	- Action should be taken to reduce the lack of opportunity recognition and limit information and limited staff (W3,W4,T5)

Above statements as strategies are reasons to implement the ideal position in the Lenngong Valley to develop tourism related SMEs in this area.

4 Conclusion

This study has explored on the SWOT analysis of SMEs in tourism related business in Lenggong Valley. Lenggong Valley as a new emerging and developing tourism sites will have to empower their SMEs to support the development. Synonyms with tourism, among the popular business activities need to cover are accommodation, food and craft, transport and hotel businesses. Having a rural site and agricultural as a main economic activities provide natural resources for third level development of economic activity. Lenggong Valley is an interesting example of new developing world rural tourism sites in Peninsular Malaysia.

SWOT analysis performed to assess the potential business of tourism related SMEs which are initiatives on the area with entrepreneurs and managers. Careful inspection of tourism strategies are critically considered when creating public policy that benefits the area and the local community. Thus, opportunities and threats in the case of sustainable SMEs tourism development in Lenggong were identified and evaluated by SWOT analysis. Sustainable SMEs tourism infrastructure can be making in the area to fulfil tourists needs and desire and attracts more tourists to make more business in the area. This development in the region will defiantly change local residents' life condition and bring satisfaction to them due to its job creation and income making.

Therefore, an integrated plan in relation to country rural planning and management are needed for the development of Lenggong Valley tourism by focusing on involvement of local community to sustain the development programme and overcome the impacts of tourism.

5 Acknowledgement

The authors would like to extend their appreciation to the Universiti Sains Malaysia (USM) for the research grant entitled (Heritage Awareness and Interpretation) [Grant No 1001/PTS/8660012] that makes this study possible.

Reference

1) P.M. Mshenga & G. Owuor. Opportunities for Micro and Small Scale Businesses in the Tourism Sector: The Case of The Kenya Coast. *KCA Journal of Business Management*, **2**,2, 52- 56 (2009)

2) C. Avcikurt. Auditing managerial training needs of Turkish small and medium-sized hotel enterprises. Managerial Auditing Journal, **18**,5, 399-404 (2003)

3) L. Cernat & J. Gourdon. Paths to success: Benchmarking cross-country Sustainable Tourism. *Tourism Management*, **33**, 1044–1056 (2012)

4) B. Lane. What is rural tourism? Journal of Sustainable Tourism, **2**,1-2, 7-21 (1994)

5) L.M. Campbell. Ecotourism in rural developing communities. Annals of Tourism Research, **26**,3, 534-553 (1999)

6) C. Wild, C. P. Cooper & A. Lockwood. Issues in ecotourism. Progress in tourism, recreation and hospitality management. **6**, 12-21 (1994)

7) R. MacDonald & L. Jolliffe. Cultural rural tourism: Evidence from Canada. Annals of Tourism Research, **30**,2, 307-322 (2003)

8) F. Brown & D. Hall. Case studies of tourism in peripheral areas. Research Center of Bornholm, Bornholm (1999)

9) W. Irvine & A.R. Anderson. Small tourist firms in rural areas: agility, vulnerability and survival in the face of crisis. International Journal of Entrepreneurial Behaviour & Research, **10**,4, 229-246 (2004)

10) D.D. Dimitrovski, A.T. Todorović & A.D. Valjarević. Rural Tourism and Regional Development: Case Study of Development of Rural Tourism in the Region of Gruţa, Serbia. *Procedia Environmental Sciences,* **14**, 288-297 (2012)

11) *List of Business Licensing Code for January-February 2012.* Lenggong District Councils Perak, Malaysia (2012)

12) M. Jaafar, N. Dahalan & S.A Mohd Rosdi (2014). Local community entrepreneurship: A case study of the Lenggong Valley. *Asian Social Science*, **10**,10,(2014)

13) Ministry of Information, Communication and Culture. Department of National Heritage. Archaeological Heritage of the Lenggong Valley. Nomination Dossier for Inscription on the UNESCO World Heritage List. Malaysia (2011)

14) P. Othman & M.Rosli (2011). The Impact of Tourism on Small Business Performance: Empirical Evidence from Malaysian Islands. International Journal of Business and Social Science; **2**,1, (2011)

15) S. Haber & A. Reichel. Identifying Performance Measures of Small Ventures—The case of the tourism industry. Journal of Small Business Management, **43**,3, 257–286 (2005)

16) F. Hassan, M. Rindam, N. Abdul Hamid, Z. Zakaria & F.H. Yahya. Peningkatan Daya Saing Tempat Berdasarkan Keunikan dan Kekuatan Elemen-elemen Setempat: Kajian Kes Lembah Lenggong. In Z. Zakaria (Ed.), Proceedings of Seminar Kajian Pelancongan Tentang Kesedaran Warisan & Interpretasi: Kes di Lembah Lenggong Perak (pp. 1-18). Penang: Universiti Sains Malaysia (2012)

17) R. Eftekhari & A. Mahdavi. Rural tourism development strategies using SWOT analysis; small Lavasanat Village. Journal of Agricultural Science. **10**,2, 1-30 (2006)

18) J. Nouri, A. Karbassi & S.Mirkia. *Environmental management of coastal regions in the Caspian Sea. International Journal of Environmental Science and Technology,* **5**,1, 43-52 (2008)

19) T.L. Wheelen & D.J. Hunger. *"Concepts in Strategic Management and Business Policy"*, Pearson Education, New Delhi, 110-114 (2004)

11

Medical Tourism Destination SWOT Analysis: A Case Study of Malaysia, Thailand, Singapore and India

Kee Mun Wong[1] , Peramarajan Velasamy[2], Tengku Nuraina Tengku Arshad[3]

[1]School of Business and Accountancy, University of Malaya, 50603 Kuala Lumpur, Malaysia
[2,3]Research and Informatics Department, Malaysia Healthcare Travel Council, 59000 Kuala Lumpur, Malaysia

Abstract. The growth of global medical tourism in the recent years had spurred the interest of many governments to join in the bandwagon, particularly from Asia. Using the SWOT analytical model, this paper provides pertinent comparative analysis of the medical tourism destinations here being Malaysia, Thailand, Singapore and India. Each destination possesses its own value propositions to convince the demands of medical tourists. Malaysia and Thailand have a good mixture of elements (medical, tourism and wellness) to be an excellent medical tourism destination while Singapore and India need further development in some of these elements. Meeting or exceeding the medical tourists' expectations and requirements are the priority of medical tourism destination marketers in ensuring a successful medical tourism industry development.

1 Introduction

The global flow of patients across borders has changed the patterns of demand and supply of healthcare services over the recent decades [1]. This phenomenon is often described as medical tourism or medical travel. The global medical tourism industry is forecasted to generate a revenue between USD 38 to USD 55 billion [2] annually. While the definition of medical tourism is frequently contested by scholars and medical tourism enthusiasts, Musa et al. (p. 630) defined precisely the phenomenon as "All the activities related to travel and hosting a tourist who stays at least one night at the destination region, for the purpose of maintaining, improving or restoring health through medical intervention" [3]. The medical intervention may cover a wide range of medical services such as dental, cosmetic, fertility and elective procedures. The movement of these services further accelerates the trade liberalisation in health services [1].

Medical tourists are motivated to seek healthcare outside their area of residence by many factors, including cost, time, regulation, medical preferences and availability, quality, leisure tourism and information availability [4]. Hospitality and tourism companies, as well as local governments and destination marketers, are positioning themselves to capture share in the global medical tourism market [5]. In Asia, the main players include Malaysia, Thailand, India and Singapore, where these destinations are expected to control at least 80% of the Asian market share by 2015 [6]. However, the existing literatures offer little direct comparison between these destinations, thus the competitiveness of each destination remains unclear. Hence, the objective of this paper is to provide a descriptive, yet meaningful comparison of the four medical tourism destinations: Malaysia, Singapore, Thailand and India, through the use of SWOT analysis.

SWOT analysis is an analytical model that considers and determines the external environmental issues (opportunities and threats) along with internal issues of the examined organisation (strengths and weaknesses), so it allocates the proper strategy on considered situations. To perform the SWOT analysis, we have gathered information and relevant findings from the secondary data published in various research journals, articles, leading newspapers, websites and government reports. The strengths and weaknesses of each medical tourism destination will be first discussed before the opportunities and threats of medical tourism in the region is highlighted.

2 Malaysia Medical Tourism

Malaysia has been reputed as one of the preferred medical tourism destinations by its modern private healthcare facilities and highly efficient medical professionals [7]. The nation's 2020 medical tourism target is to hit RM 9.6 billion (approximately USD 3.2 billion) in revenue from 1.9 million foreign patients [8]. In determining to achieve this target, the Malaysian government had initiated the establishment of Malaysia Healthcare Travel Council (MHTC) within the Ministry of Health since 2009. Malaysia received 770,134 foreign patients in 2013, generating USD 216 million (approximately RM 690 million) in revenue [2]. As a Muslim country, Malaysia has all it takes to attract medical tourists from the Middle East and North Africa (MENA) nations whilst currently attracting the highest number of foreign patients from Indonesia [2, 4].

MHTC nurtures active Public-Private Partnership (PPP) through its local and overseas promotional activities (e.g. trade shows, networking sessions, packaging workshops, health talks, familiarisation tours, etc), and by bringing in relevant stakeholders to work together to promote medical tourism through packaging [9]. A dedicated medical tourism website, a call centre, medical tourism concierges and lounges at international airports and overseas representative offices have been established to provide relevant information and value-added services (e.g. hospital appointments, handling medical enquiries, tourism recommendations, etc) to potential medical tourists.

The Malaysian government provides flexible ease of entry for foreign patients entering Malaysia for treatment where visa for medical tourists are extended if needed, from 30 days to 90 days. The facility also allows four accompanying persons to travel with the patient under the same visa conditions [10]. Permits issued by the Commercial Vehicle Licensing Board allow the ministry recognised hospitals to ferry patients to and from the airport and hospital or hotel [11], further enhancing the logistics experience of the medical tourists in Malaysia. Among the popular advanced treatments offered in Malaysia for foreign patients are cardiac procedures, orthopaedic, cancer treatment, fertility treatment, cosmetic surgery and general health screenings. In addition, Malaysia also offers traditional and complimentary medicine (TCM) as alternative medical treatments [4].

Affordable cost, less waiting time, relative political stability, minimal language barrier and various tourism attractions lend Malaysia a distinct comparative advantage [4, 12]. In addition, private healthcare facilities in Malaysia are also driven to attain international accreditation. To date, there are 13 healthcare facilities which had obtained the Joint Commission International (JCI) accreditation [13], where ten of them had also obtained the Malaysian Society for Quality in Health (MSQH) accreditation [14]. While Malaysia is a strong contender in the regional medical tourism scene, it is reported that the country is failing to attract high spending patients as compared to Thailand and Singapore [2]. One contributing factor may be that the Malaysian medical professional's capability may be less convincing to medical tourists as the information about their professionalism is scarce and difficult to locate on the internet.

3 Thailand Medical Tourism

International tourists are flocking to Thailand for its unique Thai hospitality, exotic beaches, entertainment opportunities and medical treatments. In fact, the Thai medical tourism started since the 1970s [4]. Thailand reported to have received about 2.53 million medical tourists, generating a revenue of between THB 121 to 140 billion (approximately USD 4 to 4.6 billion) in 2012 [15]. Even though the statistics are reported to include wellness and spa receipts [2], Thailand is still known as a medical tourism leader globally. While the majority of the medical tourists in Thailand are Japanese, Americans, Britons, Middle Easterns and Australians [15], Chantal and Siripen [16] estimated that about 35% of the medical tourism receipts is contributed by patients from South East Asian nations. Medical tourists to Thailand can generally enter the country quite easily. Visa on arrival is available for most nationalities. Medical tourists are able to apply for a non-immigrant visa for medical reasons, which grants them 90 days of stay in the country. To lure the medical tourists from the Middle East, Thailand has offered a 90 days visa free stay since 2013 [17].

Besides cosmetic surgery [18], dental treatment is also the most popular treatment among the foreign patients in Thailand [4]. In addition, a number of medical facilities in Thailand offer fringe medical procedures (e.g. gender reassignment) [19] which may not be available elsewhere in the region. Thailand also provides integrated wellness centres and facilities, including the Thai massage, spa, wellness activities and restorative activities [20]. Thai hospitals are among the first in Asia to be internationally accredited. To date, there are 37 hospitals accredited by JCI in Thailand [13], where a majority of them are located in Bangkok [4]. While medical tourists appreciate Thailand's excellent service experience, most of them face language barriers during their stay in Thailand. To overcome the issue, Thai hospitals hire multilingual speaking staffs (e.g. English, Arabic, Japanese, etc). The doctors in Thailand are trained in reference to western training and certification, mostly in the United States or United Kingdom [18]. Similar to other destinations, foreign medical professionals with recognised qualifications are allowed to practice in Thailand, but they are required to pass an examination in Thai language [16]. The stringent requirement sets a barrier for foreign medical professionals to obtain a practicing license from the relevant authorities (e.g. Thai Medical Council, other professional councils).

Historically, Thailand medical tourism is much promoted overseas by independent high-profile private hospitals (e.g. Bumrungrad International Hospital, Bangkok Hospital, Samitivej Hospital). The Tourism Authority of Thailand (TAT) is also currently promoting Thai healthcare services actively by creating worldwide awareness through e-marketing and media campaigns [4]. Familiarisation tours are organised for international media and potential buyers. However, the recent political instability dampened much of its promotional efforts.

4 Singapore Medical Tourism

Singapore is a city-state with a small population, hence enabling it to be more decisive in implementing the privatisation of healthcare financing and corporatisation of healthcare provision. While the Singapore government targets to bring in 1 million medical tourists, the statistics reported by the Singapore Tourism Board (850,000) in 2012 has been critically evaluated by medical tourism enthusiasts. IMTJ argued that the numbers are inclusive of accompanying family members and local expatriates, hence, the actual number of medical tourists to Singapore perhaps is only about 200,000, of which 47% of them are from Indonesia and 12% are from Malaysia [21].

Similar to Malaysia, the Ministry of Health Singapore had established Singapore Medicine, a government-industry partnership, in 2003. Its objectives are to enhance the medical tourism industry and to strengthen its image as the leading medical hub in Asia [4]. However, the Singaporean government had not indicated its support on medical hub policy explicitly. In fact, the support for medical tourism has become unnoticeable in the recent years, perhaps due to potentially conflicting goals of trade and health policies that may spark controversial public opinions [16].

Singapore's medical tourism strategies are built on its high quality medical care, trustworthy and internationally accredited hospitals [4]. With 21 JCI accredited hospitals [13], Singapore endeavours to provide top notch healthcare delivery system and facilities to its citizens, hence, possessing some of the most advanced diagnosis equipment available in the market [22]. English is widely spoken, clean and safe environment and a stable political scene attract tourists to Singapore [23]. In Singapore, foreign doctors made up more than half of the 836 new doctors in the year 2011 and its stated that more than one in three doctors in the public sector is a foreigner [24]. While this may benefit the international patient market, over reliance on foreign doctors may be a threat to the country when the doctors return to their home countries or shift elsewhere due to social and/or economic reasons.

Singapore's positioning on high end complex quality healthcare [25] eventually weakens its price competitiveness in the region (refer Table 1). Besides, while most medical tourism destinations actively promote and position itself in the much contested medical tourism market, Singapore is somehow lacking in its efforts to further expand its medical tourism industry [25]. In addition, the shortage of beds in public hospitals continues to be a problem for Singapore [24] which causes its citizens to question the emphasis of the government on medical tourism over public health equity.

5 India Medical Tourism

India has emerged as one of the world's most cost efficient and fastest growing medical tourism destinations today [26]. The uniqueness of India is its ability to offer holistic medical services such as unani, yoga, meditation, ayurveda, and homeopathic treatments [4, 26]. Despite the advantage of having low medical costs (refer Table 1), the Indian government is taking a different approach in promoting its medical tourism industry by highlighting its wellness elements.

The Indian Ministry of Tourism is actively promoting medical tourism through overseas roadshows where market development assistance (MDA) is provided to medical and wellness tourism service providers to encourage overseas promotion. The government had introduced medical visa to govern medical tourism [26]. In order to further expand the healthcare system and enhance its quality, the government also actively provides incentives and giving special approvals to foreign firms for direct investments. Vice versa, some of its large hospital groups (i.e. Apollo Hospitals, Fortis Healthcare) are expanding overseas, creating a strong global brand name and building referral opportunities. Among the most popular sought after treatments by the medical tourists in India are cardiac surgery, orthopaedic, dental care, cosmetic surgeries, organ transplant and surrogacy [27], where the latter two may not be easily available in other destinations. The Indian Ministry of Tourism reported that 171,021 foreign tourists visited India for medical purpose in 2012, an increase of about 23% from the previous year. Most of the medical tourists are from South Asia, Africa and Middle East [28]. While a majority of them prefer India due to the low cost factor, the destination also offers less waiting time in the hospital, personalised services, medical specialisation and highly trained doctors [4, 29]. As a world-renowned medical study destination, India produces more than 30,000 medical graduates annually [4]. India has 21 JCI accredited hospitals [13] where the majority of them are situated within the cities of New Delhi and Mumbai [4].

Despite the growth of medical tourism, the infrastructure system (e.g. flight connectivity, roads, public transport) and general hygiene conditions in India are still lacking far behind by the Western standards [30, 31]. Foreign patients are reported to have less trust of Indian hospitals, particularly when there is a lack of uniform pricing policies and standards across hospitals [30]. The recent rape cases of foreign tourists and increasing crime rates in India further tarnished its tourism destination image [32]. The negative image may cause medical tourists to practice extra cautions before deciding to seek treatment in India.

6 Opportunities and Threats of Medical Tourism in the Region

The global healthcare spending is expected to escalate by 5.3% from 2014 to 2017 and account for an average of above 10% of gross domestic product (GDP) [33]. Healthcare is the second highest government spending among the developed nations (i.e. 17.4% of GDP in the United States (US), 10.7% of GDP in Western Europe) [33]. The rising medical costs eventually drive the people from the developed nations (e.g. the US, United Kingdom, Australia) to seek treatment overseas, particularly for treatments which are not covered by their insurance (e.g. eye, dental, cosmetic and fertility treatment). Although the current ex-change rate of Asian currencies is least favourable as compared to the late 90s, a comparison of a few popular treatment costs between the US and the Asian medical tourism destinations still indicates a cost savings of between 40% to 95% (refer Table 1). The medical tourism insurance policy offered by insurance firms in the US and Australia further ensure medical tourists have peace of mind when seeking treatment overseas [34, 35].

Treatments that require long waiting periods (e.g. open heart surgery, joint replacement, cancer treatment) or treatments that are simply not available in their home countries (e.g. surrogacy, organ transplant, stem cell therapy) is also a motivating factor for them to go overseas [4]. The rising role of medical travel facilitators and second home retirement tourism in Asia further support the surge of cross-border healthcare services demand [36, 37]. These factors create opportunities for the Asian medical tourism destinations to take advantage of. In the perspective of healthcare excellence in medical tourism, Malaysia and India seem to excel better as several of their healthcare facilities had won international medical tourism awards introduced by the MTQUA and IMTJ recently [38, 39].

Table 1. Average Medical Cost Comparison (in USD).

Treatment	United States	Malaysia	Thailand	Singapore	India
Heart Bypass (CABG)	136,000	14,000	13,000	23,000	7,000
Angioplasty	57,000	8,750	3,800	27,750	3,300
Knee Replacement	45,000	10,900	11,400	16,700	6,800
Gastric Bypass	33,000	8,600	16,700	20,000	5,500

Source: Authors, August 2014, compiled from healthcare providers, medical tourism providers and online resources

Postoperative complications and aftercare at the patient's country of residence remain a major deterrent of medical tourism [40, 41]. Besides, the recent political instability and surrogacy scandal in Thailand, the aviation disasters in Malaysia and the rising crime rate in India further impact the tourism sector of these countries. While it is a threat to these countries, it is also an opportunity for others in luring medical tourists from these competing destinations. The imposing of Indian medical visa and the lack of Singapore government's interest in further promoting medical tourism globally is also seen as an opportunity by other regional players. As the medical tourism industry continues to develop in Asia, several ethical issues were raised. Illegal organ trades have been reported in India, while gender reassignment surgery is becoming a norm in Thailand [4]. From a bioethical point of principle, under certain conditions, these surgeries and treatments are morally non-acceptable and cannot be categorised [42, 43].

While the opportunities and threats can be generalised to all destinations, certain threats can be destination specific. For example, the destination's image is affected due to political instability (in Thailand), aviation disasters (in Malaysia), lack of government focus on medical tourism (in Singapore) and increasing crime rate (in India). The comparative SWOT analysis of the medical tourism destinations is summarised in Figure 1.

7 Conclusion

Medical tourism destinations are developed mainly for economic reasons. Different destination offers unique value propositions in attracting this lucrative and growing market. Malaysia offers a value for money experience while Singapore highlights their sophisticated medical technology. India uniquely positions itself with the holistic medical services and Thailand's hospitality services are no match to its competitors in the region.

The SWOT analysis suggests that Malaysia needs further value creations in niche treatment, advanced technologies and medical excellence in order to attract high spending patients. Thailand, being the market leader, requires strong campaigns to regain its positive destination image. India should improve its infrastructure, hygienic environment and security conditions to complement its low cost advantage. Medical tourism destination marketers should put more emphasis on the integration between medical, tourism and wellness services in order to excel in medical tourism holistically. Both Malaysia and Thailand probably have all these elements and Thailand has an advantage of being well recognised internationally for decades. India needs to develop more attractive tourism products while Singapore needs to further enhance its offerings in both wellness and tourism services.

Despite limited information, this paper provides useful insights to both the academics and practitioners on the competitiveness of Asian medical tourism destinations. While low cost is one of the Asian destination's selling points, the recent currency fluctuations in the global market depreciate their cost advantage. Besides, the rise of the European, Middle Eastern and South American medical tourism destinations in recent years post direct threat to Asian destinations in luring high spending western medical tourists. Thus, the ability of Asian destinations to meet or exceed medical tourists' expectations and requirements is essential in ensuring the sustainability of its medical tourism development.

References

1. N. Lunt, R. Smith, M. Exworthy, S.T. Green, D. Horsfall, R. Mannion, *Medical Tourism: Treatments, Markets and Health System Implications: A Scoping Review*, 1-55 (OECD, 2011)
2. T. Leong, *Malaysia tries to parlay appeal to Muslim visitors into medical tourism push*, http://www.reuters.com/article/2014/07/29/us-malaysia-medical-idUSKBN0FY2AT20140729 (2014)
3. G. Musa, D..R. Doshi, K.M. Wong, T. Thirumoorthy, J Travel Tour Mark **29**, 629-646 (2012)
4. K.M. Wong, G. Musa, *Medical Tourism: The Ethics, Regulation and Marketing of Health Mobility*, 167-186 (2012)
5. K. Wendt, UNLV Theses/Dissertations/Professional Papers/Capstones. Paper 1483, (2012)
6. Renub Research, *Asia Medical Tourism Analysis and Forecast to 2015*, http://www.reuters.com/article/2012/10/23/idUS80088+23-Oct-2012+BW20121023 (2012)
7. B.J. Shah, *An Insight into Malaysia's Medical Tourism Industry from a New Entrant Perspective*, http://www.valuenetworksandcollaboration.com/images/bhavinshahmba-medicaltourismindustrymalaysia.pdf (2008)
8. Pemandu, *Creating wealth through excellence in healthcare*, http://www.moh.gov.my/images/gallery/ETP/NKEA%20Penjagaan%20Kesihatan.pdf (2010)
9. Health and Care Bureau, *Malaysia was once known as the "Hidden Jewel in Healthcare"*, http://healthandcare.in/malaysia-was-once-known-as-the-hidden-jewel-in-healthcare/ (2013)
10. M.K. Yuen, *Malaysia competes in medical tourism*, http://www.ttrweekly.com/site/2013/06/malaysia-competes-in-medical-tourism/ (2009a)
11. M.K. Yuen, *Malaysia's visa change is a boost for healthcare tourism*, http://www.eturbonews.com/13394/malaysias-visa-change-boost-healthcare-tourism (2009b)
12. IMTJ, *MALAYSIA: Malaysia can be medical tourism hub*, http://www.imtj.com/news/?EntryId82=152011 (2009)

13. JCI, *JCI-Accredited Organizations,* http://www.jointcommissioninternational.org/about-jci/jci-accredited-organizations/ (2013)

14. MSQH, *List of Hospital With Current Accreditation Status,* http://www.msqh.com.my/msqh/ct-menu-item-19/ct-menu-item-21/ct-menu-item-33 (2014)

15. MyMEDHoliday, *Thailand's Medical Tourism Statistics: a Look at the International Patient Numbers,* http://www.mymedholiday.com/blog/2013/10/793/thailands-medical-tourism-statistics-a-look-at-the-international-patient-numbers/ (2013)

16. H. Chantal, S. Siripen, *Medical Tourism in Malaysia, Singapore and Thailand,* https://editorialexpress.com/cgi-bin/conference/download.cgi?db_name=SERC2013&paper_id=230 (2014)

17. MyMEDHoliday, *Thailand Visa Requirement for Medical Tourists,* http://www.mymedholiday.com/country/thailand/article/177/thailand-visa-requirements-for-medical-tourists (2014)

18. A. Wilson, Body Soc **17**, 121-137 (2011)

19. I. Olson, *Fringe Medical Practices in Thailand,* http://www.thailawforum.com/laws/medical-practices-thailand-stem-cell-cloning-cancer-sex-change.pdf (2010)

20. Thailandmedicaltourismcluster.org, *What Makes Thailand A Prime Medical Destination,* http://www.thailandmedicaltourismcluster.org/AboutMedicalTourism/WhyThailandNo1inMedicalDestination/WhatmakesThailandaprimemedicaldestination.aspx (2010)

21. IMTJ, *SINGAPORE: Singapore medical tourism is recovering,* http://www.imtj.com/news/?entryid82=413890 (2013)

22. AsiaOneYourHealth, *Singapore: At the forefront of medical tourism,* http://yourhealth.asiaone.com/content/singapore-forefront-medical-tourism (2014)

23. B.S.A. Yeoh, E.S. Tan, J. Wang, T. Wong, *Tourism Management Policy* (World Scientific, 2002)

24. Singapore General Hospital, *Shortage of hospital beds, so some ops delayed,* http://www.sgh.com.sg/about-us/newsroom/News-Articles-Reports/Pages/Shortageofhospitalbeds,sosomeopsdelayed.aspx (2013)

25. J. Rerkrujipimol, I. Assenov, J Tour Hosp Culinary Arts **3**, 95-105 (2011)

26. L. Singh, African J Hosp Tour Lei **3**, 1-11 (2014)

27. N. Swamy, *The Preferred Destination,* http://indiatoday.intoday.in/story/world-class-treatment-and-cheaper-deals-medical-assistance/1/347252.html (2014)

28. Ministry of Tourism India, *India Tourism Statistics 2012,* (Market Research Division, 2013)

29. Knowledge@Wharton, *Will medical tourism be India's next big industry,* http://knowledge.wharton.upenn.edu/article/healthy-business-will-medical-tourism-be-indias-next-big-industry/ (2011)

30. S.K. Dawn, S. Pal, Int J Multidiscip Res **1**, 185-202 (2011)

31. L.L. Gan, H. Song, *A SWOT Analysis of Medical Tourism: India and South Korea,* http://papers.ssrn.com/sol3/papers.cfm?abstract_id=2194856 (2012)

32. P. Rana, *Attacks on women rattle travelers to India,* http://online.wsj.com/news/articles/SB10001424052702304244904579278050017041212 (2014)

33. The Economist Intelligence Unit (EIU), *World Healthcare Outlook,* (2014)

34. S. Parnell. *Health fund NIB to offer medical tourism,* http://www.theaustralian.com.au/news/health-science/nib-health-fund-to-offer-medical-tourism/story-e6frg8y6-1226747206131 (2013)

35. MyMEDHoliday, *Medical Tourism Insurance Companies,* http://www.mymedholiday.com/providers/170/medical-tourism-insurance-companies (2014).

36. M. Ormond, R. Holliday, M. Jones, *Navigating international medical travel: A three-country study of medical travel facilitators sending patients to Malaysia* (ISA Annual Conference, Yokohama, 2014)

37. K.M. Wong, G. Musa, Tourism Manage **40**, 141-154 (2014)

38. B. Neild, *First medical tourism awards tout top treatment trips*, http://edition.cnn.com/2014/04/22/travel/medical-tourism-awards/ (2014)
39. MTQUA, *MTQUA 2013 World's Best Hospitals for Medical Tourists*, http://www.mtqua.org/providers/top-10-worlds-best-hospitals-for-medical-tourists-list/ (2013)
40. M.D. Horowitz, J.A. Rosensweig, C.A. Jones, Medscape Gen Med **9**, 33 (2007)
41. Deloitte, *Medical Tourism – Consumers in Search of Value*, 1-30 (Deloitte Center for Health Solutions, 2008)
42. M.C. Hume, Res Cogitans **2**, 37-48 (2011)
43. B. Paul, M. Valapour, D. Bartels, A. Abbott-Penny, J. Kahn, *Ethics of Organ Transplantation*, 1-48 (Center for Bioethics, 2004)

Public Tourism Infrastructure: Challenges in the Development and Maintenance Activities

Shardy Abdullah[1] , Arman Abdul Razak[2], Mastura Jaafar[3]

[1,2,3] School of Housing, Building and Planning, Universiti Sains Malaysia, 11800 Penang, Malaysia

Abstract. In Malaysia, the tourism sector is a major contributor to the nation's development and is spearheaded by the government's efforts in investing heavily towards providing sufficient and well-functioning public tourism infrastructure. This infrastructure should be ideally developed with a clear and systematic maintenance plan in hand. The challenge herein is not merely providing the necessary infrastructure to sustain tourism activities but rather a pro-active approach towards establishing and subsequently maintaining this infrastructure at its optimal level. The aim of this paper therefore is to identify critical aspects that need to be in place to further enhance the Malaysian tourism industry. The paper discusses the issues and challenges that need to be addressed as a precursor towards an effectively developed and maintained tourism infrastructure system. Development issues that have been identified revolve around the dimensions of quality, quantity and ability of the public agencies involved, particularly issues of inadequate infrastructure, quality of infrastructure and the capability of the agencies in undertaking efficient maintenance activities. These issues were found to lead towards challenges of working with resource constraints, lack of an effective maintenance culture and system as well as the need for clear and effective policies and strategies.

1 Introduction

Tourism is an important industry in many countries including Malaysia. Various studies have shown that tourism influences many things such as the quality of life, cultural development, economic growth and also infrastructure. In Malaysia, tourism industry contributes the highest revenue after oil and gas industry. In order to further develop the tourism industry, the government has spent billions ringgit to develop tourism infrastructure and facilities for tourism.

According to Grigorescu [1] public infrastructure is important for economic growth and one of the main factors of the failure to attract foreign investor is due to poor development of infrastructure. Moreover, the provision of infrastructure is one of the key factors that contribute to the increasing number of tourists.

In Malaysia, most of the developed infrastructures are funded by the government and this type of infrastructure is referred as public infrastructure. These infrastructures are referred as public infrastructures where normlally can be categorized under five groups, namely water and sanitation, telecommunications, power supply, roads, and ports.

Most of tourist destinations in Malaysia, particularly in the urban areas, have good tourism infrastructure due to the government's commitment to improve the tourism industry. According to The Saigon Times [2], Malaysia is one of the ASEAN countries with the capability to provide sufficient tourist infrastructure while Vietnam is still lagging behind. The government has always taken seriously the need to provide adequate tourism infrastructure. As an example, in the country's development plan, especially in the Seventh Malaysia Plan (7th MP) to Tenth Malaysia Plan (10th MP) a large sum of money was allocated to fund the development of tourism infrastructure in Malaysia.

As a valuable asset to the country, public tourism infrastructure should be maintained efficiently and effectively to ensure that it can be used in accordance with the original purpose of its development. The main objective of the maintenance of infrastructure is to prolong the service life of an infrastructure by delaying or minimizing the damage, obsolescence and the failure of the infrastructure to function. In addition, infrastructure is also maintained in order to protect the function, value and appearance of any asset.

Tun Abdullah Badawi, the fifth Prime Minister of Malaysia has voiced his concern on the issue of public tourism infrastructure. He stated that Malaysia has first class infrastructure but third class mentality in maintaining the available infrastructure [3]. In his speech during the NAFAM conference in Kuala Lumpur in 2007, Badawi mentioned that the government has been spending billions of ringgit to preserve public infrastructure due to poor infrastructure maintenance.

The purpose of this paper is to discuss the critical aspects that need to be addressed in order to create a positive image of Malaysia's tourism industry. Then, a discussion on the issues and challenges in maintaining public infrastructure is highlighted to serve as a catalyst to plan and implement actions to eliminate or minimize the negative impacts due to poor maintenance of public infrastructure.

2 Public tourism infrastructure in Malaysia

For tourism sector, Middleton and Hawkins [4] explained that tourism infrastructure involves a method of transporting, maintaining or preserving natural resources; construction in the natural environment; and the provision of legal services, recreational facilities and basic infrastructure such as gas, water and sewage. Tourism infrastructure can be discussed in two different contexts, namely public and private tourism infrastructure. Public infrastructure is considered as the "Economic Overhead Capital" or "Social Overhead Capital" [5].

This means that the infrastructure is one of the factors or mechanisms that influence the level of social and economic development of a country. Public tourism infrastructure is also referred to any general and basic physical asset provided by government agencies to support tourism activities at minimum or no charge (not based on profit). Typically, public tourism infrastructure consists of basic needs that serve as an initiator of a program or activity. In contrast, private tourism infrastructure is referred to the infrastructure provided or facilitated by a person or a group to generate profit.

Under normal circumstances, the government is the party responsible to provide or develop public infrastructure. This is because the development of infrastructure projects is costly and risky. In addition, the investment to develop infrastructure are not attractive due to the rate of return means long terms, do not generate profit and most of the time no income as direct forms of return [1].

In the 1970s, the Malaysian government's priority in tourism industry was to provide basic infrastructure such as highways, airports and tourism sites all over Malaysia. Government's commitment towards tourism development was shown through the increasing amount of funds being allocated in the next few years. In the Second Malaysia Plan (2nd MP), the allocated funds tourism industry including marketing and promotion stages were RM 17.2 million. Meanwhile, during the Ninth Malaysia Plan (9th MP) in 2006 to 2010, the allocation increased approximately 136% to RM 1.8 billion from the Eight Malaysia Plan (8th MP) [6].

Compare to other Southeast Asia countries, Malaysia appears to be among the top countries with first-class tourism infrastructure [7]. Malaysia's capabilities to develop tourism infrastructure should be continued in order to create a sustainable development of tourism sector. Moreover, Malaysia's popularity as a tourist destination is influenced by the ability to provide adequate tourism infrastructure. However, according to a report by World Economic Forum [8], Malaysia's achievement in tourism infrastructure is still at an intermediate stage compared to Singapore and Thailand.

Development and provision of tourism infrastructure is seen as a pre-requisite to become a popular tourist destination. An attractive tourist destination is not only relying on its natural resources, but also on its available infrastructure and facilities. tourism infrastructures are the main factor considered in choosing tourist destination. Infrastructure plays an important role in the tourism industry of an urban area as it affects the level of tourist satisfaction; and adequate and good condition of infrastructure will reduce the number of negative response received from tourists. Business Opportunities created from the development of infrastructure are also beneficial to the shareholders of tourism industry.

This is in line with the statement made by Lerner and Haber [9] as they explained that the development of infrastructure is considered as one of the key factors in developing tourism enterprise. Therefore, for the growth of tourism industry, each tourist destination must be equipped with a variety of infrastructure such as roads, airports, ports and terminals.

3 Challenge in the development and maintenance of public tourism infrastructure

The development and maintenance of tourism industry should be emphasized by researchers, academics, civil servants and also independent agencies (NGO). This is because the aspects of development and maintenance of infrastructure are interlinked with each other and both of the aspects make a huge impact on the growth of Malaysia's tourism industry. Consistent growth of the tourism sector is only possible with the provision of related infrastructure.

Hence, consistent maintenance of infrastructure is vital to preserve the functionality of infrastructure and to ensure the infrastructure remains as high value asset of the government. According to BS 3811, maintenance can be defined as all technical and administrative actions undertaken to maintain or restore the functionality of an item (physical asset). Lind and Muyingo [11] further explained that maintenance can be considered as actions taken to restore or maintain the condition of an item so it can perform a specific function as intended by the maintenance process.

In the tourism sector in Malaysia, the discussion on the maintenance of public infrastructure, specifically in the context of urban tourism, is very limited. Previous studies only discussed in the context of user's satisfaction on the available infrastructure. However, according to reports from various media and articles, there are many challenges and issues regarding the maintenance of public tourism infrastructure such as financial burden, damage that disrupts the functionality of infrastructure and the infrastructure are not being used optimally.

In terms of the development of the public tourism infrastructure, the related issues can be viewed from several dimensions which are quality, quantity and ability of an agency. The main issue that is often discussed is the quantity of the available infrastructure as it is directly related to the inadequacy of public tourism infrastructure. Typically, the government is responsible in providing various needed infrastructure.

The development of public infrastructure by the government (central, state or local government) is conducted in limited sizes and quantities; sometimes the development of the infrastructure does not meet current demand. This occurs when the development of the infrastructure takes place without understanding current market or is conducted on ad-hoc basis. Without sufficient market research, there is a possibility for insufficient development of infrastructure.

Some of the infrastructure has been built without considering the increasing demand in the future. Consequently, the infrastructure developed can only accommodate current tourists for a short period of time. The issue of inadequate tourism infrastructure is also due to the financial constraints of the government as the cost to develop an infrastructure is high. Table 1 shows the allocated funds for tourism industry in the Eight Malaysia Plan (8th MP) and 9th MP. Consequently, the government is unable to handle many development projects of infrastructure in within the same time frame. According to Meyer [12] the lack of cooperation by private agencies in developing tourism infrastructure is also one of the factors that cause the insufficiency of tourism infrastructure.

Table 1. Expenses and Provisions of Tourism Development, 2001 - 2010

Program	8th MP Expenses (RM Million)	9th MP Expenses (RM million)
	243.1	652.1
Environmental Protection and Beautification Facilities, Infrastructure and Maintenance Accommodation Other	459.4	1,034.8
	31.7	115.0
	49.4	46.0
Total	**783.6**	**1,847.9**

Source: Unit Perancang Ekonomi [11]

Private agencies are also inclined to focus on the development of profitable tourism infrastructure that can generate a profit in a short period of time. Due to this, the government has to borne the financial burden of developing public tourism infrastructure. Various responsibilities of the government have led to the development of tourism infrastructure being halted. To express the importance of private agencies to get involved in the development of tourism infrastructure, the government has established Tourism Infrastructure Fund in 2011.

The objective of this fund is to encourage the involvement of private agencies in the development of tourism infrastructure [13]. Through this, a special fund was established to enable the private sector to gain capital to fund the development of tourism infrastructure. Furthermore, rate of interest charged was reduced to 3.75 percent to reduce the burden of loans made by private agencies. In addition, inadequate infrastructure is also associated with the failure of the contractors who have been appointed by the government to build infrastructure within a given period of time. Consequently, many constructions projects are abandoned.

There is also challenge with the quality of tourism infrastructure. The main issue is the poor quality of tourism infrastructure. This occurs due to several factors such as financial constraint, ineffective monitoring by government agencies and irresponsibility of the appointed contractors. The poor quality of infrastructure will cause various problems such as premature damage, unsafe usage and problems with the functionality of the infrastructure. These problems can lead to dissatisfaction and negative reactions from tourists. This has been explained that the quality of support services (including tourism infrastructure) is one of the determining factors that influence the level of tourist satisfaction in Pulau Kapas, Terengganu [14].

The next issue of the development of tourism infrastructure is the ability of government agencies to manage the infrastructure where this situation has been mentioned by previous studies such as JBIC [15] and Vaugeois [16]. The government of Malaysia is divided into three levels, namely, federal, state and local governments. Each level of has its own department that manages the development of infrastructure in a certain region, state or province. Each agency has different size, knowledge and expertise. For large agencies, especially agencies under federal and high density state government, they are more capable in handling development projects of infrastructure. In contrast, agencies under state or local government have limited capability to handle infrastructure development projects due to financial constraint.

In the context of public infrastructure maintenance, there are various issues being discussed by researchers, academics and civil servants. The most critical issue being discussed is the lack of maintenance activities being conducted to preserved public infrastructure. Studies on the implementation of public tourism maintenance are not being emphasized. The implementation of maintenance activities has been a challenge for a long time [17]. It is often regarded as a key factor in strengthening the tourism infrastructure.

Deterioration or damage in the functionality of an infrastructure is due to the lack of proper maintenance as it causes premature deterioration of infrastructure. Generally, inadequate maintenance program can be defined as the lack of maintenance activity or program on an infrastructure or the failure to perform maintenance activities as decided during the planning stage. The development of an infrastructure must be accompanied by maintenance activities to avoid obsolescence and damage. On-going neglect of maintenance activities will lead to a severe damage of an infrastructure. However, various issues and challenges arise as different maintenance programs are needed to preserve different types of infrastructure.

The main challenge that has been highlighted from previous studies such as [15-16] on the maintenance of tourism infrastructure is resource constraint. The effectiveness and feasibility of maintenance activities depend on the available resources [17]. There are many resources that must be provided by the government to enable maintenance activities such as financial, personnel, equipment and material. Each infrastructure must be maintained properly due to a number of factors such as aging, environment, human behaviour and many other possible factors.

Thus, the increasing number of infrastructure available leads to a higher demand of maintenance activities. Consequently, government must provide more resources to support maintenance activities, especially financial resources and this will increase the financial burden of the government. However, the government is trying to cut their operating cost due to the economic downturn. In return, the implementation of maintenance of tourism infrastructure will be limited due to financial constraint as the cost to maintain tourism infrastructure is very high.

As an example, a total of RM 8.94 million was allocated for the maintenance activities of public tourism infrastructure in Segamat Johor with RM 8.83 million was used to repair roads and pavements and RM 110,000 was spent to preserve Jeram Tinggi Waterfall as the centre of recreation and tourism. From these figures, it can be concluded that the government will need to allocate a huge sum of money to maintain various tourism infrastructure in Malaysia.

Resource constraints in the maintenance of public tourism infrastructure can also be associated with an organization's capability to manage their resources. According to Alejandrino-Yap [17], governments still fail to allocate necessary funding towards maintenance activities despite having adequate resources. Failure to manage resources is often associated with incapability of maintenance staff to maintain tourism infrastructure. Without adequate skills, the process of resource management cannot be handled properly, leading to losses and wastage of resources. Furthermore, resource constraints in the maintenance of infrastructure also caused by unnecessary development of technologies related to maintenance activities. The lack of knowledge regarding the technologies involved will lead to inefficient and ineffective maintenance activities.

The lack of an effective maintenance management system is also one of the major issues in maintaining public tourism infrastructure. This is because the maintenance management process is often associated with various difficulties [15]. To ensure that all maintenance activities can be fully implemented as required in the planning stage, the management mechanism must be integrated by the maintenance team. Hence, the term of maintenance management is referred to an effective tool to carry out an effective maintenance work. The lack of management process will lead to a failure in carrying out maintenance work.

Maintenance management involves a long-term strategic planning to meet the needs of infrastructure maintenance. Through the integration of systematic management, the implementation of all maintenance activities will be based on four levels of management i.e. planning, organizing, implementing and monitoring. In addition, maintenance management enables the infrastructure to be maintained systematically as per conditions such as condition-based maintenance, time-based maintenance and performance-based maintenance. Poor maintenance management is usually due to the lack of top management support coupled with maintenance activities being conducted on an *ad hoc* basis, the absence of guidelines or specific maintenance procedures, inability of the management team and many more.

The absence of a maintenance measurement method is an issue in urban tourism. The need to evaluate maintenance programs is actually not a new concern. According to Parida and Kumar [16], factors that influence the need to evaluate maintenance programs are as value of maintenance program, investment requirements, review of resource allocation, safety, health an environment issues as well as information management. Performance measurement is vital in managing the performance of a program. A system to measure maintenance activities should be developed with clear indicators because it can be used to identify the gaps and weaknesses of a process. A system to measure the performance of a maintenance program is important to ensure the functionality and safety of an infrastructure in the long run.

Moreover, a discussion on the issues and challenges of public infrastructure maintenance in urban tourism has been linked with the lack of policies and specific maintenance strategies. According to Lee [22], the government should have a definite maintenance policy in order to develop an effective maintenance program. The maintenance policy can be also considered as an important factor in creating high quality retention programs. Maintenance policy is seen as a guideline that indicates the core mechanism of different maintenance activities. In the context of public infrastructure maintenance, maintenance policy explained the objective and method that must be considered by an organization (including government agencies) in implementing any maintenance program. Policies enacted should be able to clarify the framework of infrastructure maintenance, the method of operational management, the availability of funding for maintenance purpose and the level of priority for all maintenance activities.

Maintenance strategy is also referred as a tactic and tool used to realize the maintenance plans as well as to define the roles of the related maintenance and it is critical as it requires an understanding of the functionality of an asset; "what the assets are supposed to do and not to do, when it needs to be done and how assets interact with each other" [18]. Maintenance strategy must be adapted in a maintenance program in order to explain the maintenance approach in the development of maintenance policies. Lastly, the issue and challenge that should be discussed is the lack of maintenance culture. According to Abdullah, the money spent by the government to maintain public buildings is being wasted due to poor maintenance culture. The problem of poor maintenance due to human behaviour can be solved by adapting the concept of maintenance culture. Through this concept, people will be reminded on their role and responsibility to maintain an infrastructure. This will create awareness and ultimately lead to the culture of maintaining public infrastructure. The culture of maintenance can be regarded as an important strategy to attract voluntary participation from any interested entity to practice a good habit in maintaining infrastructure. This culture will enable the effective implementation of public tourism infrastructure.

4 Conclusion

The aim of the development of public tourism infrastructure is to attract more tourists. In developing countries like Malaysia, the government is striving to provide tourism destinations with adequate infrastructure. Infrastructure, as a man-made asset, is influenced by many factors that can lead to damage or destruction. To prolong the life and functionality of public infrastructure, good maintenance program must be implemented effectively and efficiently. Failure to practice good maintenance program will cause various problems which ultimately will affect the government's investment. This paper discussed various critical issues faced by the development and maintenance of tourism infrastructure. Even though the level of issues involved cannot be determined clearly, all parties must take the issues seriously as the loss incurred by the government is actually exhaustive and it impacts all walks of life in Malaysia.

5 Acknowledgment

This project was funded through a research grant from the Ministry of Higher Education, Malaysia under the Long-Term Research Grant Scheme 2011 [LRGS Grant No. JPT.S (BPKI) 2000/09/01/015Jld.4 (67)].

References

1. A. Grigorescua, Rev. Reg. Dev. Tourism, **4**, 1 (2006).
2. The Saigon Times. www.vietnamtravelarticle.com/articles/poor-infrastructure-impedes-vietnams-tourism (2011)
3. K. Hashim, http://utusan.com.my/utusan/info.asp?y=2008&dt=0630&pub=Utusan_Malaysia&sec=Rencana&pg=re_09.htm#ixzz2f8KsRGy5 (2008)
4. V.T.C. Middleton & R. Hawkins. *Sustainable tourism: A marketing perspective*. Butterworth & Heinemann. Oxford.(1998)
5. E.M. Bergman & D. Sun. *Infrastructure and Manufacturing Productivity: Regional Accessibility and Development Level Effects*. In Batten, D.F. & C. Kalsson (eds.). Infrastructure and the Complexity of Economic Development. Advances in Spatial Science. Springer. Berlin. 17-35 (1996).
6. Government of Malaysia. Rancangan Malaysia Kesembilan. Unit Perancang Ekonomi, Jabatan Perdana Menteri (2006)
7. J. Jusoh & B. Mohamed. Tourists Infrastructure Provision Versus Successful Destinations; Case Study: Langkawi Island. *Proceedings of 12th Asia Pacific Tourism Association & 4th Asia Pacific ChRie*. June 26-29, 2006. Hualien, Taiwan. (2006).
8. World Economic Forum. The ASEAN Travel & Tourism Competitiveness Report 2012. www.weforum.org (2012)
9. M. Lerner, S. Haber, J. of Bus. Vent. **16**, 1 (2000).
10. H. Lind & H. Muyingo, Is there anything special with building maintenance, Licentiate Thesis in Building and Real Estate Economics, Stockholm (2009)
11. Unit Perancang Ekonomi, Dokumen Rancangan Malaysia Kesembilan, www.epu.gov.my (2006)
12. D. Meyer http://www.researchgate.net/profile/Dorothea_Meyer/publication/242371864_Key_issues_for_the_development_of_tourism_routes_and_gateways_and_their_potential_for_Pro-Poor_Tourism/links/0046352d83f1db7cd1000000?origin=publication_detail (2004)
13. Department of Information. http://pmr.penerangan.gov.my/index.php/sosial/742--tabung-infrastruktur- pelancongan (2008).
14. Z.A. Nasir & F. Kari. Determinant Factors and Tourist Satisfaction Towards Pulau Kapas Tourism Destination. *Prosiding PERKEM VI*, **1** (2011).

15. JBIC.   http://www.jica.go.jp/english/publications/jbic_archive/jbic_today/pdf/td_2005july.pdf (2005).

16. N. Vaugeois.http://fama2.us.es:8080/turismo/turismonet1/economia%20del%20turismo/economia %20del%20turismo/tourism%20and%20developing%20countries.pdf

17. R. Gopal, S. Varma, R. Gopinathan. Conference on Tourism in India – Challenges Ahead, (2008).

18. G.L. Smith & F.A.C. Da Lomba.. http://www.saimm.co.za/Conferences/NarrowVein2008/12-Smith.pdf (2008).

19. Alejandrino-Yap, M. Dornan & K. McGovern. Infrastructure Maintenance in the Pacific: Challenging the Build-Neglect-Rebuild Paradigm. Sydney: Pacific Infrastructure Advisory Centre (PIAC) (2013).

20. A. Marquez. The Maintenance Management Framework – Models and Methods for Complex Systems Maintenance. (2007)

21. A. Parida & U. Kumar. *Maintenance Productivity and Performance Measurement.* Handbook of Maintenance Management and Engineering, Chapter 2, 17-41 (2009).

22. W. Lee. Msc. Thesis. Universiti of Hong Kong.Unpublished (1999).

23. NAMS   &   IPWEA.   www.acelg.org.au/upload/program4/1299554949   _AM4SRRC_ Info_Sheet__V3.pdf. (2011)

13

Rural Tourism at its Peak: Socio-Cultural Impacts towards Host Communities of Kinabalu Park, Sabah (Malaysian-Borneo)

Tania Maria Tangit[1] , Ahmad Khairuman Md Hasim[2], Akmal Adanan[3]

[1]Faculty of Hotel & Tourism Management, Universiti Teknologi MARA, Sabah, Malaysia
[2,3] Faculty of Hotel & Tourism Management, Universiti Teknologi MARA, Melaka, Malaysia

Abstract. The Kinabalu Park in Sabah (Malaysian-Borneo) represents multiple tourism opportunities for its stakeholders, host communities and tourists. Being the first World Heritage Site in Malaysia endorsed by UNESCO since 2000, this nature-based tourism destination is a popular tourism destination in Malaysia, as well as in the Asia region. The designated study area includes villages nearby Kinabalu Park. Through the popularity of the park and various other attractions within the area, tourism activities contributes to socio-cultural impacts towards its host communities. The perceptions and attitudes of the locals towards tourism are identified and evaluated. By having the input of host communities as part of conserving tourism whilst meeting certain principles of sustainable tourism, the paper aims to attain interesting findings about the perceptions of the host communities towards socio-cultural impacts of tourism on their community. The paper further aims to recommend for the continuous improvement of sustainable tourism development at Kinabalu Park and its surroundings.

1 Introduction

It should be pointed out that the people of Sabah are divided into 32 officially recognised ethnic groups, where the largest indigenous ethnic group is Kadazandusun (17.8%) and predominantly wet rice and hill cultivators [1]. Ranau, a rural district of Sabah, has a total population of 94,092 people and with slightly more than 85% are of the Kadazandusun tribe [2]. Located in Ranau, Kinabalu Park covers an area of 754 sq km and was gazetted as a park in 1964 [3-4]. The park houses Mount Kinabalu, which stands amidst 4095 meters above sea level. It also comprises of Poring Hot Springs, Mesilau, and sub-stations located at the district of Kota Belud and Kota Marudu. The Kadazandusun community reveres Mount Kinabalu as the ancient belief is that 'Nabalu' means *"place of spirits of the dead"* [5].

Sabah Parks, the main caretaker for the mountain, the park and its surroundings, aims to protect, conserve and preserve natural areas of Sabah Parks, especially areas which contains unique features with high aesthetical values as a natural heritage, so that it remains preserved for the benefit, knowledge, scientific researches and recreational sites for the present and future generations [4]. The Ministry of Tourism, Culture and Environment, the Wildlife Department, Environment Protection Department, Sabah Cultural Board as well as Sabah Tourism Board are other main stakeholders of Kinabalu Park.

As Malaysia's first World Heritage Site and a popular destination, the number of visitors to Kinabalu Park (including from various sub-stations) for the year 2012 is 715,927 visitors, where almost 40% of the total visited the park headquarters [4]. Nonetheless, in the following year, there has been a decrease of 27% on the total number of visitors (519,913 visitors) to the park. However, gathered from the Sabah Tourism Website (2014) [4], the total number of tourist arrivals to Sabah showed a 17.6% increase in 2013 from the total of 2,875,761 visitors from the previous year. With an increase of tourist arrivals to Sabah as a whole and a decrease of visitors to the park, there is a need to study on the possible socio-cultural impacts host communities whom are affected with the tourism developments as of the case of Kinabalu Park and its nearby surroundings.

The aim of this study is to identify the socio-cultural impacts of the tourism industry towards the host communities of Kinabalu Park and its surroundings. The objectives of this exploratory research are to identify different socio-cultural impacts of tourism, and to evaluate the socio-cultural impacts of tourism. It is imperative to understand how host communities perceive socio-cultural impacts of tourism, which affects them, in order for stakeholders to have insights on how the locals balance these issues in their daily lives.

2 Empirical Study

A review of the literature saw three main areas of study, which are host communities, sustainable tourism in rural areas and tourism impacts, particularly socio-cultural impacts. A summary of the following is presented.

2.1 Defining host communities

Host communities are a vital element in the success of tourist destinations, sustainable tourism is dependent upon the willingness of the host community to service tourists [6]. Swarbrooke *"all those people who live within a tourist destination"* [7]. For the purpose of this study, the study population is targeted to the people who live within the tourist destination (Kinabalu Park and its surroundings) regardless whether they are directly or indirectly affected by the tourism industry.

2.2 Sustainable tourism in rural areas

Sustainable tourism is an important concept in the tourism field. UNWTO website (n.d.) in UNEP and UNWTO (2005:11-12) [8] defined sustainable tourism as *"tourism that takes full account of its current and future economic, social and environmental impacts, addressing the needs of visitors, the industry, the environment and host communities"*. From a tourism standpoint, sustainability principles refer to the environmental, economic and socio-cultural aspects of tourism development, and a suitable balance must be established between these three dimensions to guarantee its long-term sustainability [9]. Aspinall (2006) [10] too affirms the three common components when measuring sustainability, which are economic, social and environment.

UNESCO (2004) defines sustainable tourism as *"tourism that respects both local people and the traveller, cultural heritage and the environment"*. Host communities are often the weaker party in interaction with guests and service providers [11]. The socio-cultural impacts of tourism can be both negative and positive [7]. Therefore, appropriate planning can help to prevent the negative socio-cultural impacts from affecting the host population [12-13.

In reference to defining "rural areas", authors Shaw and William (1994) [14] describe rural areas as idyllic places to escape from the pressure of modern urban-industrial life in which for some to rekindle the human spirit. Lane (1994) [15] suggests that, rural tourism should be functionally rural, small in scale, traditional in character, organically and slowly growing and controlled by the local people, apart from being located in rural areas. Further stated, rural tourism extends beyond farm-based tourism to include special-interest nature holidays and ecotourism, walking, climbing and riding holidays, adventure, sport and health tourism, hunting and angling, educational travel, arts and heritage tourism, and in some areas, ethnic tourism (Lane, 1994:9) [15]. This description is applicable to the case of Kinabalu Park and its surroundings where the main product would be Mount Kinabalu itself. Hence, this study takes the definition of rural tourism from the Organization for Economic Cooperation and Development (OECD, 1994) [16], as any *"tourism taking place in the countryside"*.

2.3 Socio-cultural impacts at tourism destinations

Murphy (1985) [17] defines tourism as a socio-cultural event for both the guest and host. Described in UNEP website (n.d.) [11], socio-cultural impacts of tourism are the effects on host communities of direct and indirect relations with tourists, and of interaction with the tourism industry. These impacts can bring changes in value systems and behaviours, hence threatening indigenous identity. Nonetheless, impacts on tourism can be positive and seen when fostering pride in cultural traditions and help avoid urban relocation by creating local jobs.

The socio-cultural impacts of tourism are basically consequences of either the development of the tourism industry or the presence of the tourists (and the characteristics of the tourist-host relationship) (Sharpley, 1994) [18]. Fox (1977) [19] suggests that the social and cultural impact of tourism is the way in which tourism contributes to the change in value systems, individual behaviour, family relationships, and collective lifestyles, levels of security, moral conduct, creative expressions, traditional ceremonies and community organizations. Also supported, by Smith (1995) [20] who states that the interaction between host and guest qualifies as a socio-cultural impact.

The relationship between the impacts of tourism and residents' attitudes toward tourism was studied by various research and several models and theories were developed. One of the most influential models is Doxey's Irridex Model (1975) [21], which is a theoretical model that states an increase in numbers of tourists and a more developed tourism industry at the destination results in irritation in the host community. In other words, the more developed tourism industry is at a particular area, local community may be irritated and resent tourism as to show incompatibility of the host and the guest.

3 Methodology

Exploratory and conclusive research designs were applied for this research. Secondary data were derived from the District Office of Ranau, where the village population and demographic profiles were considered vital internal sources for this study. For the purpose of this study, the study population is targeted to the people who live within the tourist destination (Kinabalu Park and its surroundings) regardless whether they are directly or indirectly affected by the tourism industry. Convenience sampling was applied and conducted within 6 main villages of the district, namely, Bundu Tuhan, Kundasang, Kinasaraban, Mesilau, Poring and Luanti Baru.

The survey was conducted in November 2012 where the sampling population was specifically chosen for reasons being, (1) The main workforce of Kinabalu Park and supporting services within the park are from the villages within the selected sub-districts, and, (2) The sub-districts are closest to Kinabalu Park, the area of study. These villages were selected according to its location and the available tourist attractions within the area. A sample of 378 respondents was gathered from various villages within the sub-districts of Kundasang and Bundu Tuhan.

The framework and indicators for this study is adapted from Alhasanat and Hyasat (2011) [22]. A compilation items were given a five-point Likert-type response format based on the following scale; 1=strongly disagree, 2=disagree, 3=neutral, 4=agree, and 5=strongly agree.

4 Analysis and findings

The results of the analyses show the samples' mean responses and standard deviation in answering the research objectives of this study. The analyses are divided into two sections; descriptive respondents' demographic profile and a descriptive analysis on respondents' perceptions on socio-cultural impacts of tourism.

4.1 Demographic PROFILE

The respondents (n=378) for this study were local (88.6%), female (61.4%) between the ages of 21-30 years old (31.5%) and 31-40 years old (24.3%). As shown in Table 1, more than half of the respondents attended secondary school (54.2%) and a quarter had attended tertiary education (25.1%). There are 68.3% of the respondents whom are involved in the tourism industry and almost 50% of the respondents have been involved in the tourism industry between 1-10 years. They are attached at various sectors within the tourism industry such as agriculture (18.5%) and entrepreneurs (20.6%).

Table 1. Perceptions of respondents towards socio-cultural impacts of tourism

Demographic Profile		Frequency	Percentage
Gender	Male	146	38.6
	Female	232	61.4
Age Group	18-20	23	6.1
	21-30	119	31.5
	31-40	92	24.3
	41-50	78	20.6
	50 and above	66	17.5
Education	No Formal Education	26	6.9
	Primary School	52	13.8
	Secondary School	205	54.2
	Certificate / Diploma	72	19.0
	Degree	23	6.1
Local of Ranau	Yes	335	88.6
	No	43	11.4
Involvement in Tourism	Yes	258	68.3
	No	120	31.7
Years involved in Tourism	1-3 years	75	19.8
	4-6 years	56	14.8
	7-10 years	58	15.3
	11-15 years	16	4.2
	16-20 years	14	3.7
	21-30 years	13	3.4
	More than 31 years	4	1.1
	No Response	22	5.8
	Not Applicable	120	31.7
Occupation	Farmer / Agriculture	71	18.8
	Business / Entrepreneur	80	21.2
	Government Employee	25	6.6
	Others	57	15.1
	No Response	25	6.6
	Not Applicable	120	31.7

4.2 Results of descriptive analyses

The main objective of this study is to identify different socio-cultural impacts of tourism and to evaluate them. Hence, the following analysis looks into investigating the socio-cultural impacts of tourism from the perspectives of the host communities of Kinabalu Park and its surrounding areas. The responses of the study population (measured by Mean and Standard Deviation) are perceptions of respondents towards the impacts of tourism, which can be measured by both positive and negative impacts as elaborated in Table 2.

Table 2. Perceptions of respondents towards socio-cultural impacts of tourism

Statements	Mean	S.D.
Perceptions towards the impact of Tourism		
Tourism has improved the image of Kinabalu Park and its surrounding areas	4.23	0.804
Due to tourism, infrastructure at Kinabalu Park and its surrounding areas has been enhanced such as roads, hospitals, schools, etc	3.90	1.019
Tourism increases the level of education at Kinabalu Park and its surrounding areas	3.77	0.850
Tourism has improved my behaviours with my family and society	3.65	0.939
Tourism encourages immoral behaviours of some people at Kinabalu Park and its surrounding areas	2.28	1.157
Tourism has increased crime in the local community at Kinabalu Park and its surrounding areas	1.99	1.035
Tourism is the reason of some youngsters' misbehaving	2.06	1.060
Benefits of tourism at Kinabalu Park and its surrounding areas outweigh its costs	2.84	0.983
Perceptions towards the impacts of exposure to tourist activities		
I benefit from tourism at Kinabalu Park and its surrounding areas	3.71	0.915
Tourism at Kinabalu Park and its surrounding areas improves my lifestyle	3.77	0.882
I support tourism and welcome tourists to come to my community	4.02	1.013
Women are not suitable to work in the tourism industry	2.03	1.229
The closer my residency to the tourist site the more I benefit out of tourism at Kinabalu Park and its surrounding areas	3.65	1.108
Tourism increased the cost of living at Kinabalu Park and its surrounding areas	3.32	1.063
I have more money to spend because of my work in tourism at Kinabalu Park and its surrounding areas	3.08	1.160
I deal with tourist almost every day	3.27	1.266
Earnings from tourism lure children in my community to drop out of school at an early age.	2.29	1.163
Perceptions according to seasonality, cultural differences between host and guests		
Tourism during high season contributes to issues such as crowding, inflation, etc	2.86	1.118
Working in tourism during high season is feasible, though I prefer having a permanent job in another sector	3.26	1.056
I interact with individual tourist more than I do with tourists in groups	3.07	1.177
Tourists show respect to our culture and traditions	3.97	0.836
Tourism made me understand other cultures better	4.06	0.784
Tourism increased my pride in our national culture	4.22	0.778
I encourage more tourists to come and see Kinabalu Park and its surrounding areas	4.26	0.864
I support tourism development in Kinabalu Park and its surrounding areas concerning more marketing and in site infrastructure	4.16	0.837
Community representatives at Kinabalu Park and its surrounding areas are involved in development decisions concerning Kundasang	3.71	1.062
Negative impacts of tourism may drive me to leave Kinabalu Park and its surrounding areas	2.03	1.268

Note: n=378, S.D. = Standard Deviation

Respondents perceive tourism to improve the image of Kinabalu Park and its surrounding areas (m=4.23), increase the level of education (m=3.77) and infrastructure has improved due to tourism (m=3.90). The study attempts to also identify the impacts of respondents' exposure to tourist activities. Generally, respondents support tourism and welcome tourists to their community (m=4.02). They also feel that tourism improves their lifestyle (m=3.77) and they benefit from tourism (m=3.71). Respondents' felt indifferent on having more money to spend although working in tourism field (m=3.08) as well as the increase of cost of living (m=3.32). Not all respondents deal with tourists everyday (m=3.27), nonetheless, they feel the closer they live near a tourist site, the more benefits they get out of tourism (m=3.65).

On respondents' perceptions of tourism according to its seasonality and cultural differences, they feel that tourism led them to understand other cultures' better (m=4.06), increase pride in national culture (m=4.22), hence, encourage more tourists to come and see Kinabalu Park and its surrounding areas (m=4.26). They support tourism development when it comes to marketing their area as well as the provision of in-site infrastructures (m=4.16) and somewhat agree that community representatives are involved in development decisions (m=3.71). However, respondents disagreed that negative impacts of tourism may drive them to leave Kinabalu Park and its surrounding areas (m=2.03) although tourism during high season contributes to issues such as crowding, inflation, etc (m=2.86).

Both descriptive and analytical data results were interpreted to obtain findings about the perceptions of the host communities of Kinabalu Park and its surrounding areas on tourism development. It was derived that not all negative socio-cultural impacts particularly on crime rates (m=1.99), immoral behaviors (m=2.28) and misbehaviours (m=2.06) are directly associated with the host community. Residents who are directly employed in tourism tend to be more tolerant of the impacts (Faulkner and Tideswell, 1997) [23]. It is interesting to note that respondents perceive women to be unsuitable to work in the tourism industry (m=2.03). This supports the findings by Swarbrooke (1999) [7] in a similar study in Tunisia that men occupied most of the jobs in tourism. Nonetheless, residents do feel quite indifferent on the benefits of tourism in outweighing its costs (m=2.84).

5 Conclusion and Recommendations

Mount Kinabalu, located in Kinabalu Park, Kundasang, serves as an intangible cultural heritage for the Kadazandusun communities of Sabah as they believe that the mountain is the final resting place for departed souls. As Mount Kinabalu is an important asset to the Kadazandusun community, and Sabahan and Malaysians as a whole, it is vital that socio-cultural impacts of the host communities of Kinabalu Park and its surroundings are minimized and controlled.

The overall result of this study is consistent with the literature presented and it concludes that not all tourism activities are welcomed at Kinabalu Park and its surrounding areas as there are negative socio-cultural impacts, which could deteriorate the host community's social structure and cultural traditions. Generally, respondents are still receptive in receiving tourists and welcoming tourism developments in Kinabalu Park and its surrounding areas, although, responses gained were not surprisingly high (i.e. tourists show respect to our culture and traditions (m=3.97), tourism increased my pride in our national culture (m=4.22), I encourage more tourists to come and see Kinabalu Park and its surrounding areas (m=4.26), etc). This supports the opinions of Allen, Long, Perdue and Kieselbach (1988) [24] who found that tourism is often considered beneficial in areas of lower to moderate levels of development.

In relation to Doxey's Irridex, the attitudes of the host communities of Kinabalu Park and its surrounding areas and its surroundings towards tourism development are between euphoria and apathy. The result of this study does not represent any obvious irritations towards tourism development; hence, tourism in Kinabalu Park and its surrounding areas are still being welcomed. However, to maintain tourism development at a controllable level, Faulkner and Tideswell (1997) [23] states that the socio-cultural impacts of tourism should be monitored continuously in order to maximize the benefits of tourism at the destination.

From a resource management point of view, social and cultural impacts of tourism should be considered throughout the planning process and in an environmental impact assessment procedure, so that benefits are optimized and problems minimized (Brunt, 1999) [25]. Therefore, the study has met its objectives in investigating the host communities' overall perception on socio-cultural impacts of tourism at Kinabalu Park and its surrounding areas. The findings of this investigation can assist tourism stakeholders especially government agencies as well as tourism planners in the implementation of sustainable tourism development strategies based on the input of the host communities when making decisions involving tourism at Kinabalu Park and its surrounding areas.

6 Acknowledgements

The funding for this project is made possible through the research grant obtained from the Ministry of Higher Education, Malaysia under the Long Term Research Grant Scheme 2011 [LRGS grant no: JPT.S (BPKI)2000/09/01/015Jld.4(67)]. This research is also made possible with the assistance from Universiti Teknologi MARA, Malaysia, the Ministry of Culture, Environment and Tourism of Sabah and its agencies, Sabah Parks, Sabah Tourism Board, Sabah Cultural Board and the Environment Protection Department of Sabah.

References

1. Sabah Tourist Association Website, 2014. People & Culture. Accessed on 10th March 2014 from URL: http://www.sta.my/people_culture.cfm (2014)
2. Population and Housing Census of Malaysia, 2014. Population in Malaysia based on Ethnic. Accessed on 10th March 2014 from URL: http://www.statistics.gov.my/portal/download_Population/files/population/04Jadual_PBT_negeri/PBT_Sabah.pdf (2014)
3. UNESCO, 2014. Kinabalu Park. Accessed on 10th March 2014 from URL: http://whc.unesco.org/en/list/1012 (2014)
4. Sabah Parks, 2014. Introduction – Kinabalu Park. Accessed on 10th March 2014 from URL: http://sabahparks.org.my/eng/kinabalu_park/ (2014)
5. Kadazandusun Cultural Association, 2005. Kinabalu: Kina Balu, Aki Nabalu or Ki Nabalu. Accessed on 10th March 2014 from URL: http://kdca.org.my/archives/68 (2005)
6. K. Kim, The Effects of Tourism Impacts on Quality of Life of The Residents In The Community. Unpublished doctoral dissertation, Virginia Polytechnic Institute and State University (2002)
7. J. Swarbrooke, The Host Community (11:123). Sustainable Tourism Management Wallingford: CABI Publishing (1999)
8. UNWTO, n.d. Definition of Sustainable Tourism in Making Tourism More Sustainable - A Guide for Policy Makers, UNEP and UNWTO, Accessed on 20th March 2014 from URL: http://sdt.unwto.org/content/about-us-5 , 11-12 (2005)
9. UNWTO, in European Centre for Ecological and Agricultural Tourism (2004)
10. A.J. Aspinall, Communities in change: social sustainability and tourism development. Unpublished master's thesis, University of Waterloo, Ontario, Canada. (2006)
11. UNEP, n.d. Socio-Cultural Impacts of Tourism. Accessed on 22nd April 2014 from URL: http://www.unep.org/resourceefficiency/Home/Business/SectoralActivities/Tourism/WhyTourism/ImpactsofTourism/SocioCulturalImpacts/tabid/78780/Default.aspx
12. UNESCO, Sustainable Tourism. Accessed on 22nd April 2014 from URL : http://www.unesco.org/education/tlsf/mods/theme_c/mod16.html (2007)
13. UNWTO, n.d. Sustainable Development of Tourism – Definition. Accessed on 16th May 2014 from URL : http://sdt.unwto.org/content/about-us-5
14. G. Shaw and A. Williams. Critical issues in tourism. Oxford: Blackwelln. (1994)
15. B. Lane, *What is rural tourism?*. Journal of Sustainable Tourism, ISSN 0966-9582, **2**, 1-2, 7–21 (1994)
16. OECD. Tourism policy and international tourism in OECD countries 1991-1992, Organization for Economic Co-Operation and Development, ISBN 9-26414-091-3, Paris, France (1994)
17. P.E. Murphy, *Tourism: A Community Approach*. London: Routledge (1985)
18. R. Sharpley, *Tourism, Tourists and Society*. Huntingdon: ELM (1994)
19. M. Fox, *The Social Impacts of Tourism: a Challenge to researchers and planners*, University of California: Santa Cruz (1977)
20. S.L.J. Smith, *Tourism Analysis*. Harlow: Longman (1995)

21. G.V. Doxey, A causation theory of visitor-resident irritants: methodology and research inferences, *Proceedings of the Travel Research Association, 6th Annual Conference, San Diego, California, USA*, 195-8 (1975)

22. S.A. Alhasanat and A.S. Hyasat. *Sociocultural Impacts of Tourism on the Local Community in Petra, Jordan.* Jordan Journal of Social Sciences, **4**, 1, 2011

23. B. Faulkner & C. Tideswell, *'A framework for monitoring community impacts of tourism'*, Journal of Sustainable Tourism, **5**, 1, 3-28 (1997)

24. R.P. Allen, R. Long, Perdue, and S. Kieselbach, *The Impact of Tourism Development on Residents' Perceptions of Community Life.* Journal of Travel Research **27**, 1, 16-21 (1988)

25. P. Brunt and P. Courtney. *Host Perceptions of Sociocultural Impacts.* Annals of Tourism Study, **26**, 3, 493-515 (1999)

26. Sabah Parks, Introduction (History of Establishment). Accessed on 10th March 2014 from URL: http://sabahparks.org.my/eng/public/02introduction.asp (2014)

27. Sabah Parks, Visitor Statistics. Accessed on 10th March 2014 from URL: http://sabahparks.org.my/eng/public/visitorfigure.asp (2014)

28. Sabah Tourism, Visitor Statistics. Accessed on 10th March 2014 from URL: http://www.sabahtourism.com/business/statistic (2014)

14

Cave Tourism: The Potential of Asar Cave as a Natural Tourism Asset at Lenggong Valley, Perak

Main Rindam[1]

[1]Centre for Distance Education, Universiti Sains Malaysia, 11800 Penang, Malaysia

Abstract. The Lenggong Valley, from a standpoint of natural tourism research, presents strengths, weaknesses, opportunities and challenges that can be utilized to help increase the opportunities for the local community to increase their standard of living. Asar Cave comprises one of the caves that are found in Lenggong. A series of external studies have been done on Asar Cave in order to measure its potential for natural tourism in Lenggong. The objective of this study is to discuss caves as a natural resource that has great potential in the growth of the economy of the residents of the Lenggong Valley. Marketing caves as a source of nature tourism helps the government's achievements in National Key Result Areas, apart from being a form of environmental control as well as helping to increase awareness about environmental education, specifically those associated with caves. The research results find that SWOT analysis presents huge potential for caves to become a source of nature tourism development in Lenggong. Great potential can also be seen from a standpoint of increasing the standard of living of its residents through their involvement in the tourism sector based on local natural assets.

1 Introduction

Caves are a part of nature tourism, or "ecotourism", that is capable of attracting tourists [1] and it increases in popularity in Korea [2] and even in Vietnam [3]. Caves are important to the tourism industry because it develops rapidly in developing countries, where hundreds of caves every year are developed for that purpose [4]. It could be said that caves form a complex natural resource in the large-scale tourism trade of a particular country [5]. There are more than 5,000 tourist-friendly caves around the world currently, with 10 of them being significant caves. Cave tourism successfully pulls approximately 250 million tourists every year with an estimated expenditure of USD2 billion, apart from providing employment to 200,000 people and generating a total household income of USD100 million per year [4].

The opening of Gua Phong Nha-Khe Bang, Vietnam in 1990 for instance, can facilitate to diminish the rate of poverty in the local community [6]. Taking inspiration from this experience, many countries around the world have taken initiatives to develop the caves found amongst them to be raised as important tourism products, such as the case with Brazil [19], Russia [5], Indonesia [20] and Australia [21].

The awareness behind turning caves into a source of natural tourism reaches far past the borders of mere economics. Based on the development of Malaysia, it involves the National Key Result Areas (NKRAs) o the government which seek to improve the quality of life of the local citizenry, and empower both urban and rural population [7]. Although it connects itself to the issue of eradicating hardcore poverty which itself is related to the granting of aid by the Malaysian Welfare Department, the development of women entrepreneurs and encouraging prosperity within rural communities through the increasing of various local infrastructure, it does not necessarily have to be the metaphorical 'fish', but is necessarily more akin to the same metaphor's "fishing rod".

Sustainability is described as increasing the quality of life through the increase of entrepreneurial knowledge. It's respectively, development that improves the quality of human life while living within the carrying capacity of supporting ecosystems. Developing natural resources and assets is ultimately for the sake of the sustainability of their livelihoods. The anthropocentric view focuses on the sustainable welfare of human [22].

The specialness and uniqueness of a certain cave's landscape should be shared with the general public. It is unique because caves only present the frond portion or 'gate' of itself, while most of it remains hidden [8]. The perception of the cave as a dark and foreboding place needs to be changed because in reality it comprises a landscape that is beautiful and awe-inspiring [9].

The aim of this paper is to discuss caves as a natural resource that has huge potential in the growth of the economy of the inhabitants of the Lenggong Valley. Therefore, marketing caves as natural source of tourism is important in order to help the achievement of government NKRAs, as well to serve as environmental conservation and to increase awareness of environmental education that is relevant to caves. Secondly is to explain SWOT analysis and its link to cave tourism development program in Lenggong, Perak.

2 Area Background

Asar Cave is situated to the West of Kajang Cave. It has a geographic location of 5° 07.53' North and 100° 58.82' East. This cave is situated 78 meter above sea level. In order to get to Asar Cave, visitors must travel through Kajang Cave and use a footpath as soon as they exit from the Southern gate of the aforementioned cave. The small footpath that has been layered with wood was built in bridge-form in order to ease visitors that wish to visit Asar Cave, Puteri Cave and Ngaum Cave. Moreover, this path forms a physical border between a rubber plantation and the foothills of a karst landforms that forms a complex of combined limestone caves in Lenggong, Perak.

The landscape of Asar Cave has one main gate that faces the South exactly in front of the Information Booth of the said cave, which was built by the Museum And Lenggong Heritage Authority. Visitors to Asar Cave will pass past many vents which can be entered through a variety of direction, including from the top of the cave. The inner land scape of Asar Cave is not like Kajang Cave, because it only has one main chamber and possesses a high ceiling at its Southern gate and tapers or lowers towards its Northern side. There are several vents in the East ceiling and wall of Asar Cave, but its opening is not very large. The interesting aspect of these vents is that they serve as passages that allow sunlight to enter into Asar Cave, which gives an artistic impact that is quite attractive.

Asar Cave possesses only one space or main hall. The ceiling for this space possesses many stalactites, and has no stalagmites. The stalactites of Asar Cave are unique in that their shape is sharp like the tooth of a shark (shark tooth stalactite). This fact shows that Asar Cave is a younger cave when compared to Kajang Cave or Puteri Cave. The existence of 'soda straws' and 'flowstone' on the cave walls is a natural resource that can be marketed to tourists. There are two kinds of rock present, namely tufa and travertine. Tufa is formed through the precipitation of calcium carbonate and is porous, while travertine is formed through the deposition of calcium carbonate is one of the signs that might be on Gua Kajang [10].

The description of Asar Cave from a physical geography standpoint comprises something that is interesting to produce and write out, because it itself is a field that is still new in Malaysia, even though this field has been long well-researched at the global level. Papers on this cave are hoped to give information that can be shared with the local citizenry associated with Ansar Cave, and brings communities both local and foreign to come and get to know it more intimately. It comprises the caves that must be visited in Lenggong because of its location, which is in the middle of Kajang Cave, Ngaum Cave and Puteri Cave. Landscapes such as stalactites can be found on the ceiling of Asar Cave. It has a coarse shape and slightly different from the stalagmites that are created through the dripped water, undergoing a crystallization process.

According to the locals, several vents or exist found in Asar Cave connects the said with other caves in its vicinity. These passages form added value packages that can be marketed as a tourism product that is based on a natural resource. Asar cave are fragile and should be conserved. Since cave are delicate place and almost no mechanisms for repair any cracks, scratches or even name writen on the wall, do so will stay that way perhaps idenfinitely. Asar cave provide food and shalter for animals particulary poultry such as birds and bats. They are particulary vulnerable to human interference when they are hibernating, and when they are bringing up the young. The best practice when we visit them is stick to one trail to minimize damage to the floor and wall of the cave.

3 The Potential of Asar Cave as a Tourism Attraction in Lenggong Valley, Perak

Mammoth Cave National Park has successfully raked in USD62 million for its local community in the south of Kentucky, USA [11]. If Mammoth Cave can give such a positive impact to the local economy, there is no reason why Asar Cave and its network of caves in the Lenggong Valley should not as well. Although some would says the Mammoth cave may be inappropriate as the cave resources in Lenggong cannot be compered but don't look at physical assets instead of the way people manage this cave to attract tourist.

If doubts still linger as per Asar Cave's ability to lift the local economy because of its remote location, look no further than New Zealand, which benefited greatly through placing Waitomo Cave on the tourist map. Originating from a tiny village with only 307 inhabitants, through government efforts and collaboration with tourism agencies in the country, Waitomo Cave successfully pulls 500, 000 tourists from around the world every year [12]. A 40 minute experience through the 200 meter tunnel via the limestone complex can bring numerous benefits to the local economy and the New Zealand economy in general. Even though this cave is separated from mainstream tourism, it still manages to attract hundreds of thousands of tourists to visit it. Again, it's not about what Mammoth and Waitomo have, it more towards approach requires a strategy to promote nature just like Asar cave and the others caves in Lenggong as haritage tourism product.

Tourism based on caves or *speleotourism* form a new space that involves a varied spectrum for tourists in nature [13]. The landscape of the caves (*speleothems*) such as stalagmites, stalactites and various other formations have long since attracted the interest of tourists who come to experience the view of the limestone caves around the world, as early as the beginning of the 20th Century, where caves have received more than 500,000 visitors every year [14]. This development as attracted the interest of many researchers who study the motivations that bring all these people to come and witness, and enjoy, the landscape of these caves.

According to Samuel et al. 2008, who have studied the characteristics of cave tourists, their motivations and identified them according to certain segments in Korea, one segment that is discussed is the desire to experience for themselves being in the environment of a cave itself. Paolo Forti [4] concludes that for a while now, caves have become the most important geological item to tourists and for about 20 years recently, their economic important has increased dramatically in Oman.

Cave tourists around the world are encountering an evolution and transformation in the context of tourism destinations. The focus of tourism now emphasises the issue of how interactions between tourism organisations can act as mechanisms for tourism destination management by themselves. Taking the case of Asar Cave and the other caves in the Lenggong Valley, the Local Authorit must play a pro-active role in marketing these resources in a more effective and efficient manner. Aspects that must be emphasised include efforts to increase visitor flow, the number of visitors and their duration of stay in Lenggong.

Lenggong Valley, which is a world heritage area, can become a gateway to cave tourism that already exists in the valley, especially in Asar Cave. The Ipoh-Kuala Kangsar-Grik route is a communal route from the West Coast to the East Coast of Peninsula Malaysia, which can offer economic benefits to the local community. As many as 3,421 vehicles used this route every day on 2011, or 1,248,665 vehicles a year [15]. If each vehicle carries with it an average of three people that spend an average of RM100 a day on lodging, food, petrol and other provisions, the potential for spending along this corridor is RM41,622,166 a year.

It seems the economic opportunity along the Ipoh-Kuala Kangsar-Grik route is hardly taken advantage of by the local community, especially in Lenggong. The potential for Asar Cave as a natural tourism resource in Lenggong must be motivated by taking cues from reports that state that in 2006, outdoor recreative activities were capable of generation USD730 billion for the US economy , and provided employment for 6.5 million people across the country. In this context, Lenggong must be more proactive in marketing its natural resources through various packages that can utilise collaborations with various tourism agencies.

Asar Cave if combine with other caves in Lenggong valley can also elevate its potential as a 'show cave' by giving focus to four primary areas, which are scientific research, art, technology and management. Scientific research has obviously been suggested and performed early on, which would be the first phases of aspects of hydrology, geography, biological sciences and earth sciences, which can used a platform to gather experts in these field to Lenggong to study Asar Cave as well as other caves in Lenggong Valley. The surface features of Lenggong can become a hub of cave research across the region, and even internationally. Artistry, if combined with other disciplines such as engineering can increase the potential of Ansar Cave in the tourism sector.

The artistic lighting in the cave can be used as a value added aspect in Asar Cave, as an information centre about natural caves, such as the case with Heinrich's Cave, Germany [16]. The combination of art, technology and hydrometeorology are necessary to control water, humidity and other environmental influences in the cave for the design of appropriate paths for creating an artistic landscape viewing angle for tourists. Effective and efficient management begins as early as the planning stage on paper until the phase of the project is completed. This includes managing and adding to already existing infrastructure that has already been created, such as pathways and wooden walkways, and information huts, managing it so that it is safe to us by tourists and capable of supporting the presence of many tourists at a time. The surveying of wooden paths and constructs based on wood must be done often because wood easily spoils in geographic locations that encounter heat and humidity throughout the ear. Furthermore, wood easily rots , apart from it being vulnerable to termite attacks (*Coptotermes formosanus*).

When the Perak state government targets six million tourists in conjunction with Visit Perak Year 2014, the Lenggong Valley must acquire some benefit from this campaign [17]. In 2012, Lenggong was elevated to the status of tourism cluster in conjunction with Visit Perak Year (*Tahun Melawat Perak,* TMP) and was apropos with the concept of clusters itself, which meant fusing things together, and thi placing it among 10 tourism icons of Perak, under the Belum Royal State Park pakej, itself in Hulu Perak, making it relevant. The Visit Perak Year 2014 campaign and Visit Malaysia Year (*TMM, Tahun Melawat Malaysia*) 2014 need to include Lenggong as a destination or a tourism map, be it for state or country because it is a world heritage site.

Learning from experiences with spectacular cave like Mulu cave in Sarawak, Asar Cave and other caves in Lenggong are indeed unique and can be offered to the tourism industry in Perak as well as Malaysia in general. Taking the *Blue Ocean* strategy concept, which is to say "competition is no longer relevant", the uniqueness of the caves that are in Hulu Perak, 60 km from Ipoh city and 5 kilometres from the town of Lenggong, Asar Cave and the other caves around it can be considered caves with great geological wonders because it has stalactites, stalagmites and flowstones as well as landscape walls, and cave ceilings that are interesting to watch.

Asar Cave has a landscape that makes it well suited as a shelter because it has a main chamber that is wide, but is generally unsuitable as a domicile because its ceiling has numerous vents. These physical characteristics allow Asar Cave to offer tourist activities that are more challenging, such as crystal calcite exploring, exploring the vents on the ceilings and the passages that connect Asar Cave to the other caves in the karst area in Lenggong Valley (which takes around 30 to 40 minutes). Through this package, tourists can enjoy the atmosphere, the stone chamber, with wild plants and the calls of various unique animals.

Turning Asar Cave into a show cave for visitors or tourists is bound to open up opportunities for venturing into areas that before this were unavailable to the general public, for going into the caves that has been acclaimed as a form heritage with evidence of limestone formations that have been found. At this point, there are no archaeological digs that have been recorded at Asar Cave. Information about with Asar Cave must still be deepened and expanded. With that in mind, Asar Cave should be preserved as an educational too and could turn out to be a health development in the natural tourism agency. The cave environment should be developed as an *ethnopark* [5] which should focus on the local community economy, exotic animals, wells, the farming of maze and orchards, apart from fishing activities in rivers and lakes. It is best offered as a package and not separately.

The SWOT analysis was conducted in Lenggong valley in Mac, 2014. The purpose of analysis is to be used for Asar cave self evaluation. It's a lens under which tourism program can reflect on what is currenlyt working, not working and what obstacles might occor down the pipeline, to focus on what is positive and what needs to and can be inprove upon. The analysis has been conducted individually through three step. First step is scanning which start from develop a list, long or short of strengths of Asar cave, individually or as a group. Consider all elements of the cave and has been done on a flip chart. Second step was evaluate and consolidate by constructively read throug the list and eliminate any item that are redundant.

Boil down the top concept and summarize any item that are overly wordly. Choose the best 5-10 strengths that be the top strength, weakness, opportunity and threats or chalanges. The SWOT/C analysis of Asar Cave shows that this cave has Strength (S), Weakness (W), development opportunity (O) and threats (T) or challenges (C) that must be observed. Conceptually, strength (S) and weakness (W) are internal factors while the items of opportunity (O) and threats (T) or challenges (C) on the other hand are external factors, as mentioned in Table 1.

Asar Cave and other caves in the Lenggong Valley have many strengths for fortifying their potential in the tourism industry, like S1- Ease of visit, S2- Having a protected environment, S3- That the heritage caves are under Lenggong Museum & Heritage, and PBT, S4-Being an archaeological site S5 – Scientific value (geography, geomorphology, hydrology, speleology, karstology, biospeleology, ecology, palaeontology and archaeology. In lieu of that, the local community, especially the youth and women entrepreneurs in Lenggong, must take advantage of whatever opportunities that are present in order to realize the NKRAs targeted by the government. At the same time, efforts must be made in order to overcome problems with the present weaknesses, which are W1- Weak or poor marketing, W1- Threats to the cave ecosystem, W3-Imbalanced development in the district and W4-A lack of both amenities and services.

Collaboration with various government agencies such as the PBT, the District Council and private companies are very much needed in order to achieve this objective. Entities that have the stout ability to overcome these present weaknesses include the people of the Lenggong Museum and Heritage that was formed in 2012. It was aided by the Local Authorities (*Pihak Berkuasa Tempatan, PBT*) as well as NGOs, and these groups include local farmers, tourism entrepreneurs and other members of society.

Table 1. Formatting sections, subsections and subsubsections SWOT analysis.

Strength (S)	Weakness (W)
S1 – Easy to visit S2 – Protected environment S3 – Heritage caves under Lenggong museum & Heritage and PBT. S4 – An archaelogical site S5 – Scientific value (geography, geomorphology, hidrology, speleology, karstology, biospeleology, ecology, palaeontology dan archaeology).	W1- Weak marketing W2 – threat to the cave ecosystems W3- Uneven development in the district W4- A lack of relevant amenities and services
Oppertunity (O)	Threats (T)/challenges (C)
O1. A focused strategy in developing the specific needs of tourism O2. An oppertunity to upgrade tourism resources already available O3. Operational all-year round O4. The mastery over a new market O5. New job oppertunities in local community O6. The strengthening of the entrepreneurial field O7. Insentives to develop new forms of special tourism interests	T/C1. Competition from the international market T/C2. A lack of investor interest T/C3. A lack of initiative by the locals T/C4. Few locals T/C5. No control or protection to archeological sites and formasions of dripstones.

The various opportunities that are predicted to arise can sustain and elevate the number of visitations and total amount of visitors as well as protect the ecosystem of Asar Cave and the various other caves that are found within the karst complex from non-sustainable management practices. With the presence of various opportunities, such as O1-A focuses strategy in developing the specific demands of tourism, O2- The opportunity to upgrade present tourism resources, o3-Year-long operation, O4- The mastery of a new market, O5-New job opportunities for the local community, O6- The strengthening of the entrepreneurial field and O7- Incentives to develop new forms of special interests in tourism. The local community are not able to interpret all opportunities available to opportunities specifically for increasing their standard of living without help from the PBT and the relevant authorities. At the same time, the aspect of threats (T) or challenges (C) need to have their impacts lessened to the local community. Although there is some concern over the negative impact of tourism on the environment of the cave, studies have shown that such concerns are largely unsubstantiated because the ambient heat that is produced by visiting tourists is quickly absorbed into the caves cavernous chamber [18]. This issue came about based on a report done on a research side in the heritage site of Phong Nha-Khe Bang cave in Vietnam, which also presents that the stalactites within the cave lost their colours and showed signs of dryness and mould[6]. Threats like T/C1- Competition from international markets, T/C2- A lack of investor interest, T/C3- A lack of initiative among the local community, T/C4- A small population and T/C5- No control or protection to archaeological sites and dripstone formations. The environment of a cave is dark, cold, damp and the ability to manage risky as well as dangerous situations require well-developed standard guidelines in order to ensure that the safety of the tourists is guaranteed. The PBT of the Lenggong Valley must learn from premier organisations around the world, especially in structuring tourism experiences that are challenging. Cooperation with organisations that have a great deal of experience involving rugged or challenging activities is sorely needed, especially in the form of quality training programs that follow international standards. At the same time, a formal mechanism must be present in order to satisfy the need for a 'rescue team'. Guides from exploration organisations work together in emergency situations. The question that often arises is what happens when cave tourists are faced with emergency situations. Interaction among the members of these networks is extremely critical in order to give rise to working relationships that are based on knowledge when they acknowledge their mutual co-dependence, which they both feel towards the reputation towards a particular tourist destination. The development of this capability only exists when the network is formed and interaction begins to form acknowledgement based on knowledge in an outer context.

Enabling the marketing of the caves of the Lenggong Valley is sorely needed. Market competition such as Red Ocean strategies does not suffice for Asar Cave, when compared to using a Blue Ocean strategy that places competition as irrelevant. In lieu of that, Asar Cave needs initiate a four-grid framework in order to demonstrate its presence in the nature tourism product market, via four elements, which are *eliminate, reduce, raise* and *create.*

In order to increase its potential as a tourism product, the element of weakness (W) must be eliminated; the element of strength (S) must be expanded just like how the development of the cave follows international standards in the field of tourism cave management by involving researchers (in the fields of karstospeleolog, geography, geology, archaeology, palaeontology, earth sciences, endokarst biology, vegetation, economy, karst area conservation and art), identifying the value added aspects of a cave, such as measuring the dynamics of the cave, planning the circulation of visitors and access, determining the required funding, planning a marketing strategy, identifying the cave's biota, its microbiota and its macro-ecosystem of flying cave dwellers, the mapping of the cave system, examining the quality and quantity of fresh air that is required and determining zoning when there arises a need to close a section of the cave for the purposes of academic research.

The potential of Asar Cave can also be expanded through the element of creation, especially using the aspects of opportunity (O) that are available for creating new demands within the tourism industry. Creativity and innovation must be adapted in order to enrich Asar Cave (in the form of products, services and presentation). Creativity in the form of interactivity, for example, seeks to see marketing groups that are structured into three groups, the first group being local stakeholders, where the focus of this group is to penetrate the local supply chain. Secondly, cooperation with tourism agencies can bring benefits to Asar Cave, and thirdly, with tourism agencies that have a dominant presence in the national tourism industry, such as a relationship with Malaysian Airlines (MAS), Berjaya Air, Firefly, Malindo Air and AirAsia as icons that have a direct relationship with good tourists from within and outside the country.

4 Conclusion

The main goal of this paper is the spread the knowledge about the uniqueness of the caves of the Lenggong Valley, especially Asar Cave, to the local community and also to international tourists. These special qualities, or uniqueness, become the basis to Asar Caves potential as a natural asset to be elevated as a major destination in the tourism agency. This effort is tightly tied to the desire to initiate the NKRA requirements for increasing the quality of life of low income groups and also through the empowerment of infrastructure in the rural areas. As such, the local community must involve themselves directly with ecotourism not just for increasing their income but also for doing rehabilitation work. Secondly, it is hoped that with this paper, it will increase public awareness about how important it is to preserve environmental heritage, especially the caves in this valley, so that they can persist as an abundant resource for the future generations of Lenggong. Considering the competition faced by tourism destinations that ever increase within the economy, both locally and globally, Asar Cave's potential as a natural tourism asset in Lenggong must be seen from an angle of its uniqueness.

5 Acknowledgment

The authors wish to thank Universiti Sains Malaysia for the Research University Grant managed by the Sustainable Tourism Research Cluster (1001 / PTS / 8660012)

References

1. Zsuzsa Tolnay, Interpretation in Cave Tourism – A little utilised management tools", http://www.i-s-c-a.com/documentloader.php?id=663&filename=35-tolnay-interpretation-in-cave-tourism.pdf. Cited at 5 November (2013).

2. Seongseop Samuel Kim, Miju Kim, Jung Woong Park, Yingzhi Guo."Cave Tourism: Tourists' Characteristics, Motivations to Visit, and the Segmentation of Their Behavior". Asia Pacific Journal of Tourism Research.**13**:3, 299-318 (2008).

3. Pang Nguyen Hong, Quan Dao Thi, Quynh Le Kim Thoa. Ecotourism in Vietnam: Potential and reality. Featured in October (2012) http://kyotoreview.cseas.kyoto-u.ac.jp/issue/issue1/article_167.html. Cited at January 16, 2014.

4. Paolo Forti. "Caves: The most important features geotouristic in the world", *3rd International Conference on Geotourism.* (2013) http://www.geotourism.om/geo/presentation/2%20Paolo%20forti%20Geoparchicarsici.pdf Cited at 5 November 2013.

5. Knezevic & Renata Zikovic Grbac, "Analysis of the condition and development of cave tourisn lucre in Primorsko-goranska Country", Turizm, **15**: 1,11-25 (2011).

6. Thanhnien News. Com., "Researcer say tourism is ruining Vietnam's worl famous caves", *Thanhnien News*, 16 Dicember (2012). http://www.thanhniennews.com/2010/pages/20121216-researchers-say-vietnam-grand-caves-need-to-rest-from-tourism.aspx. Cited at 6 November 2013.

7. 1 Click. The success of the 2014 Six areas NKRA (2014). http://pmr.penerangan.gov.my/index.php/nkra/4808-pointers-6-bidang-keberhasilan-utama-negara-nkra.html. Cited at 8 January 2014.

8. Patricia Kambesis, "The Importance of cave exploration to scientific research", Journal of Caves and Karst Studies, **69**: 1, 46-58 (2007).

9. Bahamas Caves Research Foundation, "Research and conservation of blue holes and flavor of the Bahamas" (2013). http://www.bahamascaves.com/. Cited at 6 November 2013.

10. Main Rindam, Fatimah Hassan, "The Potential of Lenggong Valley as a Natural Tourism Resources in a Rural Setting" viewed. *Proceedings of the 3rd Regional Conference on Tourism Research*, Bayview Hotel, Langkawi, Malaysia. October 29-31 (2013).

11. Vickie Carson, Mammorth cave pumps $ 62 million/year into local economy. *The Amplifier.* (Thursday, February 23, 2012)

12. Kathryn Pavlovich."The evolution and transformation of a tourism destination network: the Waitomo Caves, New Zealand", Tourism Management, **24**: 2, 203-216 (2013).

13. Heros Augusto Santos Lobo, Eleonora Trajanoc, Maurício Marinho de Alcântara, Maria Elina Bichuettee, José Antonio Basso Scaleante, Oscarlina Aparecida Furquim Scaleantef, Bárbara Nazaré Rocha, Francisco Villela Laterza."Projection scenarios onto fragility of tourist maps: Framework for determination of provisional tourist Carrying capacity in a Brazilian show cave". Tourism Management, **35**, 234-243 (2009).

14. A. Baker, D. Genty. Journal of Environmental Management, **53**(3), 165-175 (1998)

15. Ministry of Transport Malaysia. 2012 Transport Statistics 2011 http://www.mot.gov.my/my/Publication/Official/Statistik%20Pengangkutan%20Malaysia%202011.pdf. Accessed on January 14, 2014.

16. *Cave Lighting*. Light up your show cave. Made by cave lighting: Heinrich's cave. http://www.cavelighting.com/index.php?area=1. (2014) Cited at January 13, 2014.

17. Silver News. "Silver target of 6 million tourists for 2014" in the. Silver News, 10 September 12:15 Tuesday (2013). http://www.peraknews.com/berita-utama/49-utama/9689-silver-target-6-million-visitors-to-2014. Cited at 7 November 2013.

18. Science Daily, "Tourist does not harm all caves, study suggest", *Science Daily*, 11 April. (2011). http://www.sciencedaily.com/releases/2011/04/110411111036.htm. Cited at 6 November 2013.

19. Heros Augusto Santos Lobo & Edvaldo Cesar Moretti. "Tourism in Caves and the Conservation of the Speleological Heritage: The case of Serra da Bodoquena (Mato Grosso do Sul State, Brazil)". Acta Carsologica 38/2-3, 265-276, POSTOJNA (2009).

20. Eva Rachmawati & Arzyana Sunkar. "Consumer-Based Cave Travel and Tourism Market Characteristic in West Java, Indonesia". Tourism and Karst Areas, 6(1), (2013).

21. Dragovich, D. & Grose, J. "Impact of tourists on carbon dioxide levels at Jenolan Caves, Australia: an examination of microclimatic constraints on tourist cave management". Geoforum, Vol. **21(1),** 111-120 (1990).

22. Barret, C.B & R.E. Grizzle. "A holistic approach to sustainability based on pluralistic stepwardship ". Environmental Ethics. **21** :23-42.

15

Evaluating the Impact of Regional Marketing Projects on the Development of Regions from Different Stakeholder Perspectives

Kim-Kathrin Kunze[1] , Hanna Schramm-Klein[2]

[1]Department of Marketing, University of Siegen, 57068 Siegen, Germany
[2]Department of Marketing, University of Siegen, 57068 Siegen, Germany

Abstract. In the competition for economically attractive stakeholders, regions have to implement strategies to gain and adhere those interest groups. Empirical studies concerning the migration motivations show that it is not only labor market but also soft locational factors of the social environment, nature and landscape that are of high importance: A majority of the population is willing to move or rather stay at a special place because of such soft locational factors. This study examines the impact of regional marketing projects on the development of regions from the perspectives of inhabitants and tourists as well as general attributes to measure a region's attractiveness from the perspective of high potentials. We argue that those projects that fit to the region and its unique selling propositions contribute to positioning and building location brand value. We show that projects have a socio-economic effect on the attitude towards regions and contribute to building location brand value. An analysis of group differences shows that the project influence on the region and region attractiveness are perceived in significantly different manner depending on the knowledge level of the stakeholder group. Consequently, one should increase the awareness of marketing activities and regions and focus on soft locational factors while establishing and positioning a region brand.

1 Introduction

The competition between regions and cities concerning attractive stakeholders, e.g. investors, inhabitants, tourists and human capital increases [1]. Demographic change and the urbanisation of the younger generation cause an aging and decline of the population as well as an increasing skill's shortage. Especially rural areas and old working-class regions have to implement strategies to gain and adhere inhabitants, manpower and external stakeholder groups. These regions started to develop proactive and responsive strategies to communicate their potential for increasing investments and quality of life [2]. Empirical studies concerning the migration motivations show that besides the labor market the soft locational factors of the social environment, nature and landscape are of high importance: A majority of the population is willing to move or rather stay at a special place because of such soft locational factors. Regional marketing projects shall increase the attraction of a region and thereby attract different stakeholder groups [2-4]. However, the effectiveness of establishing and promoting destination uniqueness has declined dramatically during the past few years. Many destinations rely on the promotion of similar quality characteristics such as scenery, history and culture and lose sight of the relevant and unique destination attributes [5]. In this paper, we address the issue of regional brand image. We argue that regional marketing projects that fit to the region and its unique selling propositions contribute to positioning and building location brand value. Most studies focus on tourism marketing alliances and possible marketing activities such as communication and campaign design which could strengthen a region, but almost no study analyses the influence of existing regional marketing projects. Usually, the investigations do not differ between diverse stakeholder perspectives and reproduce only in rare cases the whole process of attitude and behavior formation. Therefore, the aim of this study is to fill these gaps in empirical research and to investigate how to positively influence the perception, attitude and behavior towards a region. We focus our research on a specific regional marketing project – a wildlife conservation project – that can be understood as a soft locational factor to increase the value of leisure and nature of a region.

2 Background

A region becomes a recognizable and recallable location for the target group with the help of regional marketing which is used to develop regions and build relationships between the region, its market partners and target groups. It supports a strategic positioning and profiling of a region within the competitive environment between regions wherefore it includes the analysis, planning, implementation and control to identify and realize site-related factors, which provide competitive advantages to target groups [6]. Therefore, regional marketing has to fit with the requirements of the target groups with regard to cultural, demographic and economic relations [6].

Altered global and local challenges shifted the priorities in the field of regional marketing: Global challenges concern the macroenvironment of a region, e.g. as a result of globalization; local challenges relate to the microenvironment, thus, changes inside of a region such as demographic change. These changes force regions to identify and improve those factors that form their region attractiveness to gain and adhere the required stakeholders with whom the continuity of the region may be ensured. Regions have to adjust their profile to the particular needs of their interest groups to make them want to migrate, visit and stay in the region in which they are needed to limit the results of demographic change and provide manpower that ensures future economic security. A region's attractiveness reflects the opinions, beliefs and emotions that individuals hold about a region's perceived ability to provide satisfaction in relation to one's specific needs [7]. It can be understood as the result of a comparison process relating to the relative importance of individual benefits and the perceived ability of the region to deliver these individual benefits. It is incidental that the stronger the belief in a region and its satisfaction of individual needs are, the more attractive that region will be and the more likely it will be selected as a potential domicile, place of work, or travel destination. For all types of relations towards a region, the region represents a package of facilities and services consisting of various multidimensional attributes that altogether determine its attractiveness to a particular individual. Some individuals want to stay and live in the region because of these attributes, others will be drawn away from their homes and visit or move to the region [7].

Regional marketing projects in particular focus on the conception and establishment of strong local brands and need to consider the diverse demand of a region's different stakeholders. Previous literature has shown that regional marketing activities influence a region's image and associated behavior such as a visiting purpose in a positive way. Regions have to differentiate between two target group orientations: a) internal stakeholders are mainly the inhabitants as well as intraregional service providers and decision-makers in the fields of economy, science, education, culture, politics and leisure; b) external target group orientation alludes for instance to potential inhabitants, investors, companies, manpower and tourists [6-8].

In this study, we focus our research on a specific regional marketing project – a wildlife conservation project – that can be understood as a soft locational factor to increase the value of leisure and nature of a region. The special feature of this project is its location: Imbedded in the rural area of Bad Berleburg in North Rhine-Westphalia, Germany, it is very close connected to the supervising district Siegen-Wittgenstein which itself consists of two regional parts. An urban city builds the center of reference which is surrounded by many rural villages and towns. The relationship between the project and the involved cities and regions is full of interdependencies and raises expectations in the context of social, demographic, touristic and economic development within all stakeholder groups. This project includes a socioeconomic component which influences different stakeholders like inhabitants and tourists. Within the group of inhabitants, acceptance should be build because they live and stay close to the project and are confronted with it in their daily live. It is necessary to inform and integrate them in the process of establishing such a regional marketing projects. Tourists should be attracted with the help of diverse marketing activities and image campaigns to increase the knowledge of the project and region as tourist destinations.

3 Conceptual Background and Research Design

We base our study on these general aspects of regional marketing with the focus on how regional marketing projects can help building strong regional brands both for internal as well as external stakeholders. Our aim is to investigate how to positively influence the stakeholder's perception, attitude and behavior towards a region, regional loyalty and regional image. With our study we consider the two major problems regions have to deal with: (1) informational problems based on the lack of integration of different stakeholders in the decision process and (2) informational problems based on perceptions and attitudes towards a region and its service offers of different stakeholders. On the supply side, a region tries to differentiate and separate itself from others by profiling its economic and living space. On the demand side there are different stakeholders with different needs and interests. Taking these groups into account, a region has to consider different views on itself: Internal stakeholders are 'locals' that know the region from their own perception and opinions, relying on their own impressions and experiences, whereas external stakeholders have a distorted view, which often arises from secondary information. Regions or destinations pursue the goal of increasing their stakeholders' awareness level and thereby try to enhance the attitude towards their service offer and to improve their images [8]. The specific objectives of our study are therefore to contribute to the knowledge on the impact of regional marketing projects on the development of regions and destinations from the perspective of (a) internal stakeholders and (b) external stakeholders.

The conceptual framework of our study is based on the theory of reasoned action (TRA) that suggests that an individual's attitude towards the behavior and subjective norms form and influence the behavioral intention. Individuals and groups make decisions with respect to their own attitude towards that behavior and take account of the social desirability [9]. Transferred to our research context, we propose that regions have to build a consistent regional image to avoid a lack of integration of supply and demand side tasks. According to TRA, attitudes are formed based on consumer evaluation of the destinations' characteristics [10-12]. They are regarded key antecedents in attitude formation. We therefore propose:

> *H1: Consumer evaluation of a regional marketing project has a positive impact on the attitude towards this specific project.*

For that reason, regions have to identify their target groups and have to align their supply with their stakeholders' needs. Concerning these target group orientations, regions have to consider different perspectives on themselves. Locals or visitors know the region and/or the regional marketing project and can rely on their own impressions and experiences, whereas external stakeholders posses secondary information.

Attitude towards a region reflects individual mental pictures and associations that individuals hold with regard to a specific region, to delineate it from competing regions. Besides this cognitive dimension, however, attitudes also hold an affective dimension that includes a regional bonding, i.e. internal stakeholders such as inhabitants identify themselves with the region and external stakeholders develop interest in the region and its offers. If a region is able to produce positive attitudes, according to TRA this should result in positive behavioral intentions towards the region. For internal stakeholders, this might mean a decrease in migration and an increase in commitment with the region. For external stakeholder, for example, this would lead to increasing tourism, investments and migration into the region and would state an incentive for businesses to locate in the region.

Regional marketing projects are embedded in the specific region. Thus, there should be an intercorrelation of images both of the region itself and the regional marketing project. Attitude is an effective predictor of participation and satisfaction. We assume that individuals transfer their positive or negative attitude from one object to another, providing that there is a fit between the subject matters [13-14]. Thus, in addition to the effect of the individual's evaluation of a regional marketing project, attitude formation towards these projects is based on the general attitude that consumers hold towards a region. However, because of the nested constellation of regional marketing projects as elements that altogether form the attitude towards a region, we also expect that the attitude towards the regional marketing project influences the attitude towards the region. We therefore propose:

H2a: The attitude towards a region influences the attitude towards a regional marketing project in a positive way.

H2b: The attitude towards a regional marketing project influences the attitude towards a region in a positive way.

Following TRA, perceptions and attitudes of the attractiveness of objects may lead individuals to develop an attachment to it. With respect to regional marketing, this implicates that attractive marketing activities such as regional marketing projects cause commitment with the project and lead to positive behavioral intentions with regard to the regional marketing project [15]. However, we also suppose an influence of social norm and therefore assume, that individuals form their attitude towards regions and regional marketing projects with respect to social desirability. We expect them to behave in a way that matches with their attitude towards this behavior and subjective norms [9].

This is in line with TRA, we therefore propose that an individual's attitude towards a regional marketing project acts as a predictor of its satisfaction which affects the behavioral intention [13, 16]. With respect to regional marketing, this implicates that attractive marketing activities such as regional marketing projects cause commitment with this project and lead to positive behavioral intentions with regard to the regional marketing project [15]. However, we also suppose an influence of social norm and therefore assume, that individuals form their attitude towards regions and regional marketing projects with respect to social desirability. We expect them to behave in a way that matches with their attitude towards this behavior and subjective norms [9]. This is in line with TRA, we therefore propose that an individual's attitude towards a regional marketing project acts as a predictor of its satisfaction which affects the behavioral intention [13,15-17].

H3:   The attitude towards a regional marketing project has a positive influence on the behavioral intention with regard to this project.

To test our hypotheses, we conducted a series of consumer surveys in a central German region. As environmental stimuli we included a) a region's general attributes such as quality of life, labor market, leisure time activities and b) a wildlife conservation project (the reintroduction of European bisons to the wild) as a specific marketing project within the region that offers a range of services that fit to the region like hiking, walking, etc. A prestudy and focus groups showed that there is a fit between the considered region and the corresponding regional marketing project.

Our first study was the start of a long-term study to analyze the changes in evaluation, attitude formation and behavior. This first investigation was executed during the establishment of the regional marketing project. Therefore, we included intentional behavior as outcome variable. The second investigation was executed after the opening of the project which entails the measurement of real behavior.

Our first quantitative consumer survey was conducted following a broad qualitative study, consisting of 26 in-depth focus group discussion which were conducted in the observed region. The sample of Study I (N=676) represents the demographic structure of the region, 49,9% were male and 50,1% female inhabitants. To avoid problems of social desirability bias in the measures, we administered questionnaires to consumers in the pedestrian areas of 26 cities and villages in the region, conducted face-to-face interviews (78% of respondents) and an online survey (22% of respondents). In Study II, we administered it to 141 consumers in the region under review, who had not answered it in the first period, and 98 consumers outside of the observed region (N=196) to detect possible differences between an internal and external sample. This internal sample showed the same demographic structure as in Study I and the external sample was adapted to represent demographics of Germany.

In this study four main constructs were analysed both for the region and for the regional marketing project: perception/awareness, image, attitude and behavioral intention. The items were adapted from previous studies. To measure perception or awareness, we adapted a 3-item scale from Bigné, Sànchez & Sànchez [15], such as "What do you know about the region?". Attitude was measured with 10 items from Batra and Ahtola [18], e.g. useful, nice, safe. To analyse the behavioral intention, we used items such as "I would recommend the city to my family and friend" [13]. We used almost the same items to analyse the perception, attitude, image and behavioral intention towards the region marketing project to see if they fit together. All constructs are measured with a seven point scale ranging from strongly disagree (1) to strongly agree (7).

4 Analysis and Results

Measure validation and model testing for the model were conducted using Smart PLS. Because we expected bidirectional effects between our latent constructs, we conducted two separate pathways each with one hypotheses system (following suggestions of [19]).

The results for Study I are presented in Table 1 and Table 2. The endogenous variables are well-explained by the endogenous variables. The significant path coefficient of .768 with high effect size of $f^2 = 1.527$ shows that the evaluation of the regional marketing project has a very strong influence on the attitude towards the region. Thus, we can confirm H2b. In contrast, the attitude towards the region has no substantial influence on the attitude towards the project. H2a, therefore, cannot be confirmed. Thus, the better evaluation of the regional marketing project, the better is the attitude towards the project ($\beta = .768$). A positive attitude towards the project induced the consumers more likely to visit it ($\beta = 0.719$). Hypotheses H1 and H3 are supported by our data, however, we cannot find support for H2b. A possible reason for this might be that the regional marketing project was not yet opened during the first data collection. This result may change within the second questioning.

Table 1

exogenous, latent variables	endogenous variables	ß	f^2	R^2	Q^2
image of regional marketing project	attitude towards regional marketing project	0.768***	1.527	0.652	0.462
attitude towards region		0.105**	0.028		
attitude towards regional marketing project	behavioral intention towards the regional marketing project	0.719***		0.517	0.510
*** p ≤ 0.001; ** p ≤ 0.01; * p ≤ 0.05; n.s. p > 0.05					

In our second path model, we reveal that the influence of the attitude towards the regional marketing project has no explanatory power for the attitude towards the region ($R^2 = .120$), but the path coefficient indicates that the relation between the two constructs is substantial ($\beta = .347$). Hypothesis H2b can be supported. The Stone-Geisser-Criterion which assesses the predictive quality of the model indicates a satisfactorily model specification [20].

Table 2

exogenous, latent variables	endogenous variables	ß	R^2	Q^2
image of regional marketing project	attitude towards regional marketing project	0.801***	0.642	0.456
attitude towards regional marketing project	attitude towards region	0.347***	0.120	0.074
attitude towards regional marketing project	behavioral intention towards the regional marketing project	0.719***	0.517	0.514
*** $p \leq 0.001$; ** $p \leq 0.01$; * $p \leq 0.05$; n.s. $p > 0.05$				

In Study II, we distinguish between the internal (N=141) and the external sample (N=98).

Table 3

exogenous, latent variables	endogenous variables	internal sample			external sample		
		ß	R^2	f^2	ß	R^2	f^2
image of regional marketing project	attitude towards regional marketing project	0.796***	0.681	1.793	0.683***	0.597	0.925
attitude towards region		0.084^{ns}		0.019	0.169*		0.057
attitude towards regional marketing project	behavioral intention towards the regional marketing project	0.750***	0.563	0.514	0.660***	0.436	0.514
*** $p \leq 0.001$; ** $p \leq 0.01$; * $p \leq 0.05$; n.s. $p > 0.05$							

Table 4

exogenous, latent variables	endogenous variables	internal sample		external sample	
		ß	R^2	ß	R^2
image of regional marketing project	attitude towards regional marketing project	0.821***	0.674	0.758***	0.575
attitude towards regional marketing project	attitude towards region	0.329***	0.108	0.472***	0.223
attitude towards regional marketing project	behavioral intention towards the regional marketing project	0.750***	0.563	0.660***	0.435
*** $p \leq 0.001$; ** $p \leq 0.01$; * $p \leq 0.05$; n.s. $p > 0.05$					

Generally, the results show that the project is significantly better known in the internal sample. In the analysis of the data subsets with the moderator variable 'regional affiliation', it is to accentuate that the path coefficient ß of the relation between the image of the project and the attitude towards the project in the internal sample is higher than in the external one. The effect size of the influence of regional project evaluation on the attitude towards the regional project is also stronger than in the external sample. Thus, there are differences in awareness of the project and otherwise that the awareness has an influence on the image.

Although in the internal sample there is higher knowledge with regard to the project, the attitude towards it is significantly higher than in the external sample. However, a t-test shows that the path coefficient and R^2 in the external sample are significantly higher than in the internal sample ($ß^{internal}=0.329$; $ß^{external}=0.472$; $R^{2internal}=0.108$; $R^{2external}=0.223$). Thus, these results show that there is a different impact of regional marketing projects on internal and external stakeholders.

The comparison of the two path models reveals significant differences, especially with regard to H2b in path model II. Differences in consideration of the significance of the path relations exist in path model I, whereas the influence of the construct 'attitude towards region' on the construct 'attitude towards the regional marketing project' is not significant in the internal sample, however it is in the external one. A possible reason for this effect may be that some respondents of the internal sample indicated that they do not associate the regional project with the region. Nevertheless hypothesis H2b shows that the attitude towards the project influences the attitude towards the region significantly positive. This effect is considerably and significantly higher in the external sample.

5 Conclusion and Implications

This study examines the impact of regional marketing projects on the development of regions and destinations from the perspectives of inhabitants and tourists. While previous studies focused on migration motivations and soft locational factors, this study shows that regional marketing projects have a significantly positive effect on the attitude towards regions. Our results of the PLS models show that the behavioral intention is significantly and substantially influenced by the attitude towards this project. This attitude is in turn significantly and substantially influenced by the evaluation of the project's characteristics. However, the comparison of the region-internal and region-external respondent groups shows that perception and evaluation of the regional marketing project depend on the awareness of the project. Consequently, regional marketing managers should increase the awareness of marketing activities within the different stakeholder groups.

The most important result for regional marketing managers is the positive effect of the attitude towards a marketing project on the attitude towards a region. This can be understood as an indication that such projects have positive socio-economic effects on the attitudes towards a region. An analysis of group differences provides the result that the project influence on the region is more significant within an external sample. This implicates that regional marketing should focus on soft locational factors while establishing and positioning a region brand and corresponding strategies.

References

1. R.L. Florida, *The flight of the creative class: The new global competition for talent,* HarperBusiness, HarperCollins, NY (2008).
2. R. Paddison, *City Marketing, image reconstruction and urban regeneration,* Urb. St., **30,** 2, 339-349 (1993)
3. P. Pellenbarg, W. Meester, *Regional Marketing to change regional images: The examples of the Groningen Province Campaign,* ESRP, **16,** 1, 23-39 (2009)
4. K. Knickel, H. Renting, *Methodological and conceptual issues in the study of multifunctionality and rural development,* Sociol. Rural., **40,** 4, 512-528 (2009)
5. C. Blain, S.E. Levy, J.R.B. Ritchie, *Destination branding: Insights and practices from destination management organizations,* JTR **43,** 3, 328-338 (2005)
6. M. Kavaratzis, *Place Branding : A review of trends and conceptual models,* MR **5,** 4, 329–342 (2005)
7. Y. Hu, J.R. Ritchie, *Measuring destination attractiveness: A contextual approach,* JTR **32,** 25, 25-34 (1993)
8. L. Birgit, *Image segmentation : The case of a tourism destination,* JSM **15,** 1, 49–66 (2001)
9. M. Fishbein, I. Ajzen, Understanding attitudes and predicting social behaviour, *Prentice Hall, Englewood-Cliffs, NJ* (1980).
10. C.B. Castro, E.M. Armario, D.M. Ruiz, *The influence of market heterogeneity on the relationship between a destination's image and tourist's future behaviour,* TM **28,** 175–187 (2007)
11. C.F. Chen, D.C. Tsai, *How destination image and evaluative factors affect behavioral intentions,* TM **28,** 1115–1122 (2007)
12. A. Beerli, J.D. Martin, *Tourists' characteristics and the perceived image of tourist destinations: A quantitative analysis*—a case study of Lanzarote, Spain, TM **25,** 623-636 (2004)

13. T.H. Lee, *Ecotourism behavioral model of national forest recreation areas in Taiwan*, Int. Forestry Rev. **9**, 3, 771–785 (2007)

14. M.G. Ragheb, R.L. Tate, A behavioural model of leisure participation, LS **12**, 1, 61-67 (1993)

15. J.E. Bigné, M.I. Sanchez, J. Sanchez, Tourism image, evaluation variables and after purchase behavior: Interrelationship, TM **22**, 6, 607-616 (2001)

16. I. Ajzen, *The theory of planned behavior, organization behavior and human decision processes*, **50**, 179–211 (1991)

17. I. Ajzen, B.L. Driver, *Application of the theory of planned behavior to leisure choice*, JLR **24**, 3, 207-240 (1992)

18. R. Batra, O.T. *Ahtola, Measuring the hedonic and utilitarian sources of consumer attitudes,* Marketing Letters **2**, 2, 159-170 (1990)

19. M. Wetzels, G. Odekerken-Schröder, C. van Oppen, *Using PLS path modeling for assessing hierarchical construct models*, Mis Quarterly 33, 1, 177–195(2009)

20. C. Fornell, J. Cha, Partial Least Squares, *Blackwell Publishers, Cambridge,* MA (1994)

16

Length of Stay and Tourism Facility Assessment: The Viewpoint of Malaysian Tourists at Langkawi

Mastura Jaafar[1] , Mana Khoshkam[2]

[1,2]School of Housing, Building and Planning, Universiti Sains Malaysia, 11800 Penang, Malaysia

Abstract. This investigation employed partial least square analysis to scrutinize factors influencing the social perceptions of Malaysian tourists of tourism facilities at an island tourism destination. It focuses on the effect of one particular socio-demographic variable, length of stay, on consumer satisfaction. Data was collected from a major tourism destination at Langkawi, Malaysia. The results indicate that length of stay has an effect on tourists' social perceptions and contributes to their dissatisfaction with the destination. Tourists who stayed more than 10 days were less satisfaction than those who stayed for less than 10 days. The implications of this finding and recommendations for further study are discussed as well.

1 Introduction

Langkawi is considered as a major tourism destination in Malaysia which plays an important role in the country's tourism industry. Ever since the Sixth Malaysia Plan (1991 – 1995), efforts had been undertaken to improve and promote Langkawi's tourism facilities [1]. But while increasing the volume of tourists and ensuring their satisfaction is a priority, various problems exist in relation to the quality of attractions, including issues with safety, poor maintenance, vandalism of facilities, and other issues [2].

One of Langkawi's more popular tourist attractions is the Oriental Village. Owing to this popularity, the Oriental Village was chosen as the focus of this study, the aim of which is to examine how length of stay (LoS), social perceptions (SP), and social facilities (SF) affect customer satisfaction (CS). The research model and hypothesized relationships were tested using the Partial Least Squares (PLS) approach.

2 Literature

2.1 Length of stay

There are few studies that have used duration models in the context of tourism [3]. LoS is concerned with the duration of a tourist's stay at a destination [4]. However, tourists are often unsure about how long they should spend at a destination and this is often a decision best made when planning ones travel [5]. In part, the determination about LoS is guided by external demands (esp. necessity to return to work), but is also be informed by economic considerations. Economic factors also influence the range of activities that tourists undertake while visiting a destination and their choice of accommodation. Tourist socio-demographic information and their expectations regarding the quality of the facilities and services is best recorded when the tourist is departing. This information tells us about tourist profiles, their destination experiences, and their expectations [5, 6]. Davis and Mangan (1992) [7] suppose that LoS determines what activities a tourist engages in and their economic impact on the host community. Therefore, LoS can be considered predictive of tourist spending [7-9].

Additionally, Butter (1975) [10] identified five tourist-related factors that influence tourist interactions with local residents; including the number of visitors, LoS, ethnic characteristics, economic and socio-cultural characteristics, and activities undertaken during their stay. Chen and Hsu (2000) [11] reported that LoS, among other variables, affects how Korean tourists' measure the attractiveness of a destination. But despite the growth of the tourism literature, few studies have investigated LoS and tourism facilities in Malaysia. This study seeks to examine the relationship between several variables to better understand CS in relation to the facilities at Langkawi's Oriental Village. Therefore, the primary research hypothesis for this study was as follows:

H1: LoS has a positive effect on SP

Whilst LoS pertains to the amount of time that a tourist spends at a destination, it does not include the time spent travelling [12]. Furthermore, LoS does not include time spent at other destinations. For example, LoS at Langkawi is calculated separately from LoS at Penang; although both could be combined to determine LoS in Malaysia. Ascertaining LoS allows for key stakeholders to develop appropriate tourist infrastructure [12]. Based on the literature review above, we hypothesized that:

H2: LoS has a positive effect on SF

Previous studies have demonstrated a positive relationship between LoS and CS with a destination [13]. Beachside destinations tend to be favoured by tourists and receive a high number of repeat visitors [14]. Therefore, satisfaction with a previous visit positively influences the decision to return [15], and this sense of satisfaction is itself influenced by aspects of the destination [16]. Therefore, we hypothesized that:

H3: LoS has a positive effect on CS

2.2 Tourism facilities

In the context of tourism, satisfaction refers to the perceived sum of the relationship between ones expectations of a tourism product and one's actual experience of consuming said product. If a product does not meet expectations, dissatisfaction results [17]. Previous studies suggest that perceptions of service quality are correlated with value satisfaction, and that satisfaction affects loyalty and post-consumption behaviors [18]. Accordingly, we hypothesized that:
H4: SP will influence CS

2.3 Customer satisfaction

With reference to some researchers, CS has its origin within the individual, in how they compare their expectations of a product or service with the actual product or service that was delivered. Furthermore, it has been hypothesized that CS can be measured behaviorally. To illustrate, definitive satisfaction or dissatisfaction with a product might be expressed through the voluntarily writing a letter to complain or compliment a product. Similarly, a tourist might be complimentary of their experience of a product, but be dissatisfied with the facilities. Satisfaction might be expressed though repeat visits to a destination or through "word-of-mouth" recommendations [2].

Sharpley [4] notes that satisfaction plays an important role in the planning of marketable tourism products and services. However, despite the apparent importance of tourist satisfaction, few papers have defined the concept. In one paper, tourist satisfaction was described as the total sum of the quality of a visitor's experience; the psychological state or outcome produced as a result of the visitor's interaction with the various aspects of a tourist product or service [19]. With this definition of tourist satisfaction in mind, there is a paucity of research concerning the relationship between tourist satisfaction and tourist facilities. In one of the few studies of its kind, Sekaran and Bougie (2010) [20] report that SF, such as friendly/quality services, and physical facilities (i.e. lodgings) are significant contributors toward a tourist's overall satisfaction. Therefore, we hypothesized that:

H5: SF will influence CS

3 Research context and research model

In this particular study, we investigated the contribution made by the tourism facilities at Langkawi's Oriental Village to CS, using how much a customer was willing to pay for these products as a behavioral measure of CS. To this end, we proposed five research hypotheses to be tested:

H1: LoS has a positive effect on SP
H2: LoS has a positive effect on SF
H3: LoS has a positive effect on CS
H4: SP will influence CS
H5: SF will influence CS

The hypothetical relationships between these variables, IV (Demographic characteristics), DV (Tourism Facilities), and DV (Willingness to pay), are illustrated in Fig. 1, noting that satisfaction is the product of the interaction between SP and LoS, and between SF and LoS. LoS itself, however, leads more directly to the experience of satisfaction.

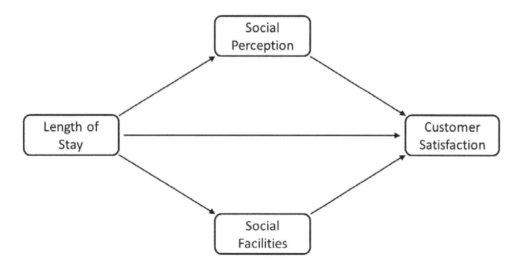

Figure 1. Research Model

4 Research Method

We targeted domestic Malaysian tourists visiting Langkawi in this study. While Langkawi receives a number of international tourists, cluster sampling allowed us to focus our attention on domestic tourists. For the first step, we divided Langkawi into five regions based on the points of the compass. Secondly, a list of tourist attractions was developed for each region, including the identification of a "hot spot" attraction that saw the most visitors. For the Northern region of Langkawi, the "hot spot" attraction was the Oriental Village. In the final step, one on of these five "hot spots" was chosen at random.

4.1 Data Collection

The self-report questionnaire used in this study was divided into four sections; the first section collected demographic information, including LoS. The second section sought to investigate the respondent's SPs. The third section inquired about their views on the Oriental Village's SF. In the final section, respondents were asked about their satisfaction and willingness to pay for various attractions. Data collection was conducted over two weeks during March 2014. Of the 800 questionnaires distributed, only 366 questionnaires were returned as complete.

4.2 Measures and Assessment of Goodness of Measures

The questionnaire contained 49 question items, 35 of which used a six-point Likert-type scale, to gather data on each construct. The items were adapted from the existing literature and modified for the purposes of measuring the facilities at the target location.

4.3 Goodness of Measures

Table 1 describes the factor loadings for the research model. Using multivariate analysis, we assigned a cut-off point to the factor loadings to regard a loading of 0.5 as significant [21]. Moreover, the questionnaire items tended to load highly on the target variables and lowly on other constructs, thereby confirming the construct validity. Convergent validity was determined based on a combination of composite reliability (CR), factor loadings, and the average variance extracted (AVE) [21]. All values loaded above 0.6.

CR indicates the degree to which a construct's indicators relate to the latent variables and should ideally exceed 0.7 [21]. We determined that the CR of our construct indicators ranged from 0.857 to 0.919 (Table 2), which was statistically acceptable.

Table 1. Factor Loading.

Indicator	SP	CS	SF
Social_B2	0.732		
Social_B4	0.787		
Social_B6	0.736		
Social_B7	0.841		
Social_C4			0.922
Social_C5			0.912
Social_C7			0.855

Willing.to.pay_D1_1		0.766	
Willing.to.pay_D3_1		0.795	
Willing.to.pay_D4_1		0.820	
Willing.to.pay_D5_1		0.835	
Willing.to.pay_D6_1		0.800	
Willing.to.pay_D7_1		0.837	

Table 2. Results of measurement model

	AVE	Composite Reliability	R^2	Cronbach's Alpha
SP	0.601	0.857	0.009	0.783
LoS	-	-	-	-
CS	0.654	0.919	0.106	0.895
SF	0.804	0.925	0.007	0.878

AVE measures the amount of variance a construct indicator relative to measurement errors. The AVE should be more than 0.5 to justify the inclusion of a construct [21]. In the present study, the AVE was in the range of 0.601 and 0.804 (Table 2). We used the Cronbach's alpha coefficient to test the reliability of the indicators. The Cronbach's alpha coefficient, AVE, and R^2 indicating the reliability of the measurements and their internal consistency is summarized in Table 2.

Discriminant validity ensures that the construct indicators are sufficiently different from one another. We describe the discriminant validity of our indicators in Table 3, where the diagonal elements are larger than the off-diagonal elements on the same row and column, alluding to discrimination. In short, our measurement model showed both convergent and discriminant validity.

Table 3. Disciminant validity

	SP	*LoS*	*CS*	*SF*
SP	**0.775**			
LoS	0.094	**1.000**		
CS	0.232	-0.130	**0.809**	
SF	0.346	-0.086	0.254	**0.897**

Table 4 summarizes the results of testing the validity of the model's constructs. The result shows that all three constructs (i.e. SP, social facility, and willingness to pay) were valid indicators according to the parameter estimates and their statistical significance [22].

Table 4. Results of the Construct Model.

	Original Sample (O)	Standard Error	T-statistics	P Values
	0.238	0.072	3.322	0.001
	0.325	0.061	5.324	0.000
	0.293	0.073	4.011	0.000
	0.421	0.058	7.197	0.000
Social_C4←SF	0.405	0.047	8.569	0.000
Social_C5←SF	0.368	0.038	9.604	0.000
Social_C7←SF		0.052	6.507	0.000
Willing.to.pay_D1_1←CS	Social_B2←SP	0.034	5.122	0.000
Willing.to.pay_D3_1←CS	Social_B4←SP	0.033	8.157	0.000
Willing.to.pay_D4_1←CS	Social_B6←SP	0.032	8.033	0.000
Willing.to.pay_D5_1←CS	Social_B7←SP	0.023	7.519	0.000
Willing.to.pay_D6_1←CS	0.173	0.035	4.973	0.000
Willing.to.pay_D7_1←CS	0.185	0.023	8.034	0.000

**p<0.01

4.4 Hypothesis Testing

A path analysis of the hypotheses was generated to test the relationships between the variables (Table 5 and Fig. 2). The R^2 for the relationships between the three variables and satisfaction was 0.106, suggesting that 10.6% of the variance of satisfaction was explained by respondent's SP, their perception of SF, and their LoS. SP and SF (b = 0.185, b = 0.181, p<0.0.1) were positively related to CS, whereas LoS was not significant. Also, the relationship between LoS and SF was not significant. Therefore, hypotheses H1, H3, and H5 were supported, while H2 and H4 were not supported.

Table 5. Path Coefficient, β and Hypothesis Testing

	B	(F²)	Standard Error	T-statistic	P-values	Supported
SP→CS	0.185	0.033	0.062	2.995	0.003	YES
LoS→SP	0.094	0.007	0.061	1.390	0.165	NO
LoS→CS	-0.129	0.017	0.056	2.254	0.025	YES
LoS→SF	-0.086	0.008	0.078	1.131	0.259	NO
SF→CS	0.181	0.031	0.052	3.455	0.001	YES

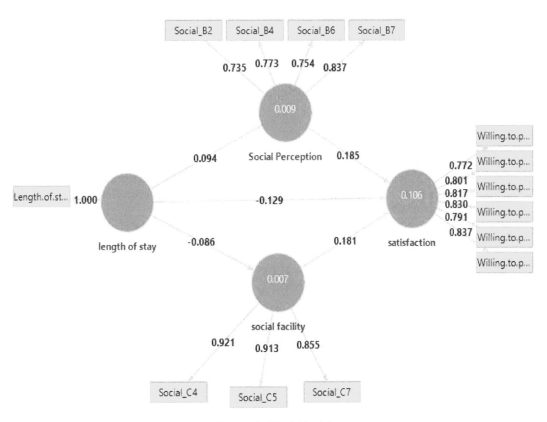

Figure 2. Final Model

These result indicate a positive and direct relationship between SP and CS (ß = 0.185, Std = 0.062, f^2 = 0.33, *t*-statistic = 2.99, *P*-value <0.05). Furthermore, LoS and SP were negatively related, a finding not supported by any previous studies. Also, LoS and CS were positively related (ß = -0.129, Std = 0.056, f^2 =0.017, *t*-statistic = 2.254, *P*-value <0.05). This indicates that LoS has an effect on SP and contributed toward the dissatisfaction of visitors; those respondents who stayed for more than 10 days being less satisfied than those who stayed for less. Also, there was negative relationship between LoS and SF (ß = -0.086, t-statistic = 1.131, P-value <0.05). Furthermore, the relationship between SF and CS was significant (ß = -0.181, Std. = 0.052, f^2 = 0.031, t-statistic = 3.455, P-value <0.05).

5   Discussion and Conclusion

In particular, the results of this study allude the imperative for improvements in the SF of Langkawi's Oriental Village. Previous studies have indicated that understanding tourist LoS might help policy-makers and planners to develop appropriate tourism infrastructure and packages [16]. This study expands on our existing knowledge in regard to tourism facilities and satisfaction by examining the issue in the context of Malaysian domestic tourism. Therefore, Langkawi's Oriental Village was the subject for this investigation.

We found that the LoS had a significant effect on SP, which was supported the by a previous study [16]. However, we also found dissatisfaction among the visitors to the Oriental Village; those who stayed for more than 10 days were less satisfied than those who had stayed for less. This finding was in contrast to previous studies finding a positive relationship between LoS and CS [13-16]. We also identified a negative relationship between LoS and SF, again in contrast to previous studies [23].

Consequently, we argue the importance of improving the tourism facilities, particularly the SF, at the Oriental Village in Langkawi. It is noteworthy to examine CS and CP in regarding to trip duration in the area and experiences with different tourist facilities. Again, this highlights the imperative to continue developing the tourism industry in this area.

We demonstrated a positive and significant link between LoS in relation to SP, SF, and CS (esp. willingness to pay). It is crucial to understand the various perceptions and perspectives of tourists visiting an area for the first or second time. For further study, the relationship between these variables during subsequent visits might be examined.

References

1.   J.A. Ibrahim, M.Z. Ahmad, *Pelancongan Langkawi 1987 – 2010: Pencapaian dan cabaranmasadepan*. In: Persidangan Kebangsaan Ekonomi Malaysia, Hotel Everly Resort, Melaka. (Didapati, Malaysia, 2011)
2.   S. Abdullah, A.A. Razak, A. Marzuki, M. Jaafar, Assessing tourist satisfaction with the facilities provided at Langkawi island gateway jetty terminals, Liburna, **2**, 2 (2013)
3.   C.P.Barros, L.P.Machado, The length of stay in tourism Ann. Tour. Res, **37**, 3, 692-706 (2010)
4.   R. Sharpley, *Tourism, tourists and society* (ELM Publications, Huntingdon, 1999)
5.   A. Decrop, D.Snelders, Planning the summer vacation: an adaptable and opportunistic process, Ann. Tour. Res **31**, 4, 1008-1030 (2004)
6.   B. Bargeman, V. Poel, The role of routines in the decision making process of Dutch vacationers, Tour. Manage **27**, 4, 707-720(2006)
7.   B. Davies, J.Mangan, Family expenditure on hotels and holidays', Ann. Tour. Res **19**, 4, 691-699 (1992)
8.   P. Legoherel, Toward a market segmentation of the tourism trade: expenditure levels and consumer behavior instability, J. Travel Tour. Mark **37**, 1, 19-39 (1998)
9.   C. Mok, T. Iverson, Expenditure-based segmentation: Taiwanese tourists to Guam, Tour. Manage **21**, 3, 299-305 (2000)
10. R.W. Butler, Tourism as an agent of social change, *Proceedings of the international geographical union's working group on the geography of tourism and recreation*, 85-90 (Trent University, Ontario, 1975)
11. J.S. Chen, C.H.C. Hsu, J. Measurement of Korean tourists' perceived images of overseas destinations , Travel Res **38**, 4, 411-416 (2000)
12. G.E. Santos, R. Vicent, J. Rey-Maquieira, Length of Stay at Multiple Destinations of Tourism Trips in Brazil, J. Travel Tour. Res **21**, 1-13 (2014)

13. L. Festinger, A theory of social comparison processes, Human Relations **7**, 117-140 (1954)

14. A. Beerli, J.D. Martin, Factors influencing destination image, Ann. Tour. Res **31**, 4, 657-681 (2004)

15. M. Kozak, Repeaters' behavior at two distinct destinations, Ann. Tour. Res **28**, 3, 785-808 (2001)

16. M. Kozak, 'Measuring tourist satisfaction with multiple destination attributes, Tour. Anal **7**, 229-240 (2003)

17. R.L. Oliver, Whence consumer loyalty? J. Mark **63**, 33-44 (1999)

18. C.F. Chen, D. Tsai, How destination image and evaluative factors affect behavioral intentions? Tour. Manage **28**, 1115 -1122 (2007)

19. M. Meng, Y. Tepanon, M. Uysal, Measuring tourist satisfaction by attribute and motivation: The case of a nature-based resort, J. Vac. Mark **14**, 1, 41-56 (2008)

20. U. Sekaran, R. Bougie, *Research Methods for Business: A Skill Building Approach* (Wiley, London, 2010)

21. J.F. Hair, W.C. Black, B.J. Babin, R.E. Anderson, *Multivariate data analysis* (Prentice-Hall, Upper Saddle River, 2010)

22. W.S. Chow, L.S. Chan, Social network and shared goals in organizational knowledge sharing, Inf Manag **45**, 7, 24-30 (2008)

23. C. Thrane, E. Farstad, Tourists' Length of Stay: The case of international summer visitors to Norway, Tour. Econ **18**, 5, 1069-1082 (2012)

17

The Diversity of Ecology and Nature Reserves as an Ecotourism Attraction in Jordan

Jamal El-Harami [1]

[1] Al-Zaytooneh University of Jordan, Amman, Jordan

Abstract. This article aims to explore ranges of mountains in Jordan which contain various types of tourist attractions exemplified by high green mountains in the Central Region, Ajloun, which are covered by many different trees. Alongside these mountains there is a large animal reservation and a tourist lodging built by using wood. This article will examine the effects of eco-tourism on the local community economically and socially. A completely different range of desert mountains in the South Region, in Wadi Rum, which is an eco-tourism attraction, will be tackled in this paper to discuss various components of tourist attractions such as mountain climbing, hiking and desert exploration. The article shows the influence of such tourism in improving life standards of local community and the sustainability of tourism in both geographical areas and their proximity to archaeological sites which can be included in tourist programs. The methodology of this article is descriptive and supported by field trips and meetings with members of local communities.

1 Introduction

Jordan is known for its rich assortment of historical, religious and geographical attractions which are spread throughout the country. These tourist attractions include Petra, Jerash, Ajloun, Baptism Site at the Dead Sea and other Islamic sites, such as; Qasr Amra, Wadi Rum in the south, and many others. Jordan's population is around 6.2 million and the land covers nearly 89,213 thousand square kilometers, approximately 75% of that space being taken up by desert. Most of the country occupies a plateau of between 700m. and 1000m. above sea level, with a few mountainous areas. Plant species that can be found include Cedar, Cactus, Eucalyptus and Pine, Olive trees and fruit producing trees, such as; apricot, plums, figs, pomegranates, grape vines, etc. Fauna in Jordan includes mongoose, lynx, striped hyenas, gazelles, various foxes and wolves, different kinds of birds.

Tourism is of vital importance to the national economy of Jordan. It is the Kingdom's largest export sector, its second largest private sector employer, and its second highest producer of foreign exchange. Tourist number in 2013 reached around 8 million in 2013 and tourism receipts reached 2883.6 JD million, more than 13% of GDP.

Jordan is keen on diversifying types of tourism by including mountain tourist attractions which are spread in areas in the north and south of the country, where each has its own characteristic. Ajloun mountains in the north are the largest mountains covered by many kinds of trees, such as: pine and eucalyptus and cedar. In the vicinity of these mountains many cultural and religious monuments dating to thousands of years do exist. In the south there is Wadi Rum mountains rising hundreds of meters among desert sandy areas where many sports are performed around the year, such as: mountain climbing, trekking and camping. In the middle in Tafilah region there is Dana Nature Reserve which combines breathtaking mountain views and wild life tourism products in Jordan and a well known ecotourism destinations. Jordan has recently became very popular for international tourists and local inhabitants.

2 Literature Review

Ecotourism has been a major topic for researchers concerned with tourism and its wide range of products in many parts of the world. Ecotourism has grown as a consequence of dis-satisfaction with conventional forms of tourism which have, in a general sense, ignored social and ecological elements of foreign regions in favor of a more anthropocentric and strictly profit centered approach to the delivery of tourism products [1].

The terms ecotourism and nature-based tourism are often used interchangeably in the published literature. Popular tourism literature and marketing materials offer many other terms that are used interchangeably with ecotourism and nature-based tourism [2], such as; green tourism, sustainable tourism, alternative tourism, ethical tourism, responsible tourism, conservative tourism and others. These terms create confusion for what they mean.

2.1 Study Problem

The interest in Ecotourism in Jordan is relatively recent in comparison with other countries in the world. The Ministry of Tourism and Antiquities in Jordan began to diversify tourism products by including natural reserves whose number reached seven supervised by Wild Jordan, a branch of RCSN. The study includes three major reserves starting from north to south of Jordan. They are Ajloun Reserve, Dana Biosphere Reserve and Wadi Rum Reserve.

2.2 Study Importance

The main motivation of the study is focusing on the components and characteristics of these reserves which make them sustainable ecotourism's attractions which will add to various tourism products in Jordan.

2.3 Study Aims

The study aims toward knowing the importance of natural reserves in Jordan and their role in improving the life style of local communities and the protection of nature and sustainability of sites, by providing an economic incentives for conservation and raising awareness of environment.

3 Methodology

This work adopts the descriptive methodology where it traces the major concepts and origins of ecotourism discussed in the published literature by many researchers. Thoughts on eco-tourism in Jordan are a result of previous studies, personal communications with those in charge of tourist attractions and material collected upon many visits and observations of the components of these mountain tourist attractions in Jordan.

4 The Concept of Ecotourism: Origins and Definitions

The first appearance of the word "ecotourism" in English language as a hyphenated term (i.e., 'eco-tourism') was used by [3]. Hector Ceballos – Lascurian used the Spanish word ecotourism earlier in the decade where he is accredited to be the first to coin the phrase in the early 1980s [4]. He defined it as a 'traveling to relatively undisturbed or uncontaminated natural areas with the specific objective of studying, admiring and enjoying the scenery and its wild plants and animals, as well as any existing cultural manifestations (both past and present) found in these areas'.[5]

Most recently Fennel says that the term ecotourism has been traced back to the work of Hetzer (1965) who used it to explain the intricate relationship between tourists and the environments and cultures in which they interact. Hetzer identified for fundamental pillars that needed to be followed for a more responsible form of tourism. These included:

1. Minimum environmental impact.
2. Minimum impact on and maximum respect for host cultures.
3. Maximum economic benefits to the host country's grassroots.
4. Maximum 'recreational' satisfaction to participating tourists.

Ecotourism has been the subject of several studies by researchers who defined it in different ways ranging from the general to the specific. A chronological sample of definitions proposed by a variety of ecotourism researchers [6] reflects the intensity of articles concerning ecotourism. Goodwin offers his definition by saying that ecotourism is a low-impact nature tourism which contributes to the maintenance of species and habitats either directly through a contribution to conservation and/or indirectly by providing revenue to the local community sufficient for local people to value, and therefore protect, their wildlife heritage area as a source of income.

A close examination of the above definitions of ecotourism reveals that the concept consists of four core criteria:

1. Ecotourism is a form of tourism and a product user should therefore meet the basic criteria used to define the 'tourist' to qualify as an eco-tourist.
2. Ecotourism attractions are based primarily on the natural environment and include the cultural attributes that are associated with this environment.
3. Ecotourism provides experiences focused on learning, education and appreciation.
4. Ecotourism must be oriented to be environmentally and socio-culturally sustainable and keeping the best practice.

Fennel concludes that the literature points to the fact that ecotourism is one aspect of nature-oriented tourism which includes many other types of tourism and outdoor recreation. Ecotourism occurs in and depends on a natural setting and many include cultural elements where they occur in a natural settings. The conservation of the natural resource is essential to the planning, development and management of ecotourism.

Characteristics of ecotourism according to Honey [7] comprise of travel to natural destinations, minimize impact, build environmental awareness, provide direct financial benefits for conservation, provide financial benefits and empowerment for local people, respect local culture and support human rights and democratic movements.

Dawson [8] mentions that in the past decade ecotourism and nature-based tourism have been the subject of many conference, professional journals, books and project reports which all resulted by giving numerous definitions and varied frames of reference as to what constitutes either ecotourism or nature-based tourism.

Despite all the various definitions which share many elements proposed by scholars and organizations to define ecotourism, it remains safe to say that each natured-based tourism can offer the suitable definition according to what it contains and represents to the visitor and the geographical location. There is still no universal agreement on the definition of ecotourism. One of the most popular definitions of ecotourism is the one given by the International Ecotourism Society (TIES). The Society defines ecotourism as "the responsible travel in natural areas that conserves the environment and sustains the well being of local people". TIES Website [9].

5 Characteristics and Principles of Ecotourism

Scholars argued in various ways to clarify the major characteristics of ecotourism. Among them Wallace and Pierce (1996) suggest this tourism may be said to be true ecotourism if it addresses six principles:

1. It entails a type of use that minimizes negative impacts to the environment and to local people.
2. It increases the awareness and understanding of an area's natural and cultural systems and the subsequent involvement of visitors in issues affecting those systems.
3. It contributes to the conservation and management of legally protected and other natural areas.
4. It maximizes the early and long-term participation of local people in the decision-making process that determines the kind and amount of tourism that should occur.
5. It directs economic and other benefits to local people that complement rather than overwhelm or replace traditional practices (farming, fishing, social systems, etc.).
6. It provides special opportunities for local people and nature tourism employees to utilize and visit natural areas and learn more about the wonders that other visitors come to see.

5.1 Ecotourism in Jordan

Jordan is well known for being the place of many ancient civilization and rich in its natural, cultural, and historical heritage. Alongside this cultural richness Jordan has a bio-diversity reflected in its mountains, valleys and desert. Nature reserves constitute rich ecotourism destinations which are designated as an ecotourism sites such as Ajloun Forest Reserve, Dana Reserve, Wadi Rum Reserve and others. Ecotourism practices in Jordan have been generally limited to nature reserves.

The early history of ecotourism in Jordan is attributed to His Majesty the Late King Hussein who was behind the creation of the Royal Society for the Conservation of Nature (RSCN) in 1996 which is a non-government organization devoted to the conservation of Jordan's natural environment. Jordan signed the declaration of the International Year of Ecotourism in 2002, A World Ecotourism Summit held in Quebec. Ecotourism practice options where considered when planning for natural tourism destinations in order to improve its contribution to the local and national economic development. An ecotourism booklet was published in April 2204 by Jordan Tourism Board (JTB), with the cooperation of the Royal Society for the Conservation of Nature (RSCN) and the Jordan Royal Ecological Diving Society (JREDS). The booklet gives a brief description for all ecotourism sites in Jordan and what has been done to enhance and develop the site. The booklet contained some important and useful ecotourism guidelines for visitors to educate tourists about the main ecotourism principles. These guidelines include:

1. Respect the cultural and traditions of the local community.
2. Purchase local products.
3. Use energy conservations practices.
4. Follow directions and rules of the reserves.
5. Use water conservations practices.
6. Do not use natural water resources since they might not be clean.
7. Do not hike alone in the dark.

As part of the program, Wild Jordan in Amman was created to formulate and enforce ecotourism programs in the preserved sites in order to help local communities economics and to establish their small enterprises and sell their local products. [10]

Ecotourism practices in preserved areas include protecting sites, securing jobs, community involvement, and sustainability. Johnson [11] ecotourism has generated tremendous revenue for the country and the rural communities in the nature reserves. The RSCN has a 100% local employment policy in all their protected areas, resulting in ecotourism directly supporting around 160.000 families throughout Jordan. Through income-generating projects with ecotourism, communities living around nature reserves earned 2.3 million USD in 2012.[12]

In Jordan what makes ecotourism a success is the involvement of local communities in these nature reserves. They lead tours and hike, and work in lodges and restaurants and transport people and resources. In the past local people depended on hunting and herding for living. Wide variety of jobs became available to people living near nature reserves which decreased hunting activities. As a result animals are used as tourist attractions rather than food. USAID helped the town of Dana near the reserve to rebuild fifty-seven historic houses whose goal was to bring back the community member to left the poor town in search of work. Ecotourism effects reduce poverty, protect environment and restore heritage [13]. This study will concentrate on the following three mountain nature reserves in Jordan

5.1.1 Ajloun Forest Reserve

A beautiful nature reserve is located in Ajloun Governorate in the North of Jordan. A Mediterranean-like hill country, ranging from 600-1100m. above sea level. It consists of 13 square kilometers of mountains covered by open woodlands that are home to a diverse collection of plan and animal species. It was established in 1987 to help conserve the Evergreen Oak Forest ecosystem.

Ajloun Reserve

This nature reserve forest is important because its trees account for 1% of Jordan's forests. These trees have been important to local people for their wood, scenic beauty and medicine and food. RSCN manages this reserve who started a captive breeding program intended to reintroduce the locally extinct Roe Deer in 1989. Rich history is reflected in the many archaeological sites in the surrounding areas. A wide variety of animals inhabit the woodland such as badgers, foxes and wild bears, and also many birds like the great tit, gold finch, turtle dove, hooded crow and jay.

Deforestation and desertification over the past 200 years led to the decline in numbers of the roe deer. Three roe deer were introduced to the captive breeding enclosure in Ajloun in 1988, brought from a similar habitat in Turkey. Today there are sixteen roe deer at Ajloun.

Visitors to Ajloun nature reserve can enjoy two trails:

a. Easy Trail: It is a scenic viewpoint about (2 km) and takes 1-2 hours. This trail starts from the campsite and reaches the summit of a nearby hill overlooking the reserve. The return trip goes past the breeding enclosures of the roe deer.

b. Moderate Trail: This trail consists of a Rockrose (8 km), and needs 4-5 hours to do. The visitor passes across heavily wooded valley ridges, villages and olive orchards and offers beautiful panoramic views of the West Bank and Syria.

In 2000, Ajloun Forest Reserve was announced by, Birdlife International and RSCN as an important area in Jordan. Ajloun Forest Reserve has one of the most effective outreach and public awareness programs in Jordan which led to raise awareness of local communities, emphasizing the importance of the reserve and its maintenance.

The Reserve's Visitor Center has displays and information about the Reserve, and a shop sell locally made handicrafts. Visitors usually take hikes along the trails set up by the Reserve management. For accommodation there is 'An African Style' campsite is located near the visitors center. It is enclosed by oak, pistachio and wild strawberry trees and offer beautiful views of the Reserve and beyond. There are 10 four-person tented lodges available with small terraces and beds inside The campsite is open mid-March to mid-November. During winter season Ajloun region is the first to have snowfall with heavy accumulation.

The RSCN has launched three development projects in Rasun and Orjan, two nearby villages to the north of the protected areas in order to provide local people with new sources of income which will minimize their dependence on natural resources, promoting environmental conservation and boosting the rural economy.

1. The Soap House: Making soap out of olive oil is a long tradition in this region. Local women are employed to make soap by hand with added floral essences. The visitor can view the soap making process. Products are displayed fro sale in the house and other places in Jordan.

2. The Calligraphy House: The RSCN has supported local women to study Arabic calligraphy in Amman, then bring such skills to the countryside. There is a silk-screening workshop where visitors can print their handiwork onto a T-shirt or card.

3. The Biscuit House: Local women are employed to produce all natural biscuits, energy bars and crisps.

The reserve and the area surrounding it are dotted with ruins. The most famous is Salahidin's Ajloun Castle, *(1184 AD)* and the most intriguing is the Mar Ilyas Church which one of the oldest churches in Jordan, and sacred to Ilyas, who is known in the Bible as Elijah. There is an enjoyable, guided hike from the reserve to Mar Ilyas and onto the castle.

Recently RSCN completed the construction of Ajloun Nature Academy at an old stone quarry near Ajloun Nature Reserve. The 3,000 square meter academy at the cost of $3.9 million was funded by USAID and the E-TVET Fund. The aim of this academy is to establish an academic center to teach topics about the eco-tourism and environment, and management of eco-lodges. Courses are designed with cooperation of many European Centers and their expertise in this respect.

Jordan's first certified nature guides who finished their intensive training in South Africa will join major nature reserves in Jordan to set up training camps and deliver a training and evaluation programme for existing RSCN guides and delivering materials for the nature guide curriculum to be delivered at the Ajloun Nature Academy.

5.1.2 Dana Reserve

The Dana Reserve covers 400 square kilometers of reserve land bridging the Jordan rift valley. It was declared a reserve in 1993. It is managed by RSCN and known for its exceptional beauty, bird watching, hiking and archaeological sites. Dana Reserve is the largest and most diverse nature reserve in Jordan in terms of habitats and species. It contains more than 697 plant species, some found nowhere else, and are more than 1,000 years old and pastal cliffs stalked by sand cats, Nubian ibex and rare Syrian wolves. There are two ecotourism operations, the Rummana Campsite, and the Dana Guesthouse and Feynan is the third.

Dana Reserve
a. Rummana Campsite was opened in 1994. It offered 'camping life' with 19 permanent platforms and tents, a kitchen and chef, and permanent bathrooms.
b. Dana Guesthouse was opened in 1996. It is located at the base of the ancient Dana Village. RSCN turned this house into an ecotourism lodge with nine bedrooms.
c. Feynan Lodge was designed in the shape of an ancient caravancerai and the architecture and design of the building was inspired by Yemeni desert architecture. Its design was an eco-friendly, electricity-free getaway, light bulbs and hot water were powered by solar panels. All 26 rooms offered in suite bathrooms.

Among activities within Dana Reserve is guided hiking where one trail linked the guesthouse and the Rummana camp, a second trail linked the guesthouse and the Feynan Lodge.

Dana Nature Reserve is the largest and most diverse nature reserve in Jordan in terms of habitats and species. Over 45 species of mammals also inhabit the reserve. Dana Reserve supports a wide variety of wildlife; including several globally threatened species of birds, 180 kinds of birds exist in the Reserve. It has been therefore, designated both as Biosphere Reserve and Important Bird Area (IBA). Dana IBA provides essential habitat to breeding, wintering and migrating birds that breed in Europe and pass through the region twice a year.

The reserve directly or indirectly employs over 40 locals resident of Dana make quality local crafts (organic herbs, fruit rolls, jams, olive-oil soaps, candles and silver jewellery) that are sold by RSCN throughout Jordan.

Dana Reserve won four international awards for sustainable development and provides significant economic benefits. It has 50,000 visitors a year. *(Source Jordanian Ministry of Tourism and Antiquities).*

Feynan Eco-Lodge is located on the lower entrance of the Dana Biosphere Reserve in Wadi Araba. This lodge was built in the Wadi where a previous campsite for the Natural Resource Authority built in 1960's. Architect Ammar Khammash designed this tourist lodge in 2005 upon the request from RSCN and in 2009 it has been run by Amman-based firm Eco-Hotels.

Feynan lodge consists of 26 rooms which can accommodate 60 people. Electricity is generated through solar panels which is used only in the reception office, bathrooms and kitchen, the rest of the building is lit by candles which are made by locally by hand. Local springs are the source for water used at the lodge. Vegetarian food is only served and prepared from local natural products.

5.1.3 Wadi Rum Protected Area

Wadi Rum is a nature reserve located 290 kms. South of the capital city of Amman, or 40 kms north of Aqaba at the Red Sea. It is well known around the world for its sandstone mountains and orange sand dunes leaning against them covering 720 square kilometers of desert. Most of the scenic mountains are 400 meters high containing sheer cliff headwalls caused by running rain water from the top creating beautiful canyons.

Wadi Rum nature reserve is an RSCN Reserve – a protected area of the Royal Society for Conservation of Nature. It is considered the most spectacular natural site of Jordan for its vast desert combined with massive mountain cliffs and endless skies. The highest mountain is Mount Um Dami which rises 1840 meters above sea level. It is also known as the valley of the moon.

Wadi Rum attracts an increasing number of foreign and local tourists who find in a variety of fully-equipped camp sites. Desert tours in Wadi Rum can be taken using 4 wheel drive jeeps or on camels, and are followed by a desert banquet at a Bedouin tent.

Wadi Rum is the place for horse racing or endurance races which attracts participants from many countries in the region and the world. Other sport and adventure activities are hot-air ballooning, gliding and parachuting, full moon desert marathons which are lit with flaming torches. Recently Wadi Rum was marketed by Jordan's Tourism Board as a place for meditation which takes place on the 15th of the lunar moon. Petra and Dead Sea are also marked for this type of tourism. Wadi Rum gained popularity among tourists for being the place where the movie, "Lawrence of Arabia" was filmed in 1962. It was also used as the surface of mars in the movie, "Red Planet". Wadi Rum is a classic picture of sandy desert where visitors can spend days or weeks exploring its mountains, hills, vast landscapes and sand dunes.

Wadi Rum is a place to hike, trek, rock climbing, horse and camel safari. Camping under the stars in a desert environment is considered a none forgettable experience the tourists have where they eat local traditional food, get entertained by Bedouins songs and dances and spend the night in Bedouin tents.

Spectacular natural scenes admired by tourists and visitors are:
1. Mushroom Rock which took this name because it looks much like a mushroom.
2. Seven Pillars of Wisdom formation of columns of rock, where the name came from T.E. Lawrence's book.
3. Caves and Lifestyle: Many natural and hand-cut caves some of them date to Nabataean times. Bedouins demonstrate how they used to use plants to clean their hands in the old time.
4. Castle from "Lawrence of Arabia", which was built for the movie.
5. Inscriptions on Rocks: There are many sites in Wadi Rum where visitors can find inscriptions, paintings, graffiti, and petrographs which date Thamudic or Nabataean periods.
6. Natural rock bridges are very common and can be climbed to the top where they give a good view to the rest of the valley.
7. Lunch preparation of a traditional made by Bedouins.
8. Panoramic site best visited at sunset when the color of the desert starts to change its shades. The view from the top of the hill surrounded by some sand dunes, a lower valley view, and uniquely cut rocks and hills.

Mountain Climbing: The first climbing expedition to Wadi Rum was in 1984.[14] by a party of English climbers, before only Bedouins were able to reach the peaks of Wadi Rum mountains often by more than one route.

Wildlife: Wadi Rum holds plants both rare and endemic to its ecosystem. A baseline survey detected the existence of the Gray Wolf, Brand Ford's Fox, the Sand Cat and the Ibex within the area. The site is an ideal area for bird watching with its 120 recorded species [15]. among which are vultures, buzzards, eagles and sparrows.

The most recent project in Wadi Rum Nature Reserve was to increase the number of Arabian Ibex was done through a gift of 25 Ibexes from the United Arab Emirates. The number of visitors to Wadi Rum in 2013 reached 110.143 according to the Jordanian Ministry of Tourism and Antiquities.

5.2 Jordan's National Environment Strategy

Scarce resources and fragile ecosystems in Jordan necessitated a viable and ongoing program of action covering all aspects of environmental protection. In order to preserve the region's natural heritage, Jordan became the first country in the Middle East to adopt a national environmental strategy. With the help from the International Union for the Conservation of Nature (IUCN). In May 1992 a team of over 180 Jordanian specialists completed a practical and comprehensive working document entitled National Environment Strategy for Jordan.

The strategy is predicted on the fundamental principle of sustainable development, which the report defines as "development which increasingly meets human needs, without depleting the matter and energy of the ecosystem upon which development is founded. An economy which develops sustainably would be designed to perform at a level which would allow the underlying ecosystem to function and renew itself ceaselessly".

The plan outlines five strategic initiatives for facilitating and institutionalizing long-term progress in the environmental sphere:
1. Construction of a comprehensive legal framework for environmental management.
2. Across-the-board strengthening of existing environmental institutions and agencies, particularly the Department of the Environment and the RSCN.
3. Giving an expanded role for Jordan's protected areas.
4. Promotion of public awareness of and participation in environmental protection program.
5. Giving sectorial priority to water conservation and slowing Jordan's rapid population growth. [16]

6 Conclusion and Recommendations

Eco-tourism is a rapidly growing market in Jordan and across the world. Jordan's Board of Tourism is active in diversifying tourism products where it looked to utilize nature in Jordan as an additional source for the many tourism products which are well known such as archaeological sites, religious shrines, health and cultural tourism.

This study investigated the components of mountain tourism and their role in improving life standards of local communities, protection and sustainability of nature reserves in Jordan.

Three reserves were chosen to illustrate the diversity of mountain tourism in Jordan. First, Ajloun Nature Reserve located in the north is the most area covered by wide variety of trees spread along high mountains and hills intertwined with many archaeological and cultural sites such as Ajloun Castle *(1184 AD)*. And Mar Ilyas Church which is one of the Christian pilgrimage sites. The Ajloun Nature Reserve is a good example of eco-tourism in Jordan because it follows characteristics of eco-tourism followed in most parts of the world. In addition to its natural components it created an economic tie with the local communities. A college for eco-tourism education with open its doors this year where courses are offered to educate students in order to work in reserves in Jordan.

Second, Dana Nature Reserve is located in the Tafila Governorate where it is spread over mountains partially with many sorts of trees and shrubs combined with geological formation overlooking Wadi Arabah. This reserve contains three major tourist attractions such as Dana Guest House, the Rummana Camsite and Feynan Eco-lodge. The reserve contains many climates, Fauna and Flora, shown in different animal species, rare plants and birds. It is also surrounded by many cultural and archaeological sites dating to thousands of years. Ancient copper mines are in a proximity of the reserve.

Third, Wadi Rum Reserve is situated in the southern part of Jordan completely different location from the previous reserves.

Wadi Rum contains many mountains (highest 1840 m.) vertical sandy rock formations, described as moon like. These mountains attract many visitors specially hikers and mountain climbers. Sand dunes are another fascinating features are seen by riding in 4x4 vehicles usually with a guide. Wadi Rum Reserve is a protected area where Arabian Ibex is being reproduced along with other sorts of animals. RSCN figures indicate that its sites received 147,000 visitors in 2013, 65% of them were foreigners. More than 16,000 people from poor rural communities were supported directly and indirectly through RSCN's tourism and small business operations.

The four young Jordanians who acquired nature guidance qualifications and accreditation from the Field Guide Association of Southern Africa will form the foundation of eco-tourism guide training in Jordan. Since eco-tourism is a rapidly growing market in Jordan and in order to develop eco-tourism successfully, Jordan needs world-class, professional nature guides who have an excellent knowledge of Jordan's ecology.

Jordan is considered pioneer in eco-tourism as illustrated in the number of nature reserves spread out in various unique locations which include mountains, forests, as well as deserts.

As for recommendations:

1. Making use of modern technology in marketing such reserves on the international level despite all current efforts in order to attract visitors locally and internationally.
2. The introduction of eco-tourism education at all levels of education will definitely benefit eco-tourism sector in terms of conservation and sustainability.
3. Unified reference and control agencies will eliminate controversy found in nature reserves management and rules.
4. Explanation of the meaning benefits of eco-tourism to the general public who live around nature reserves.
5. Endorsement of laws regarding deforestation and hunting.

References

1. Fennel, O., Ecotourism, An Introduction. Routledge London and New York 30, (1999)
2. Wall, G., *Ecotourism: Old Wine in New Bottles?* Trends **31**, 2, 4-9 (1994)
3. Romeril, M., *'Tourism and the Environment – Towards a Symbiotic Relationship'*. International Journal of Environmental Studies **25**, 215-18, (1985)
4. Thompson, P., *'The Errant E-Word: Putting Ecotourism Back on Track'*, Explore, **73**, 67-72, (1995)
5. Boo, E., *Ecotourism: The Potentials and Pitfalls*. Washington, DC; World Wildlife Fund. **1**, 2, (1990)
6. Weaver, D., Ecotourism: John Wiley and Sons Australia, Ltd. 5-7, (2001)
7. Honey, M., *Ecotourism and Sustainable Development: Who Own Paradise?,* Washington, DC. Island Press 22-24, (1999)
8. Dawson, C., *Ecotourism and Nature-Based Tourism: One End of the Tourism Opportunity Spectrum?,* in McCool, S. and Moisey, R. (eds). *Tourism, Recreation and Sustainability: Linking Culture and the Environment.* (ABI Publishing). 41, (2002)
9. TIES.http://www.ecotourism.org.
10. Al-Mughrabi, A., *Ecotourism: A Sustainable Approach of Tourism in Jordan*, University of Arizona, 54-57, (2007)

11. Johnson, Chris, "Dana: Helping Nature Helping People" Al Reem (Amman, Jordan: RSCN). **60** , 15 (March 1997)

12. Namrouga, H. "Local Communities Earn 1.6 million JD from Income Generating Projects in 2012". The Jordan Times, N.P. June 2013.

13. Shaw, G. "Jordan's first 'Heritage' to be completed this year". The Art Newspaper April 2014. Web 29 April http://www.theartnewspaper.com/articles/Jordansfirst-heritage-village-to-be-completed-this -year/32391

14. Taylor, Di, Howard Tony, , Treks and Climbs in Wadi Rum, Jordan, Cicerone Press Limited. 20, (2007)

15. www.jtb.com.jo/brouchers/eco_rumhtml. Retrieved 30/06/2014.

16. www.kinghussein.gov.jo/gea_env1.html.

18

Road Infrastructure and Road User's Satisfactions: A Case Study of Motorway Route 7, Thailand

Suthathip Suanmali[1], Kasidis Chankao[2], Veeris Ammarapala[3]

[1,2,3] Transportation Research Center, Sirindhorn International Institute of Technology, Thammasat University, Pathum Thani 12000, Thailand

Abstract. The development of tourism in Thailand relies on the development of appropriate infrastructure. Road access is the key infrastructure issue for tourist destinations throughout Thailand. Each year Thailand has welcomed over 15 million travelers, accounted approximately 7% of GDP. To support tourist activities, variety types of transportation modes have designed. However, road transportation is one of the most effective modes that connect most places together. Beside high-standard vehicles, road is another mechanism that derive comfort and safety of travelling. For this reason, Motorway networks were initiated and constructed to support high speed traffic with high safety and standard. Motorway route 7 is one of major motorway networks that lies between major cities and tourist landmarks. To raise the road standard could be the key to support tourist industry and economic growth. The road developments may not be precise and accurate without knowing the needs from road users'. Therefore, a questionnaire is developed and distributed to 890 randomly selected road users along Motorway route 7. Factor analysis and *t*-test are employed to analyze the factors affecting road users' satisfaction and to compare the satisfaction level between both inbound and outbound travelers.

1 Introduction

Tourism industry is one of the major industries in Thailand which accounted 825.6 billion baht or 7.3% of total GDP in year 2012, and is forecasted to constantly rise by 6.8% of total GDP each year until year 2023 [1]. To support the expansion of this industry, infrastructure development may be needed. Department of Tourism (DOT) is an organization that is responsible for supporting and developing tourism industry under its vision to "Support and develop tourism industry to reach international standard and to be central of Asia tourism" [2]. The travel and tourism competitiveness report in 2013 has ranked the tourism infrastructure of Thailand as the 31st out of 140 countries worldwide, also reported the keys of attracting travels from around the world to Thailand are natural resources and strong affinity for travel and tourism [3]. The communication from place to another may need to rely on transportation system; such as air, marines, trains, and roads.

However, with traveling inconvenience or deterioration of transportation infrastructure may lead to reduction of attractiveness from travelers. The transportation infrastructure development of Thailand has been highly prioritized from transportation authorities to raise the standard; as a result both air and ground transportation infrastructures of Thailand are ranked in the 21st and the 62nd respectively from 140 countries worldwide [3]. For this we see the opportunity to further develop and improve on Thailand's transportation system; in particular, land transport and highway network systems. Because road and highway networks are one of the most important infrastructures for both domestic and oversea tourists as the networks connect most places together. They are the main routes in networks linking regions, provinces, and districts. However, the deterioration of road surfaces can decrease serviceability, and such deterioration is mostly influenced by traffic. The inconvenience of travel may bring the reduction of travel demand and create an unsafe situation for travelers to commute and lead to failure of creating impression for future return. Good roads are the route to promote and enhance economic development such as vacations, shopping and entertainment. Moreover, the studies of Andrijcic, Haimes, and Beatley [4] has pointed that a consequence of failing transportation infrastructure may create the following concerns: reduced safety of travelers, high transportation cost, congestion and dissatisfaction to road users. For these reasons, the assessment of road infrastructure and road users' satisfaction should be done to identify the users' perception to the service for future development.

Department of Highways (DOH) is an organization that is responsible for constructing and maintaining most of highway networks in Thailand. Both DOH and DOT work in parallel to help the DOT accomplish its mission to raise travel standard within the country. One of the more efficient highway networks in Thailand is the motorway network system. It is a high performance road that is able to support high traffic flow with safety and comfort and is very convenience to travel on this motorway. Motorway route 7 is one of the oldest motorways in Thailand; its lie between major cities passing through many tourist landmarks such as Suvarnabhumi International Airport, Pattaya City, and Bangkok. It has a minimum of junctions and allows traffic to flow at higher speeds. Under the DOH, the Inter City Motorway Division is the main highway organization that is responsible for maintaining and developing motorway network. One of their missions is to maintain roads and bridges along the motorway to enhance safety, provide mobility, and ensure a usable transportation system for everyone.

This study is the extended study on Motorway route7 road users' satisfaction assessment. The earlier study identified factors affecting road users' satisfaction by using multiple regression technique. On this research, the objective is focused on whether there is a significance difference on satisfaction between inbound and outbound road users. The result of this study is expected to be used as a guideline for highway authorities to develop a suitable plan for maintaining the service to road users at the highest level [5].

2 Literature Review

The study on tourism industry development in Mauritius, Southeast Coast of Africa, has shown that in order to gain attractiveness from travelers, one must know factors of attraction. Several methods method has been done from the study and found out that Mauritius tourism product is normal goods and the efficient of transportation infrastructure is the concern to travelers. Moreover, accommodation capacity is one of the key to influence airlines to establish routes to the country [6].

Another study has pointed out that *Prioritization of Travel and Tourism, Air Transportation Infrastructure, Ground Transportation Infrastructure,* and *Tourism Infrastructure* are factors that create nation's competitiveness [3]. Among the four factors Ground transportation infrastructure especially road transportation is one of the major concerns as the significant growth in transportation demand with maintenance failures can cause increase in transportation cost and time, reduction in traveler's safety.

The development of infrastructures from government authorities alone may not give out the accurate development direction. To impose the accurate and precise solutions, authorities do need involvement from users. Suanmali, Ammarapala, and Chankao [7] have stated "Road users are customers who use the service, and they should have involvement in improving the service level". They can identify needs, and those needs could create fulfillment of wishes called "satisfaction".

Therefore, understand and follow the needs are essentially to create satisfaction". According to Sakai, Yamada-Kawai and Matsumoto [8] have stated customer satisfaction level has to be fulfilled by the service provider.

The road satisfaction assessment may be a new topic to Thailand, while many developed countries have done similar studies and found appropriate factors to be emphasized in order to create road users satisfaction. It is important for future development to understand how road users satisfy with the road services. In addition, Wardhana, Ishibashi, and Kiyota [9] have studied about road users' satisfaction on national road number NR-203 and NR-35 of Sagam, Japan. The study examined from the two groups of short distance and long distance road users on the following categories: *safety equipment, smoothness of road surface, travel time, rest area/ road facilities, government service level,* and *overall satisfaction towards the road.* The result pointed out that factor affecting road users' satisfaction from both groups *smoothness of road surface* and *rest area/road facilities.* Moreover, the study applied statistical techniques of multiple regression and factor analysis to identify factors affecting the road user satisfaction. In addition, the study of Karnataka State Highway Improvement Project [10] emphasized on factors affecting road users' satisfaction by asking the respondents to indicate their satisfaction level on each attribute to the basis of five-point Likert scale. The result from using multiple regression indicated that *road conditions* and *road facilities* are significant factors that can create higher satisfaction from the road users in Karnataka State.

In this study factor analysis and *t-test* are employed to analyze is there is a significant different is the mean satisfaction level for both inbound and outbound road users. This result is expected to serve as a guideline for highway authorities to develop a precise strategic plan on each bound.

3 Methodology

Two research methods are employed in this study. One is documentary research from literature surveys, journals, articles, and previous research works. These data are collected from research published in credible international journals. Second is survey research. Surveys are done by means of questionnaire surveys for tourists and road users who use motorway route 7 during two periods: first period from October 28 to November 10, 2013 and second period from December 3 to December 9, 2013. Each day, the survey is conducted from 9AM to 6PM and is taken place at the service areas of both in-bound and out-bound directions. These service areas are equipped with service facilities of gas stations, public toilets, local and fast-food restaurants. In the questionnaire we have divided into two main parts; the first part is asking about the information on socio-economic (e.g. gender, age, income, etc.) and behavioral of road users. The second part is a set of closed ended questions that attempts to address the overall satisfaction of travelers in each category. The categories mentions in the questionnaire set are developed based on the characteristics of Motorways route 7 and previous studies mentioned in literature review. They are *value and time for money, safety, comfort, amenities, distance signs and road markers,* and *road conditions.* Each respondent is asked to indicate their satisfaction level in each category based on five-point Likert scale where; 5 = Very satisfied, and 1 = Very dis-satisfied.

4 Analysis and Results

This study questionnaire was randomly distributed to 890 samples randomly. Based on the samples, demographic information can conclude that 31.80% of them regularly travel during 9.01-11.00 a.m. Second, 74.83% of respondents are traveling outbound from Bangkok to Chonburi. Third, 37.19% of them indicates that they are between 18 to 27years old, and 56.29% of them drive or use regular personal vehicles, followed by 32.47% of them use public transportation (taxi, coach). Lastly, 28.76% of the respondents are traveling on this motorway once a month. Travel time reduction has rated at the highest satisfaction level on in-bound direction at the mean score of 3.49, while the outbound direction has rated at the mean score of 3.60. Public toilet is an attribute that receives the lowest satisfaction level. The average satisfaction of public toilets is 2.46 for in-bound road users and 2.63 for out-bound road users. They are dissatisfied about the cleanliness of the public toilets.

The factor analysis are done to reduce the dimensions of independent variables and its summary of is shown on table 1. Then the independent t-test is used to compare the satisfaction level between inbound and outbound road users where hypothesis is set up as

H_0 = Respondents on both directions percept the equal attitude of satisfaction

H_1 = Respondents on both directions percept the different attitude of satisfaction,

The t-test is run on each of the item indicated on table 1. In addition, Levene's test is applied to see the homogeneity of variances whether they are assumed equal or non-equal.

Table1. Statistical Information from the Analysis

Factors	Mean in-bound	Mean out-bound	Factor Loading	t-value
FACTOR 1: Signs/traffic/warning and road marking (0.887)[a]				
1.1 Number of traffic signs	3.1830	3.3970	0.694	-3.643***
1.2 Accuracy and clarity of traffic signs	3.2098	3.4367	0.720	-3.817***
1.3 Number of emergency telephone number signs	3.0807[b]	3.2322[b]	0.730	-2.613***
1.4 Warning signs when the lanes are closed	3.0402[b]	3.2644[b]	0.731	-3.624***
1.5 Visibility of road markers	3.0536[b]	3.3228[b]	0.637	-4.506***
FACTOR 2: Convenience (0.857)[a]				
2.1 Number of tollbooths at each tollgate	3.2232[b]	3.3609[b]	0.650	-2.190**
2.2 *Smoothness of road surface*	3.2188[b]	3.3113[b]	0.598	-1.410
2.3 *Number of lanes*	3.3527[b]	3.4548[b]	0.734	-1.651
2.4 Lane width	3.2960[b]	3.5285[b]	0.726	-3.814***
2.5 Location of each interchange	3.2152[b]	3.3509[b]	0.566	-2.278**
FACTOR 3: Amenities (0.874)[a]				
3.1 Number of public toilets	2.6667[b]	2.9408[b]	0.702	-3.518***
3.2 Cleanliness of public toilets	2.4570[b]	2.6343[b]	0.830	-2.203**
3.3 Convenience to reach service area	2.7783[b]	3.0061[b]	0.737	-2.955***
3.4 Safety in service area	2.9058[b]	3.1570[b]	0.615	-3.657***
FACTOR 4: Value for Time and Money (0.833)[a]				

4.1	Speed and accuracy of toll fees officers	3.4144 [b]	3.4488 [b]	0.707	-0.593*
4.2	Traveled time	3.4866	3.6033	0.717	-2.004**
4.3	Fuel consumption	3.2646 [b]	3.4438 [b]	0.673	-3.066***
4.4	Amount of toll fees	3.1205	3.2816	0.723	-2.508***
FACTOR 5: Conditions (0.833) [a]					
5.1	Traffic volume	3.0446 [b]	3.2127 [b]	0.798	-2.643***
5.2	Cleanliness of road surface	3.1607 [b]	3.4148 [b]	0.686	-4.098***
5.3	Characteristics of Motorway Route 7	3.3632 [b]	3.5204 [b]	0.562	-2.488**
5.4	Legality of other drivers	3.0897 [b]	3.2021 [b]	0.685	-1.887*
FACTOR 6: Speed of Safety Staff (0.814) [a]					
6.1	Speed in managing the accidental area by officers	3.0507 [b]	3.2524 [b]	0.778	-3.535***
6.2	Speed of emergency responses	3.0963 [b]	3.2480 [b]	0.771	-2.529**
FACTOR 7: Safety Equipment & Environment (0.721) [a]					
7.1	Controlling of transportation vehicles	3.0045 [b]	3.1762 [b]	0.511	-2.596***
7.2	Safety equipment	3.3036 [b]	3.4615 [b]	0.526	-2.550**
7.3	Light at night	3.0982 [b]	3.2674 [b]	0.639	-2.566**

[a] *Reliability score (Cronbach's α) for each factor grouping is shown in parentheses.*
[b] *The variance of satisfaction between direction is not equally assumed.*
* p<0.10, **p<0.05, and ***p<0.01

5 Discussion

The results shown in table 1 indicated that the mean satisfaction level in *Smoothness of road surface and Number of lanes* are not significantly different between in-bound and out-bound road users. These two attributes are relatively the same in both directions. Smoothness of road surface is controlled to be with in the acceptable standard. Thereby, smoothness of the road surface is not an issue for road users. In addition, both directions have four traffic lanes. However, other items, related to road user satisfaction on motorway route 7, have significance level less than 0.1, so the mean satisfaction level in those items are different between in-bound and out-bound users. Observe that the mean satisfaction levels of in-bound road users are lower than out-bound in every item.

In order to make road users equally happy in both directions, a highway authority is suggested to take a closer look at in-bound direction travelling to Bangkok. Satisfaction level of in-bound direction is suggested to be improved in each attribute. Moreover, on the descriptive statistics, the mean differences are considered in each attribute and it is found that the biggest difference of 0.27 is on *the number of public toilets*. In bound direction currently has the same number of toilets as the out-bound;

however, its traffic congestion is higher than out-bound and number of visitors is higher, so public toilets are not enough for in-bound road users.

In accordance, to the study road users' satisfaction evaluation has been prioritizing in other countries, this is an important mechanism to elevate road infrastructure and should periodically evaluate to catch up with the demands [9]. Comparing to Thailand, the study of road structure development may be a new concept that should be supporting to raise the road infrastructure serviceability.

6 Conclusion and Future Research

Motorway route 7 is one of the most important road networks that connects Bangkok and Eastern region together. The overall satisfaction from 890 samples is 3.30. The overall mean satisfaction level of out-bound direction from Bangkok – to Eastern region is higher than the in-bound direction. Two variables of *Smoothness of road surface and Number of lanes* do create the same mean satisfaction level. The collaborative between government organizations responsible for Tourism and Infrastructure Development is important. The highway authorities of motorway are responsible to create a safe environment for road users and provide service to them in order to maximize the satisfaction level since all motorway road users has to pay the toll fee of between 30 – 120 Thai Bath (approximately RM 3 – RM12). Users are expected much more when they have to pay the toll fees. Raising the serviceability level of highway authorities certainly can support the Tourism industry. In this study, the results can be served as a guideline to highway authorities to place their emphasis on improving the service on the in-bound direction first. They are suggested to invest their maintenance budget on the items that receive low level of satisfaction; in particular, the amenities such as *the cleanliness of public toilets*. Safety is also a main concern for road users as they rated the satisfaction level of less than 3 on average.

In the future, advance statistical method such as logistics regression is recommend to further investigate significant factors that influence on road users who are satisfied while use the service on motorway route 7 and determine significant factors influencing road users who are dis-satisfied.

7 Acknowledgement

This research is conducted by partially supported by Sirindhorn International Institute of Technology and Transportation Research Center (TREC). The authors would also like to acknowledge the cooperation from the Inter-city Motorway Division, Department of Highways.

References

1. R. Turner, Travel& Tourism Economic Impact 2013, Thailand, World tourism &Travel council, World tourism &Travel council, (2013)
2. Department of Tourism, Department of Tourisms Visions/ Missions, Available online: www.tourism.go.th, (2013)
3. J. Blanke, T. Chiesa, The travel and tourism competitiveness report, World Economic Forum, (2013)
4. E. Andrijcic, Y.Y. Haimes, T. Beatley, *Public policy implications of harmonizing engineering-technology with socio-economic modelling: Application to transportation infrastructure management,* Transportation Research, **50**, 62–73 (2013)
5. S. Suanmali, K. Chankao, P. Korbsanthia, V. Ammarapala, Factors Affecting Road Users' Satisfaction: the Case of Motorway Route 7. Submitted paper prepared for the publishing at Songklanakarin Journal of Science and Technology (SJST), 24 March 2014, Songklanakarin University, Thailand, (to be published).

6. J. Khadaroo, B. Seetanah, *Transportation Infrastructure and Tourism Development*, Annals of Tourism Research, **34**, 1021-1032(2007)

7. S. Suanmali, V. Ammarapala, K. Chankao, Factors Affecting Road Users Satisfaction Level on Thailand's Highway Networks: An Empirical Study on Thailand's Motorway Route 7, Proceedings of the 8th International Congress on Logistics and SCM Systems (ICLS 2013), 5-7 August 2013, Tokyo, Japan, 329-334.

8. T. Sakai, K. Yamada-Kawai, H. Matsumoto, T. *Uchida, New Measure of the Level of Service for Basic Expressway Segments Incorporating Customer Satisfaction*, Procedia - Social and Behavioral Sci., **16**, 57–68 (2011)

9. A.P. Wardhana, K. Ishibashi, M. Kiyota, *Consideration of Road Management from the View Points of Long-and Short-Distance Road User's Satisfaction*, Civil Engineering Dimension Journal of Civil Engineering Science App., **13**, 90-97 (2011)

10. Government of Karnataka PWD, Second Road User Satisfaction Survey in Karnataka, State Highway Improvement Project (KSHIP), India, (2004)

19

Tourism Development and Planning at a Local Authority Level: A Case in Manjung, Perak, Malaysia

Nor Hasliza Md Saad[1] , Siti Nabiha Abdul Khalid[2], Norliza Zainol Abidin[3]

[1]School of Management, Universiti Sains Malaysia, 11800 Penang, Malaysia
[2,3]Graduate School of Business, Universiti Sains Malaysia, 11800 Penang, Malaysia

Abstract. Due to the importance of the tourism industry in the country, it is crucial to ensure that local authorities in Malaysia implement sustainable tourism development. In the 10th Malaysian Plan, the government set a key target to be achieved for the tourism sector. One of the key parties responsible for ensuring that the set targets are achieved is the local authorities, who are responsible for providing proper maintenance because the tourism destinations fall under their area of jurisdiction. The aim of this article is to explore tourism development and planning in one of the popular tourism destination and to analyse the role that local authorities play in the development process. This paper explores the local authorities' views and opinions on their tourism development area using interview and focus group approaches. The paper also combines the analysis of government policy and planning documents with a review of tourism development literature. The findings reveal challenges and issues that are experienced by the local authorities in regard to setting the direction, development and management of tourism development. The issues of tourism development are then discussed for the government to ensure tourism development sustainability in the long term.

1 Introduction

Over the past decade, a number of countries around the world have considered the tourism industry to be one of the most important contributions to their economic and social development. In recent years, the tourism industry has been one of the world's largest industries and generated approximately 5 percent of world GDP in 2011, 9 percent of world GDP in 2012 and 12 percent of world GDP in 2013 [1]. According to Ibrahim and Ahmad [2], tourism planning is a process of managing and coordinating the tourism area to suggest the best approach that can lead to the success of and satisfaction with tourism.

Malaysia considers the tourism industry important because it has been identified as a driver of economic activity and social development. The government has played an important role in stimulating the development of the tourism industry. In the 10th Malaysian Plan, significant attention was given to the tourism sector to improve Malaysia's position in this sector, so it could be the top 10 in terms of global tourism receipts, and to increase the sector's contribution by 2.1 times, which would contribute RM115 billion in receipts and provide two million jobs in this industry in 2015 [3].

Awareness of the important concept of sustainable tourism development has been incorporated into national planning. The purpose of this paper is to provide insight into sustainable tourism development within the national planning process.

In response to the importance of the tourism industry, governments are increasingly anticipating the active role of the local authorities in the planning, management and promotion of tourism in their respective areas [4]. Though the traditional role of the local authorities has been to provide and maintain public facilities, the role of the local authorities in tourism planning is to manage certain issues related to enhancing tourism activities.

Consistent with this role, the aim of this article is to explore tourism development and planning in one of the popular tourism destination and to analyse the role that the local authorities play in the development process. This paper explores the local authorities' views and opinions regarding the tourism development area in the Manjung District of Perak, Malaysia.

2 Role of Local Authorities in Tourism Sector

In Malaysia, the government is responsible for the change of policies and strategies and for developing policies that are consistent with the country's development in promoting growth in the tourism sector. The government is responsible for preparing development plans for both the short and the long terms, identifying potential locations for tourism and regulating the development of a more systematic approach to tourism. Malaysia is a federal country in which the Federal Constitution is the supreme law. All of the laws and governmental sovereignty are subject to the Federal Constitution. The federal system contains three forms of government structure: the Federal Government, the State Government and the Local Government (Ministry of the Welfare of the City, Housing and the Local Government, 2011), as shown in Figure 1.

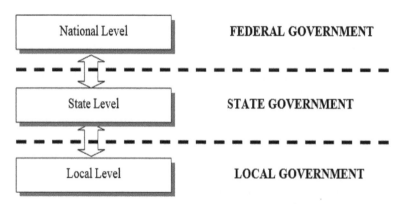

Figure 1. Malaysian Administrative Structure

Currently, the total number of local authorities across the country is 149. Their main task relates to the development and use of land in their respective areas. The duties of the local planning authorities are as follows:

   a.   to regulate, control and plan the development and use of all of the land and buildings in the area;

   b.   to undertake, assist and promote the collection, maintenance and publication of statistics, bulletins, monographs and other aspects that are related to town and country planning

   c.   to perform any other duties that are assigned to them by the Authority of the State or the State Planning Committee.

3 Research Methodology

The research method used for the study is the case study. This method well suited to an exploratory study to get deep understanding of surrounding situation. The case and the unit of analysis for this study is the Manjung Municipal Council. . A case study protocol was developed to guide the case study processes by identifying the relevant questions to be gathered.

The use of such a protocol can further strengthen study reliability. The protocol derives from review of the literature relating to tourism development practices in local authorities. Data collection was divided into two parts of qualitative research was conducted to obtain feedback and experiences from representative of Manjung local authority.

Part one was for the purpose of identifying the responsibly of local authority in dealing with tourism development in their area. In this stage the interview session was done in July 2013 from two representative of Manjung local authority who are responsible about tourism development. Part two was to gain a better understanding of their experience in terms of issues, challenging area and future direction of their responsibility in tourism development. Areas explored included how they plan and management their tourism area, what are the issues that come across with the tourism development, and how they deal with the challenging problems. .

In this stage, three administrative departments in the Manjung Municipal Council were invited and discussed about their overall strategy in tourism development. This is accomplished by prompting the group with pre-specified topics in the tourism development, allowing the discussion to evolve around these open-ended question. Using focus groups allows the interaction and extract insights from the participants [5-7].

4 A Case Study of Coastal and Island Tourism Development by the Manjung Municipal Council

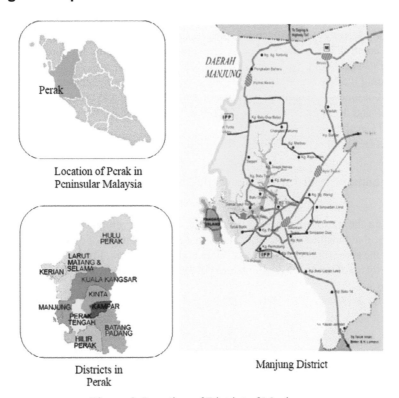

Location of Perak in
Peninsular Malaysia

Districts in
Perak

Manjung District

Figure 2. Location of District of Manjung.

This case study is related to the tourism development of the island and the coastline that is under the jurisdiction of the local authorities in the Manjung Municipal Council (MMC). The district is located in Perak, as shown in Figure 2. The beauty of nature's rich beaches and islands that are ringed with coral reefs and marine life make the drive to the Manjung District a major tourist attraction for the state of Perak.

Consistent with the concept of development and the development plan, the MMC is able to fulfil the goal of developing the tourism sector in its area of administration. There are many tourist attractions in this area that can improve the economy and safeguard the income of local residents. However, the local authorities also face issues and challenges in developing the MMC's role in the tourism sector.

4.1 Background Manjung Municipal Council (MMC) Local Authority

The Manjung Municipal Council (MMC) is one of the local authorities that has the status of a municipality and is located in the State of Perak. Before being recognised as a municipality on 1 August 2001, it was previously known as the Manjung District Council (MDC). The Manjung District Council was established on 1 January 1980 due to the merger of several Local Government Management Boards.

Most of the Manjung District is located in the administrative area of the MMC. The major cities in the MMC area include Setiawan, Lumut, Seri Manjung, Beruas, Lekir, Pantau Remis and Pangkor Island.

4.2 The Role of Manjung Municipal Council in Tourism Development

The MMC plays a key role as the local authority that is responsible for the administration of the area, collecting, controlling, and planning according to the development plan. It is also responsible for the work, as contained in Act 171 of the MPM has a clear vision of tourism, that will cause "Manjung City Tourism and Maritime to be advanced, progressive, prosperous and leading by 2015", with the aim of creating comfortable urban areas that are safe and harmonious through continuous capacity building in all of its areas.

When creating the tourism sector, the MMC created special units and parts for the management and development of tourism . There are two departments/ divisions and units:

- Travel and Research Division under the Department of Community Development and Social Development
- Lumut Development and Management Unit

4.3 The Development Plan for the Tourism Sector of the Manjung Municipal Council (MMC)

When determining the plans and development for an area, a development plan is a key instrument. The MMC for local authorities adopts instruments based on a number of development plans that have been enacted by the authorities at the national, state and local sectors. Figure 3 shows the development plan that is directly involved in the direction and development of tourism by the MMC.

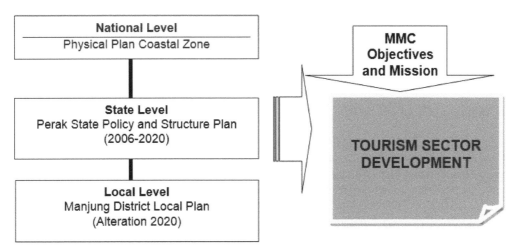

Figure 3. Location of District of Manjung.

Each plan has a content development policy and a comprehensive strategy and serves as guideline for the development of MMC.

4.3.1 The National Physical Coastal Zone Plan (NPCZP)

This is a national physical plan that was prepared by the Department of Town and Country Planning in Peninsular Malaysia as a guide for planning along the coastal areas in Malaysia. NPCZP also involves local authorities in MMC due to its coast and the Pangkor Island. This plan details the physical planning and physical development of the comprehensive and sustainable management and protection of coastal and island ecosystems. For the MMC, the area that is involved in the physical plan is Planning Unit 3 (PU3):

PU3: Pantai Remis (according to the A179 road that cuts straight towards the coast) - Sungai Perak (page 68, RZFPPN). According to the physical plan, the study area includes UP3 coastal ecosystems and the sandy beach of Pangkor Island (Pulau Pangkor and SEV), seaweed (in Teluk Nipah, Pangkor Island), sea turtle nesting sites (SEV) and coastal forests (SEV), which contains different species of plants and animals that are rarely found. The main responsibility of the MMC is to implement the physical plan for developing the tourism sector of the island and coastline to protect and preserve the natural resources sustainably.

4.3.2 Perak State Policy and Structure Plan

At the state level, development planning is more specific to the specific requirements of each state. The MMC for local authorities must consider the planning and development of policies and strategies that are outlined by the Perak State Government and the Review of the Structure of the State of Perak from 2006 to 2020.In the structure plan that was adopted, the Balanced and Integrated Development Strategy (BIDS) was used as the basis for development. The State Government identifies two main strategies:
   • the Sustainable Development Strategy of the State of Perak
   • the Balanced and Integrated Development Strategy (BIDS)

The strategies that are outlined in the main strategy are clear and consistent with the main goal of the MMC, which is to make Manjung a tourist town. This strategy accounts for the divided areas of the development planning zones. The areas in the MMC are categorised in the Kinta Valley Metropolitan Planning Zone. This zone includes the main focus areas of development, particularly the development of residential, municipal, industrial and tourism sectors.

4.3.3 Manjung District Local Plan

A development plan at the local level, which is known as the Manjung District Local Plan (Alteration) 2020, was gazetted on 4 August 2011 and includes overall of Manjung District. The requirements of Manjung District Local Plan (Alteration) 2020 are to coordinate four existing local plan reports:

      i. Local Plan Lumut-Seri Manjung 1999-2010
      ii. Local Plan Sitiawan-Ayer Tawar 1999-2010
      iii. Local Plan Pulau Pangkor 1999-2015
      iv. Local Plan Manjung 2002-2015

The local plan must also translate the development policies and strategies that had identified in the Kinta Valley Metropolitan Planning Zone of the Manjung District. At the same time, the needs of the local plan are adopted into the current policy at the national level, as shown in the national physical planning and economic development in the corridor region. The local plan contains details of a comprehensive plan that allows the development in MPM to be controlled effectively. The contents of this document are consistent with the goals and the vision of the MPM, which focus on making tourism a major development in the Manjung District. The strategies that are consistent with the development of tourism include the following:

- the Economic development strategy
- the Social development strategy
- the Physical and environmental development strategy
- the Pangkor Socio-Economic Development Strategy

The strategies discussed above were developed based on the issues of potential development that have been identified. They will also help the MMC provide guidelines for monitoring and a planning framework that focuses more specifically on development. Separate from this strategy, development concepts that include more detail, clarity and focus are also included in the local plan. Concept development is intended to ensure balanced development between urban and rural areas. This is known as the concept of integration and focus. This concept is divided into three zones of physical planning, which aim to ensure a balanced development between urban and rural areas. The physical planning zones are as follows:

- Physical planning zone of the island - a focus on Pangkor Island, Pangkor Laut and Pulau Gagasan Sembilan.
- Physical planning zone of coastal and river areas - along the walls up to the Jambatan Tuanku Permaisuri.
- Physical planning zone of land - covering the Central Region of Semi Lumut, Seri Manjung, and Sitiawan-Ayer Tawar.

Concept development and the integration of this focus is supported by comprehensive infrastructure systems to boost development. Improved road communication systems are a part of this focus, particularly in remote areas and rural growth centres. Overall tourism development in the area of MMC is considered to be consistent with development at the national, state and local levels. However, local authorities also are credited with the goal and vision to make the city centre of Manjung a leader in municipal tourism by 2015.

4.4 Issues and Challenges of Island and Coastal Tourism in the Manjung Municipal Council (MMC)

In addition, there are a range of issues and challenges regarding sustainable tourism development in relation to the Manjung township's vision. The issues and challenges that are faced include the following:

- There is a lack of development funds. Funds that are dedicated to tourism development are required to develop a tourism product. For example, there is no provision for promoting the development of tourism on the island of Giam. Funds are required for developing the old city and river tourism attractions. There is also no provision of funds for developing a water taxi that can take visitors to activities on the river walls or for developing the old town in Pangkor Island and Beruas.
- Weaknesses in tourism infrastructure are observed in the tourist destination area in Manjung District. Highway development from Teluk Batik to Teluk Rubiah should be created because it would make a huge impact on the development of tourism products, particularly in small economies.
- Overlaps occur between the operations of the local government areas in regard to tourist destinations. Overlaps in the area of operations are also a challenge faced in the development of tourism in the MMC. For example, Pantai Teluk Senangin is not within the area of operations according to the Manjung Municipal Council. Additionally, tourist destinations in Beruas (Air Terjun Ulu Licin) are included in the operations of local governments because the location of the entrance to the area is under the Manjung District; however, the area that is under the waterfall in Kuala Kangsar is outside this area.
- There is a lack of activities in the tourist attractions, which is included in the area of operations. Annual activities to attract tourists, especially domestic tourists, are needed and have been created in Pulau Pangkor and Lumut.
- Infrastructure problems - There are infrastructure problems that need to be improved, such as the lack of road signs on the main road to the tourism product and problems of an inadequate electricity supply in the tourism areas.
- There is a shortage of skilled workers who are involved in the tourism industry. Skilled human resources in the tourism industry, particularly boat operators and operators of similar sports in Pangkor Island, Teluk Batik, need to be improved through training.

5 Conclusion

The MMC in Perak is a tourist destination that has numerous attractions. It has the huge responsibility of ensuring that their efforts are effective and that they continue to be committed to the success of the tourism sector. Although many of the challenges have been described, MMC has identified actions that need to be implemented to achieve its mission of making Manjung City tourism superior in Malaysia. It is evident that the success of tourism activities requires the close cooperation of various stakeholders, such as the government, the tourism industry and local residents.   The importance of planning and management of the tourism sector is very clear and also an important role in ensuring that this development goes according to requirements and established plan. There are a variety of tourism-related development plan in place to ensure that all development in accordance with the criteria and that would meet the needs of sustainable development. . It is clear that tourism planning and development in Malaysia applies the traditional top-down approach, which starts with national goals and attempts to have them implemented at the local level. It shows that the planning undertaken by the government is very rigorous and detailed and balanced to ensure that the physical, social and economic upliftment of life, generate income, contribute to the economy and preserve the environment in line with national goals.

6 Acknowledgement

The authors would like to extend their appreciation to the University Sains Malaysia for the Research University Grant entitled 'Tourism Planning' [Grant No. 1001/PTS/8660013] that makes this study and paper possible.

References

1. UNWTO (United Nations World Tourism Organization), Tourism Highlights, 2013 ed., United Nations World Tourism Organization, Madrid (2013)
2. J.A. Ibrahim, M.Z. Ahmad, *Perancangan dan Pembanguna Pelancongan*. Kedah: UUM Press (2012)
3. GOM (Government of Malaysia) *Tenth Malaysia Plan*, Government of Malaysia Printers: Kuala Lumpur (2011)
4. A. Hamzah. *Policy and Planning of the Tourism Industry in Malaysia*, Proceedings, The 6th ADRF General Meeting, Bangkok, Thailand, 1-21 (2004)
5. S.G. Sutton, D. Khazanchi, C. Hampton, V. Arnold V. Risk analysis in an extended enterprise environment: identification of key risk factors in B2B e-commerce relationships. J Assoc Inf Syst **9**, 3 ,153-176 (2008)
6. C. O'hEocha, X. Wang, K..Conboy, The use of focus groups in complex and pressurised IS studies and evaluation using Klein & Myers principles for interpretive research, Information Systems Journal: An International Journal Promoting the Study and Practice of Information Systems, **22**, 3, pp. 235-256 (2012)
7. S.G. Sutton, J. Reinking, V. Arnold, On the use of grounded theory as a basis for research on strategic and emerging technologies in accounting. Journal of Emerging Technologies in Accounting (2011)

20

Entrepreneurship as a Catalyst for Rural Tourism Development

Norhafiza Md Sharif[1] , Ku Azam Tuan Lonik[2]

[1,2]School of Distance Education, Universiti Sains Malaysia, 11800, Penang, Malaysia

Abstract. The tourism industry is seen as capable of being an agent of change in the landscape of economic, social and environment of a tourist destination. Tourism activity has also generated employment and entrepreneurship opportunities to the local community as well as using available resources as tourist attractions. The tourism sector has the potential to be a catalyst for the development of entrepreneurship and small business performance. Through the development of tourism, the rural community has the opportunity to offer services or sell products to the both local and foreign tourists. To fulfill this purpose, local community participation in entrepreneurship is very important in order to develope the economic potential and to determine the direction of a development in rural areas. In the context of entrepreneurship, local participation is important not only as an entrepreneur and labor in this sector as well as complementary sectors of the others, but they can serve to encourage the involvement of other residents to join together to develop this entrepreneurial. This article aims to discuss the extent of entrepreneurship as a catalyst to the development of tourism in rural areas. Through active participation among community members, rural entrepreneurship will hopefully move towards prosperity and success of rural development.

1 Introduction

The tourism industry has been identified as one of the leading industries to drive development and economic transformation in developing countries [1]. In Malaysia, tourism is the second largest contributor to the economy after manufacturing sector. The sector is also one of the 12 National Key Economic Areas under the Economic Transformation Programme. In the Eighth Malaysia Plan (2001-2005), the tourism industry has experienced impressive growth where it contributes to foreign exchange contributing to economic growth, investment and employment opportunities as well as strengthening the services account of the balance of payments. Identifies five key benefits to be derived from the development of the tourism industry namely the contribution to the balance of payments, the non-industrial development, new job opportunities, increase revenues to the economy through the impact multiplier and social development. It is also argued that the sector could reduce unemployment by creating new jobs [2]. [3]also see the sector could reduce unemployment by creating new jobs [2].

Currently, Malaysia is ranked 16th in terms of global tourism receipts, which is being estimated at about 2% of global market share in 2008 providing opportunities for 1.7 million jobs, or about 16% of total employment in 2008 (The Tenth Malaysia Plan, 2006-2010). Therefore, tourism activities are seen as capable to create employment opportunities to the rural communities. For example in 2009, a total of 204,000 people or 5% of the rural population engaged in the hotel and restaurant sector, compared with 2.2% of labor force participation, or 74,000 people in the fisheries sector [4].

This helps rural tourism to be recognized as an effective catalyst in the socio-economic development in many rural areas. The increase in rural tourism development is due to the increased demand from tourists who want to enjoy nature found only in rural environments as well as to experience cultural heritage that is still preserved by the rural communities [5]. All these lead to the growth of the nature based tourism (eco-tourism), agro tourism and homestay. According to [6], the homestay program, for example, encourages rural communities to participate in the tourism industry, increase their income and create tourism entrepreneurs in the rural areas. The increasing demand for tourism products will indirectly encourage new investments in infrastructure, communications and transport [7] and develop rural areas through other social support.

According to [8], the resilience of this sector is the result of the active participation of the public and private sectors in promoting and enhancing the competitiveness of tourism products that attract tourists to visit Malaysia. Continuous efforts are made towards realizing the potential of the rural tourism sector to increase its contribution to the service sector in particular and the economy as a whole. Facilities provided by the government helps to improve the performance of the tourism industry [9]. In order to ensure the sustainability of the sector, the government is moving one step forward with the creation of the Master Plan for Rural Development (2010) as a key policy in support of rural development policies and national programs and outlines strategies for comprehensive development of rural areas until 2020. It will be a general guideline to all the parties involved in the rural development activities, including government agencies, private sector, NGOs and others.

Nonetheless, in the context of rural tourism development, questions that are often being raised are whether the local rural communities are being marginalized by development projects in their areas without them involving in its planning. If that is so, the development of the tourism sector will be less effective in the absence of a balanced emphasis on human resource development of the local rural communities which are a vital component of the tourism industry. In terms of entrepreneurship, the local entrepreneurs often face problems in business because they could not compete with many other entrepreneurs due to certain reasons. This article aims to discuss the extent the local rural tourism entrepreneurs acts as catalyst to the development of tourism sector in the rural areas. Through active participation among community members, rural entrepreneurship will hopefully move towards prosperity and success of rural development.

2 Rural Development

The countryside is an area other than an urban area. It is a settlement that covers all types of villages and small settlements of less than 10,000 people and is characterized by areas of agriculture and natural resource areas. According to [5], communities in rural areas still do the job traditionally which are based on farming and livestock activities mainly subsistence.

The rural areas are often associated with areas of life that are not advanced, low level of education, community involvement is limited, the potential suspicious and various other characteristics backwardness. Thus, [10] states that the rural communities are often depicted as a group of community that are frozen, slow and lack the initiatives to advance. [11] adds that rural areas are synonymous with the area that are well behind in much of the modern amenities such as the lack of infrastructure, location of shopping facilities and new technologies such as internet access and a mobile communication device.

Constrained by the characteristics of the isolated and backwardness, rural areas have limited options for economic development. To stimulate the economic development of rural communities, rural communities must find alternative use of existing resources to improve their living standards [12]. Hence, the rural areas have the potential to be developed as a tourist attraction and to generate economic growth.

Rural development is crucial to provide an effective delivery system that are beneficial to the local community as well as to develop a sustainable rural economy through the diversification of the economy, particularly relating to the tourism sector [13, 14]. Efficient planning of rural development is capable to activate the involvement of the local communities in programs and projects in rural areas. Such as by enhancing their training that provide opportunities to generate income to the community, especially the youth [9]. Recent planning in rural development emphasizes empowerment of rural communities [15], which enable it to be dynamic and resilient, and are able to face the challenges of the future and achieve economic status equivalent to a national level.

3 Concepts of Rural Community Participation

Local participation is an important aspect in the development of tourism [16]. According to [17], community participation is about empowering local people to determine their own goals and in consultation with local residents to determine their hopes and fears for the development of tourism in their area. In the development plan, it is important to ensure that economic development have a huge impact on the local community occupational structure [18, 19]. Analyze the employment patterns of society in Pulau Dayang Bunting, Langkawi by focusing on the level of labor participation and unemployment problems, the structure and type of employment and their implications on the level of income of the community. Community involvement in tourism is crucial to the development and sustainability of the economy in the affected areas [20].

As stated in the tourism charter of Asia Pacific Economic Cooperation (2010), Community Based Tourism (CBT) should be able to create jobs and to increase incomes and reduce poverty in rural areas [21, 22]. In addition, community involvement is able to educate local communities about tourism [16,18,20,23] and raise their living standards [24]. [25] added that the development of rural tourism brings benefits in rural areas such as reducing the migration of the local population, providing vocational training, eradicating gender discrimination and other social categories, improving the social and cultural coexistence, providing opportunities for social interaction, and involving local population in decision making [26, 27] as well as promote the arts and crafts practiced by the community [25]. [28] also stressed that local community involvement in tourism sector can provide opportunities for them to improve their economics well-being and quality of life through the opportunities arising from the development of tourism activities such as in transportation, accommodation, handicrafts and so on. According to him, the involvement of local communities in tourism activities can be viewed from two perspectives, namely:

1. Involvement of local communities in decision making whereby through the participation of the local community, there exist an opportunity for them to express their hopes and desires to develop the area.
2. Sharing of the profit or benefit as a result of tourism activities that provide opportunities for the community to improve the economy and standard of living.

This perspective is also supported by Akama and [20]. They also urged that the local community be given the chance to recommend or prescribe a tourism development programs appropriate to their environment. To achieve sustainable tourism development, local residents should also take an active part in the transformation process because they serve as advocates to the prosperity and development of the tourism industry as well as serve as a workforce that will provide economic returns in the sector and the complement of the other. This is because the community is not only acting as a catalyst to tourism activities, but they are a crucial asset that can empower tourism activities more robust and efficient.

According to Arnstein , in the context of tourism planning, community participation is a process that involves all interested parties (stakeholders) comprising local government officials, local communities, architects, developers, business people, and planners in decision making together. [29] emphasized that with the support and cooperation of various parties, the developments planning will be more meaningful and the community marginalization issue would go away. This recommendation is made to allow local communities guidance and support necessary to involve them in the tourism sector. Without these guidance and support it is feared that they can be easily exploited by certain parties who want to profit from the ongoing development of the local community by marginalizing or sidelining them itself from the progress.

The exploitation of rural tourism sector can help in the growth, sustainability and diversification of the rural economy. To meet this goal, entrepreneurship is seen as a major catalyst for the tourism sector, which is believed to be able to boost the economic activities in the rural communities [30]. The active participation of the population in entrepreneurship is deemed necessary and significant in invigorating the economic activities in the lcoal communities. According to [31], the issue of participation of communiy in the field of entrepreneurship should be viewed in the broader context as it has a good potential to be further developed and expanded in the future.

4 Entrepreneurship as a Catalyst for Rural Tourism Development

By far there is no one definite definition applicable to the entire term entrepreneur. The meaning attached to the word entrepreneur is growing along with the development of the theory. By definition, entrepreneurs turn out to be someone who was willing to bear the risk of profit and loss as a result of a contract with the government at a fixed price in the 17th century [32]. According to him, entrepreneurs in Malaysia, entrepreneurs may be referred to as those trying to various incentives provided by the government which may include entrepreneurs looking for opportunities in an organization, entrepreneurs seeking their own without the aid of any party and finally the emergence of entrepreneurs through interaction among operators.

Entrepreneurship is one of the strategies in the development of a country, the support element and the development of rural tourism [25]. Thus, it is seen as a catalyst that can overcome the problems associated with economic growth, social inequality and job opportunities [1]. Nearly 99.2% of the entrepreneurs in Malaysia are Small and Medium Enterprises (SMEs) which accounted for 32% of Gross Domestic Product (GDP) [33]. In addition, the Ministry of Rural and Regional Development and its agencies have churned 205,081 entrepreneurs under the Ninth Malaysia Plan (9MP). In many developing countries, the number of entrepreneurs in the tourism sector are increasing with the help from the government that strengthen and build the strength of small and medium industries (SMIs) which indirectly reduce the unemployment rate among local communities [2] and contribute to the alleviation of poverty [22].

[34] incorporates a theory of the development of tourism, which is a catalyst for the development of entrepreneurship and small business performance. The development of tourism can provide opportunities for local communities by offering the services or sell products to local and foreign tourists. According to [30], through rural tourism, tourists were taken on visits to the several centers of SMEs business consisting of the production of food products such as chips worked villagers, traditional cakes, shrimp paste, *cencaluk*, batik products, rattan, wood carving products, marble items and so on. As a result, tourists have the opportunity to buy these products and participate in the producting of these local village produce such as in batik painting and rattan goods production etc with the able assistance from the local community.

The rural communities participating through SMEs such as in making handicrafts, souvenirs, etc. are able to receive orders and favorable market throughout the year. This provide evidence that all the facilities provided by the government to advance the involvement of entrepreneur in rural areas is fruitful. Throughtout the years, the government has provided a variety of support and help to promote the development of SMEs and provide many opportunities for the development of entrepreneurship in local communities. This move were undertaken to drive the economy to achieve the high income status by 2020 .

Many research have been carried out in relation to the contribution of the rural tourism sector through entrepreneurship. A study conducted by [35] found that the development of tourism activities contributes to the existence of various service sectors such as rest homes, hotels, services, other handicraft business growth centers or travel agents. As a result of these growth , employment opportunities is opening up to the various levels of society. This directly catalyzes the process of urbanization, the growth of the resort prompted by the local people, an increase of Small and Medium Enterprise (SMEs), increase state income and population, and the development of communication systems and road networks.

The development of tourism for example in Pulau Tioman is successful in involving local community participation in the accommodation, catering (restaurants), tourism support services and so on. However, a study by [36] found that incentives are less help in developing tourism entrepreneurship. This is because there are many entrepreneurs who do not realize the existence of these incentives, in addition to not knowing the requirements to get it. After giving information about it, many entrepreneurs view these incentives are beneficial to them. However recommended that the government provide financial assistance easy to tour operators, particularly in sub-sectors of accommodation and transport that involves so many operators.

[37] explores the issues and challenges faced by the Batek community as a result of tourism development in Kuala Tahan, Pahang. The study found that community involvement in tourism economic activities are divided into two categories which as employees (tour guides and boat drivers) as well as the subject of a tourist attraction in itself (a cultural icon). The women of the Batek community produce handicrafts while men help market their product. Even so, their involvement in the tourism industry is highly dependent on their good relations with the outside community, as well as communication skills while dealing with foreign tourists.

The factors that influence the participation of Bumiputera entrepreneurs in the tourism sector in the Bandar Hilir, Malacca is addressed by [38]. The study found that most respondents are those who want to succeed in entrepreneurship. They are also the most forward-looking and confidence. The spirit can help them be successful in the field of tourism entrepreneurs, but it is often restricted by the lack of support from family members . Problems faced by the respondents include difficulty in obtaining capital as well as extensive competition from other entrepreneurs. This problem is a major obstacle to the development of Bumiputera entrepreneurs in the Bandar Hilir, Malacca.

[13] describe the level of participation of the population and explain the factors that influence the level of community participation in the study of the Kubang Pasu District, Kedah. The findings shows that the level of participation of the community in the field of entrepreneurship in the study area is moderate. Among the factors that influence the level of local communities participation include capital or finance and training. Most importantly, the findings also showed that cronyism and political relations also have a significant impact in influencing the level of participation of the population in the study area.

[39] discuss the potential of women as household heads in rural areas or known as single mothers to become entrepreneur as a way to get out of poverty. This is in line with effort made bythe Minister of Women, Family and Community Development, to urge women to venture into business. In addition, the ministry is also working with non-governmental organizations in implementing programs to increase women's skills in particular areas of entrepreneurship so that they can be independent and become increasingly competitive in the future. Nowadays, many schemes have been trained, being assisted especially the single mothers. However, the challenges are great and many of them failed to succeed without the government assistance. Due to this problem, there are many single mothers in rural areas who were below the poverty line.

[33] identifies factors driving the transformation of Malay entrepreneurs in Johor Bahru.This study analyzes the performance and the factors that affect it. The results generally shows that the individual initiatives, family and religious motivation are key factors that drives them to venture into entrepreneurship while their background factors, business management skills, networking skills and institutional or government support are significant factors affecting their business performance. The study found that there are four important factors that influence the performance of Malay entrepreneurs and SMEs in Johor Bahru namely background factor, management skills, business skills and support networks or government institutions.

The government remains committed to explore the potential of SMEs, including in rural areas in order to create successful entrepreneurs at the national, regional and global levels. Among the strategies proposed, including the development of SMEs as the engine of growth and innovation by reducing regulatory costs incurred by the SME, SME capacity building, support the creation of a culture of entrepreneurship, strengthening and enhancing access to financing [4]. [40] noted not only the policy, but also personal skills, motivation and initiative is important to start a new business. Entrepreneurship policies appropriate to create a conductive environment and provide a comfortable environment for other potential entrepreneurs who want to start a new business.

5 Conclusion

It is believes that entrepreneurship is a key catalyst in the economic sphere in rural areas. Naturally entrepreneurship is developed towards the further prosperity of the economic potential of rural areas. To realize this goal, all the good among the villagers, the entrepreneurs nor the agencies concerned should cooperate and work together to strengthen and further develop rural entrepreneurship. For this purpose, the rural population should be aware and have their own initiatives towards enhancing their economies. There are various incentives and support such as access to capital, opportunities to attend courses and entrepreneurial training, marketing aspects of a broader and deeper exposure to entrepreneurship should be assisted to cultivate interest and inclination to participate in entrepreneurship. In addition, each rural development agency should play a more effective and efficient in helping and encouraging the participation of communities and further developing entrepreneurship in rural areas. It is hoped that the close cooperation established between population and development agencies will be able to strengthen and highlight the potential of entrepreneurship in rural areas. The main role of the Ministry of Rural and Regional Development is to provide exposure and knowledge of the rural tourism sector in order to make rural areas attractive as a tourist destination, to provide knowledge and skills to become entrepreneurs in the field of rural tourism, provide exposure and knowledge of rural tourism as an activity which can give additional sources of income for rural communities and provide exposure, knowledge and skills that can promote environmental beautification and preservation of cultural beauty of the countryside. Ministry of Rural and Regional Development has always placed a priority to integrate rural development strategy with programs that increase income and quality of life. Efforts still need to be improved to ensure that the poverty rate in rural areas is not only reduced, but is able to achieve the targeted level of income by the government in 2020.

6 Acknowledgments

The authors would like to thank the Ministry of Higher Education for the fund provided through STRC for this research.

References

1.   Taskov,   Nako and Metodijeski,   Dejan and Dzaleva,   Tatjana and Filiposki,   Oliver. Entrepreneurship in Tourism Industry Lead to Business Benefits, *2nd Biennial International Scientific Congress* 27-29 April, 2011, Skopje, Macedonia, (2011)
2.   P.Sheldon, & T. Var. Resident Attitudes To Tourism In North Wales, Tourism Management, **5**, 1, 40-48, (1984)
3.   E. Tatoglu, F. Erdal, H. Ozgur & S. Azakli. Resident Perception Of The Impacts Of Tourism In a   Turkish   Resort   Town.   Retrieved   from http://www.opf.slu.cz/vvr/akce/turecko/pdf/Tatoglu.pdf, (Mei 15 Mei 2014), (2000)
4.   Pelan Induk Perancangan Luar Bandar. Portal Rasmi Kementerian Kemajuan Luar Bandar dan Wilayah. http://www.rurallink.gov.my/pelan-induk-pembangunan-luar-bandar-piplb- (2014)
5.   Y. Yusnita, M.M Shaladdin, W.A Aziz . Rural Tourism in Malaysia: A Homestay Program, China-USA Business Review, **12**, 3, 300-306, (2013)

6.   R. Merican Abdul Rahim Merican, M. Ruzian and A. Azrol. Homestay Industries: Surviving the Legal Challenges, Pertanika Journal of Social Sciences & Humanities, **22**, 309-328, (2014)

7.   A. Milman & A. Pizam. Social Impacts of Tourism on Central Florida, Annals of Tourism Research, **15**, 2, 191-204, (1988)

8.   A. Rosniza, A. Mustaqim, A. Rahim, Rosmiza, Novel Lyndon and Mohd Azlan. Persepsi PelancongTerhadap Agensi Pelancongan Di Langkawi Geopark. Journal of Society and Space, **8**, 7, 147-154, (2012)

9.   D. Getz & J. Carlsen. Characteristics and Goals of Family and Owner-Operated   Businesses in The Rural Tourism and Hospitality Sectors. Tourism Management, **21**, 547-560, (2000)

10.   A. Talib & H. Jusoh, Penyertaan Komuniti dalam Bidang Keusahawanan Luar Bandar. Kajian di Daerah Kubang Pasu, Kedah, *Prosiding PERKEM VII*, JILID 2, 738-749, (2012)

11.   H. Fatimah & B. Nurwati. *"Pembangunan Luar Bandar: Ke Arah Peningkatan Produktiviti dan Kepelbagaian Asas Ekonomi"* dalam Pembangunan Wilayah dan Alam Sekitar: Cabaran dalam Merealisasikan Rancangan Malaysia Kesembilan, diselenggara oleh Asan Ali Golam Hassan. Sintok: Penerbit Universiti Utara Malaysia, 79-92, (2008)

12.   A. Liu. Tourism in rural areas: Kedah, Malaysia, Tourism Management, **27**, 5, 878-889, (2006)

13.   F.J. Blancas, M. L. Oyola, M. González, F.M. Guerrero, & R. Caballero. How To Use Sustainability Indicators for Tourism Planning: The Case of Rural Tourism in Andalusia (Spain). Science of The Total Environment, **412**, 413, 28-45, (2011)

14.   J. Briedenhann & E. Wickens. Tourism Routes As a Tool For The Economic Development Of Rural Areas-Vibrant Hope or Impossible Dream? Tourism Management, **25**, 71–79, (2004)

15.   K. Kalsom & N.M. Ashikin. Penglibatan Ahli Komuniti Dalam Program Pembangunan Komuniti: Program Homestay Di Kedah. Akademika, **67**, 77-102, (2006)

16.   C. Tosun. Limits to community participation in the tourism development process in developing countries. Tourism Management, **21**, 1, 613-633, (2000)

17.   J. Brohman. New Directions in Tourism for Third World Development, Annals of Tourism Research, **23**, 1, 48-70, (1996)

18.   T. Cengiz, F. Ozkok, & C.K. Ayhan. Participation of the local community in the tourism development of Imbros (Gokceada), African Journal of Agricultural Research, **6**, 16, 3832-3840, (2011)

19.   K. Lindberg, J. Enriquez, & K. Sproule, K.. Ecotourism questioned: Case studies from Belize. Annals of tourism Research, **23**,3, 543-562, (1996)

20.   N.Y. Hafizah & A.A. Rahimah. Kelestarian Langkawi Geopark: Penglibatan Komuniti Kuala Teriang, Langkawi. Akademika, **78**, 95-101, (2010)

21.   M. Akunaay, F. Nelson. & E. Singleton. Community Based Tourism in Tanzania: Potential and Perils in Practice, *Second Peace through Tourism Conference*, Tanzania (2003)

22.   J.W. Ashe. Tourism investment as a tool for development and poverty reduction. The experience in Small Island Developing States (SIDS). [Online] http://www.tanzaniagateway.org/docs/tourism_investment_as_a_tool_for_development_and_p overty%20reduction.pdf, (February 16, 2014), (2005)

23.   A. Norzaini, A.H. Sharina, L. O. Puay & K. Ibrahim. The Langkawi Global Geopark: Local community's perspectives on public education, International Journal of Heritage Studies, **17**, 3, 261–279, (2011)

24.   S. Akis, N. Peristianis & J. Warner,. Residents' attitudes to tourism development: the case of Cyprus, Tourism Management, **17**, 7, 481-494 (1996)

25.   C.Surugiu. Development of Rural Tourism Through Entrepreneurship, Journal of Tourism, **8**, 65-72, (2009)

26.   F. Aref, S.S. Gill & F. Aref. Tourism Development in Local Communities: As a Community Development Approach. Journal of American Science, **6**, 2, 155-161, (2010)

27.   M. Chapman & K. Kirk. (Julai 2001). *Lessons for Community Capacity Building: A Summary of The Research Evidence. School of Planning and Housing Edinburgh College of Art/Heriot-Watt University. Research Department, Scottish Homes.* Retrieved at 23 Mei 2014, dari laman sesawang: http://docs.scie-socialcareonline.org.uk/fulltext/scothomes30.pdf (2011)

28.   D.J. Timothy. Participatory Planning: A View of Tourism In Indonesia. Annals of Tourism Research, **26**, 2, 371-391, (1999)

29.   I. Yahaya. Komuniti Pulau dalam Era Pembangunan: Terpinggir atau Meminggir? Akademika, **70**, 57-76 (2007)

30.   I.A. Johan & A.M. Zaki. Program Homestay Pemangkin Pertumbuhan Ekonomi Luar Bandar, Kajian Kes: Negeri-Negeri Utara Semenanjung Malaysia, *Prosiding PERKEM IV*, Jilid 2, 227-242 (2009)

31.   T. Azlizan, J. Hamzah, I. Yahaya & A. Habibah. Penyertaan komuniti dalam bidang keusahawanan luar bandar, Malaysia Journal of Society and Space, **8**, 9, 84-96, (2012)

32.   A.L. Mohd Abdullah Jusoh, Y. M. Azlan, J. Osman, Syahira Hamidon., 2012, *Asas Keusahawanan dan Pengurusan Perniagaan Kecil dan Sederhana*, Universiti Malaysia Kelantan: Kelantan.

33.   A.G.M. Asri & D. Zaimah. Transformasi dan Prestasi Perniagaan Usahawan Melayu Perusahaan Kecil dan Sederhana (PKS) di Johor Bahru. *Prosiding PERKEM VII,* JILID 1, 696-708 (2012)

34.   O. Pazim & M. Rosli. The Impact of Tourism on Small Business Performance: Empirical Evidence from Malaysian Islands, International Journal of Business and Social Science, **2**, 1, 11-21, (2011)

35.   K.T. Lee & O.S. Suriani. Pertumbuhan dan Pelestarian Industri Eko-Pelancongan: Kajian Pulau pulau Peranginan Sekitar Pantai Timur Sabah, Sosiohumanika, **3**, 2, 273-294 (2010)

36.   N.H.M. Salleh, R. Othman, S.H.M. Idris. Penglibatan Komuniti Pulau Tioman dalam Bidang Keusahawanan Pelancong dan Peranan Insentif Pelancongan, Journal of Tropical Marine Ecosystem,   **2**, 2, 57-71, (2012)

37.   M. Zanisah, Z.N. Fatanah & O. Mustaffa. Kesan Ekonomi Pelancongan Terhadap Komuniti Batek Di Kuala Tahan, Pahang, Journal e-BANGI, 4, 1, 1-12, (2009)

38.   H. Shahrin and L.K. Goh. Penglibatan Usahawan Bumiputera dalam Sektor Pelancongan: Satu Kajian Kes Di Kawasan Bandar Hilir, Melaka. Universiti Teknologi Malaysia Institutional Repository,   [online] http://www.fp.utm.my/ePusatSumber/pdffail/ptkghdfwP2/p_2009_9183_5c99079fdf3342b391 38ec251cbb0832.pdf (2010)

39.   Roddin, Rohayu and I. Mukhtar, Marina and Esa, Ahmad and Warman, Sarebah and Mohamed, Maziana and Mohamed Yusof, Anizam and Ab Rahman, Azmanirah. Pendidikan kemahiran keusahawanan dalam kalangan wanita ketua isi rumah luar bandar, *Seminar Majlis Dekan Pendidikan IPTA*, 2-3 Ogos 2010, Shah Alam, (2010)

40.   M. Lordkipanidze, H. Han Brezet & M. Mikael Backman. The Entrepreneurship Factor in Sustainable Tourism Development, Journal of Cleaner Production, **13**, 8, 787-798 (2005)

The Impact of Sustainable Tourism and Good Governance on Biodiversity Loss in Malaysia

Badariah Din[1] , Muzafar Shah Habibullah[2] , W.C. Choo[3]

[1]College of Law, Government and International Studies, Universiti Utara Malaysia, 06010 UUM Sintok, Kedah, Malaysia
[2,3]Faculty of Economics and Management, Universiti Putra Malaysia, 43400 UPM Serdang, Selangor, Malaysia

Abstract. The importance of forest in providing the natural habitat for plants and animals; storing hundreds of billions of tons of carbon; buffering against flood and drought; stabilizing soils, influencing climate change and providing food and home for the indigenous people has led the international community to protect them from further destruction in the future. In addition, the sustainable tourism is a key source of income and employment for local communities, which, in turn, provide strong incentives to protect biodiversity. For such reasons, and given the capacity limits of environmental resources coupled with the quantitative growth of tourism, there is an urgent need for the development of tourism to take biodiversity seriously. In this study we investigate the impact of sustainable tourism and good governance indicators on biodiversity loss in Malaysia for the period 1996 to 2012. In this study we employed the Ordinary Least Squares (OLS), Dynamic OLS (DOLS) and Fully-Modified OLS (FMOLS) which is efficient in small sample to estimate the long-run model of biodiversity loss (proxy by deforestation rates). Interestingly, our results found that good governance and sustainable tourism do contribute in mitigating biodiversity loss in Malaysia.

1 Introduction

Malaysia is one of the fastest growing economy among the ASEAN countries where the manufacturing sector being the main driver for economic growth. For the last two decades the tourism sector has been showing significant contribution to the Malaysian gross domestic product. As shown in Table 1, the share of the tourism industry to total national output hovering about 5 percent for the period 2005 – 2012. Another important contribution of the tourism sector is in terms of job opportunities it created for the Malaysian population. In 2012, the share of employment in the tourism industry to total employment in Malaysia is about 16.4 percent showing an almost 10 percent increase from its share in 2005. Table 1 also suggests that the demand for tourism in Malaysia is increasing over time. Tourist arrivals increased from 16,431 thousands in 2005 to 25,032 thousands in 2012 and tourist expenditures has doubled from RM32 billion in 2005 to RM61 billion in 2012. Furthermore, the length of stay by the visitors has also increased from 6.1 nights in 2005 to 7 nights in 2012.

Table 1. Some statistics on tourism in Malaysia

Year	Tourist Arrivals ('000)	Tourist Receipts (RM Million)	Average Length of stay (Nights)	No. of hotels supply	No. of rooms supply	Average occupancy rates of hotels (%)	Share of employment in the tourism industries to total employment (%)	Share of tourism sector to gross domestic product (%)
2005	16,431.1	31,954.1	6.1	2,269	155,356	63.6	15.0	4.7
2006	17,546.9	36,271.7	6.2	2,336	157,251	65.5	15.1	4.7
2007	20,972.8	46,070.0	6.3	2,360	160,327	70.0	14.9	4.9
2008	22,052.5	49,561.2	6.4	2,373	165,739	66.3	15.7	4.9
2009	23,646.2	53,367.7	6.7	2,373	168,844	60.9	16.1	5.4
2010	24,557.2	56,492.5	6.8	2,367	168,497	59.3	15.5	5.3
2011	24,714.3	58,315.9	7.0	2,707	193,340	60.6	16.2	5.2
2012	25,032.7	60,556.7	7.0	2,724	195,445	62.4	16.4	5.3

Sources: Department of Statistics, Tourism Satellite Account, Malaysia, 2005-2012.

Although we recognized the great benefits of the tourism sector to the national income, the tourism activities has also been connected to the negative impact on the economy in particular to the environment. One crucial aspect of the negative impact as a result of increase tourism activities is on the loss of biodiversity. The term biodiversity or biological diversity refers to the totality (numbers) and variability (types) of living organisms in the ecosystem, region and environment [1]. Human will eventually perish without biodiversity. According to the Convention on Biological Diversity (CBD) the definition of biodiversity includes diversity at the gene, species and ecosystem levels; the types of species; and the habitats and ecosystems within which they live. This includes the terrestrial rainforests, the freshwater lakes, the river systems, the coral reefs and the marine ecosystems. The healthy ecosystems provide food, clean air and water for human to consume and survive. The rainforest, although cover less than 2 percent of Earth's surface, support the greatest diversity of living organisms on Earth – housed more than 50 percent of the plants and animals on the planet [2]. Therefore, the loss of biodiversity among other things; threatens our food supplies, interferes with essential ecological functions, reduces the productivity of ecosystems, and destabilizes and expose the vulnerability of the ecosystems to natural disasters such as floods, droughts, hurricanes etc [3].

In a study led by the Conservation International (CI) and United Nations Environment Programme (UNEP) on the threats of tourism on biodiversity conservation [4] point out that the tourism-related for loss of biodiversity can be due to: (i) habitat disruption due to the total landscape transformation for tourism development (infrastructure and facilities) in a rapid and unplanned manner that led to deforestation and drainage of wetlands; (ii) depletion of scarce resources for the indigenous and local people (e.g. water and electricity consumption); (iii) problems associated with littering and water pollution; (iv) sewage pollution from hotels, recreation and other tourism-related facilities; and (v) damage to coral reefs by the activities of careless tourists. Nevertheless, according to [5] tourism can be an incentive for the protection of the environment. For example, tourism tends to create an awareness that the country needs to be attractive, air needs to be cleaned, and sea needs to be unpolluted. In the long-run, without appropriate policies and incentives to mitigate the negative impact of tourism activities on the environment, tourism can destroy itself. For the last two decades, national policies for tourism have been targeted for achieving economic growth and social development while protecting the environmental aspect of a country [6]. Relating to the concept of "sustainable tourism", [7] urges nations to make optimal use of environmental resources for tourism development while maintaining essential ecological processes and helping to conserve natural heritage and biodiversity [8]. [9] for example defines sustainable tourism as "tourism which is developed and maintained in such a manner and scale that it remains viable in the long-run and does not degrade the environment in which it exists to such an extent that it prohibits the successful development of other activities."

Thus, the purpose of the present study is to investigate the impact of sustainable tourism on biodiversity loss in Malaysia for the period 1996 – 2012. We also include income and measures of good governance as additional determinants of biodiversity loss, and the model is estimated using three estimators – ordinary least squares (OLS), dynamic OLS (DOLS) and fully-modified OLS (FMOLS). Both DOLS and FMOLS are efficient in small sample.

The paper is organized as follows. In the next section we review briefly the empirical work related to biodiversity loss, sustainable tourism and good governance as well as the method used in the study. In section 3, we discuss the empirical results. The last section contains our conclusions.

2 Methodology

In this study, we modeled biodiversity loss as follows:

$$biodiversity loss = f(income, sustainable\ tourism, governace)$$

(1)

Specify in a stochastic form as

$$BioLoss_t = \alpha + \beta income_t + \theta sus\_tourism_t + \gamma govern_t + \varepsilon_t$$

(2)

where $\alpha, \beta, \theta,$ and γ are parameters to be estimated, and ε is the error term. It is expected that $\beta > 0$, and $\theta, \gamma \leqslant 0$. $BioLoss_t$ is the loss of biodiversity that will be measured by deforestation rates. $income_t$ represent the level of economic development and/or national income and is measured by gross domestic product. $sus\_tourism_t$ is sustainable tourism and will be measured by constructing an index for sustainable tourism indicator, while $govern_t$ represent institutional variables that measure the quality of the government.

The increase in the level of economic development or national income increases the loss of biodiversity as a result of deforestation that give way for agriculture, infrastructure and buildings etc. For example [10] found that income (GDP) affect positively the rate of deforestation for a panel of the African, Latin American and the Asian countries. [11] on the other hand, the African and Latin American show positive relationship between deforestation and income, but for the Asian countries, income and deforestation is negatively related.

In recent years several studies has been investigating the role of governance affecting biodiversity loss and deforestation. It has been recognized that better institutions are related to better environmental management, forward-looking behaviors, higher efficiency and better enforcement of public policies. Thus, it can be conclude that better institutions are related to lower deforestation. More recently [12-13] explore the hypothesis that improving good governance is able to mitigate deforestation. In their study, six governance measures – voice and accountability, political stability, government effectiveness, regulatory quality, rule of law and control of corruption were used which was based on the database - World Governance Indicators provided by the World Bank. The indicators were constructed by Kaufman and his colleagues based on several different sources and using the linear unobserved components model to aggregate those various sources into one aggregate indicator. [14] define governance as, "Governance consists of the traditions and institutions by which authority in a country is exercised. This includes the process by which governments are selected, monitored and replaced; the capacity of the government to effectively formulate and implement sound policies; and the respect of citizens and the state for the institutions that govern economic and social interactions among them." Accordingly, the six governance measures taken from the World Bank (see info.worldbank.org/governance/wgi/index.asp) are as follows:

- Voice and accountability: measures *perceptions of the extent to which a country's citizens are able to participate in selecting their government, as well as freedom of expression, freedom of association, and a free media.*

- Political stability and absence of violence: *measures perceptions of the likelihood that the government will be destabilized or overthrown by unconstitutional or violent means, including politically-motivated violence and terrorism.*

- Government effectiveness: *measures perceptions of the quality of public services, the quality of the civil service and the degree of its independence from political pressures, the quality of policy formulation and implementation, and the credibility of the government's commitment to such policies.*

- Regulatory quality: *measures perceptions of the ability of the government to formulate and implement sound policies and regulations that permit and promote private sector development.*

- Rule of law: *measures perceptions of the extent to which agents have confidence in and abide by the rules of society, and in particular the quality of contract enforcement, property rights, the police, and the courts, as well as the likelihood of crime and violence.*

- Control of corruption: *measures perceptions of the extent to which public power is exercised for private gain, including both petty and grand forms of corruption, as well as "capture" of the state by elites and private interests.*

[12] investigate the relationship between deforestation and six governance indicators for a cross-section of 90 countries. However, they conclude that the evidence do not support a direct beneficial of good governance on deforestation but an indirect of governance on deforestation through increasing income. They suggest that good governance may act a catalyst to increasing income, and rising income are likely to reduce the rate of deforestation. According to [12], "the lack of support for a direct impact of governance variables on deforestation is consistent with the notion that governance is a macro-level variable, and as such its impact on the forestry sector a priori is expected to be diffuse and uncertain."

On the other hand [13] tested the impact of good governance on deforestation for 120 countries. The correlation analyses clearly indicate a negative relationship between the rate of deforestation and the governance indicators. It implies that globally a country with a better quality of governance tends to have a lower rate of deforestation. Further analysis with multiple regression analysis, their results support the contention that an increase in the quality of governance corresponds to a lower level of deforestation.

The tourism industry is no doubt beneficial to the nation providing job opportunities, foreign exchange earnings and infrastructure development that is related as well non-related tourism activities. Nevertheless, the rapid growth in the tourism industry has been recognized of being responsible for a considerable negative local community and environmental impact. The natural resource depletion and environmental degradation that is associated with tourism activities pose severe problems to many regions favored by tourists [15]. Tourism development negatively impacted the community in term of traffic congestion, increase cost of living, crime rates, waste water generation, pollution etc [16]. Therefore, recent strategies for tourism development are to maximize the economic benefits to the local community while minimizing the environmental and social costs [17]. Implying "sustainable tourism development", [18] promotes "tourism that takes full account of its current and future economic, social and environmental impacts, addressing the needs of visitors, the industry, the environment and host communities." Nevertheless, [19-20] and [21] point out that sustainable tourism as a concept is meaningless without indicators that can measure the impact of tourism. According to [7, 22-23] sustainable tourism indicators are time series information that is expected to respond to economic, social, cultural, environmental, institutional, technological, management issues, both within and tourism sector and broader destination.

To construct an index for sustainable tourism for Malaysia, we have selected three sustainability indicator variables – ratio of tourism expenditures to GDP (*tourismy*) [8, 24], ratio of tourist arrival to population (*touristpop*) [8, 25] and rainfall (*rain*) [26]. Both *tourismy* and *touristpop* can be considered as the driving forces indicators representing the social dimension, while *rain* can be considered as the pressure indicators representing the environment dimension [21, 26]. Following [26], by using factor analysis, we select the first principal component and by normalizing the sum of the loading factor equal to one, we have the following sustainable tourism index (*sus_tourism*) for Malaysia:

$$sus\_tourism_t = 0.336 tourismy_t + 0.392 touristpop_t + 0.272 rain_t \qquad (3)$$

We would expect that an increase in sustainable tourism will reduced the loss of biodiversity.

3 Results and discussions

In this study our main interest is to investigate the impact of sustainable tourism and good governance on biodiversity loss in Malaysia. We hypothesis that better governance will lead to lower rate of deforestation and this will also implies that good governance mitigate biodiversity loss in Malaysia. The adoption of sustainable tourism practices will also expected to reduce biodiversity loss. Following [27], in this study, the deforestation rate (proxy for biodiversity loss) was calculated as the ratio of change in forest area using data from United Nation Food and Agriculture Organization for the period 1996 to 2012. For the governance indicators, we used all six measures of governance – voice and accountability, political stability, government effectiveness, regulatory quality, rule of law, and control of corruption. All these variables are taken from the World Bank Governance Indicators constructed and compiled by the World Bank. On the other hand, data for GDP and tourism related are taken for World Development Indicators (WDI) download for the World Bank database. In this study all variables are transformed into natural logarithm except the governance indicators.

Estimating Equation (2) using Ordinary Least Square (OLS) is not without problems. The parameter estimates can be biased in small samples as well as in the presence of dynamic effects, and this bias varies inversely with the size of the sample and the calculated R^2. According to [28] estimating Equation (1) is subject to the so-called spurious regression results as the equation contains non-stationary economic variables. Furthermore, there is the problem caused by the likely endogeneity of the regressors which would prevent OLS estimating the true values of the parameters.

These problems associated with the OLS approach have led to the development of alternative procedures which is more recent and more robust, particularly in small samples. [29] propose the dynamic OLS (DOLS) while Phillips and Hansen [30] propose the fully-modified OLS (FMOLS). DOLS procedure corrects for possible simultaneity bias and small sample bias amongst the regressors by regressing one of the $I(1)$ variables on other $I(1)$ variables, the $I(0)$ variables, and lags and leads of the first difference of the $I(1)$ variables. Incorporating the first difference variables and the associated lags and leads will eliminates simultaneity bias and small sample bias inherent among regressors. On the other hand, the FMOLS procedure correct for endogeneity and serial correlation effects as well as eliminates the small sample bias. The FMOLS needs two conditions to be fulfilled. First, there needs to be only one cointegrating vector. Second, the explanatory variables should not be cointegrated among themselves [31].

As usual when dealing with time series economic variables, we test for the order of integration of the series involved for future analysis. In this study we employed the traditional Augmented Dickey-Fuller (ADF) unit root test popularized by [32], by testing the series in levels and then in their first differences. The results for the test for the order of integration are presented in Table 2. As shown in Table 2, we can safely conclude that all the series are said to be of the order one, that is, they are $I(1)$ variables. In other words these economic variables are said to achieve stationarity after differencing once. As shown in Table 2, all series in first differences are statistically significant at least at the 10 percent level (the critical values are provided by [33]).

Table 2. Results of unit root tests for biodiversity loss, income, sustainable tourism and governance indicators

Variables	ADF unit root tests:	
	Levels	First-differences
Biodiversity	-1.73 (1)	-3.06* (0)
Income	-1.96 (0)	-3.71** (0)
Sus_Tourism	-2.90 (0)	-3.81** (0)
Voice and accountability	-2.93 (1)	-3.57** (1)
Political stability	-1.95 (1)	-3.37** (1)
Government effectiveness	-1.07 (1)	-4.09*** (0)
Regulatory quality	-3.00 (1)	-3.46** (1)
Rule of law	-2.95 (1)	-2.76* (1)
Control of corruption	-2.09 (1)	-3.78** (0)

Notes: Asterisks ***, **, * denote statistically significance at the 1%, 5% and 10% level respectively. Critical values are taken from [33]. Series in levels were estimated with constant and trend, while series in first-differences were estimated with constant only. Figures in parentheses denote lag length.

For completeness we report the regression estimates using OLS in Table 3 as a guide. As shown in Table 3, in most of the cases income and sustainable tourism are significant and show correct signs. The governance indicators are significant only for political stability and rule of law. Nevertheless, we are cautious of these results as they are spurious.

Table 4 presents the results of estimating equation (2) using DOLS. To check for spurious regression we test for cointegration using Hansen [34] instability test. According to [34], the L_c statistics is an LM test statistic and can be used to test for the null of cointegration against the alternative of no cointegration. The L_c statistics at the bottom row in Table 4 clearly suggest that the variables are cointgerated and therefore the DOLS regression estimates are non-spurious. Income is significant and positively related with biodiversity loss in equations with voice and accountability, regulatory quality and control of corruption. Similarly, in these three equations, sustainable tourism indices clearly suggest that increase in sustainable tourism reduce biodiversity loss. On the other hand, the three governance indicators - voice and accountability, regulatory quality and control of corruption are significant and negatively related with biodiversity loss, implying that good governance can mitigate the loss of biodiversity in Malaysia.

Table 3. OLS results of the impact of income, sustainable tourism and good governance on biodiversity loss

Variables	Voice & Accountability	Political stability	Government effectiveness	Regulatory quality	Rule of law	Control of corruption
constant	0.6844***	0.6867***	0.6853***	0.6856***	0.6827***	0.6864***
	(187.37)	(270.51)	(188.36)	(198.82)	(250.64)	(134.61)
income_t	0.0020**	0.0015**	0.0014	0.0024***	0.0024***	0.0019**
	(2.5131)	(2.9394)	(1.7655)	(3.0781)	(4.1858)	(2.5053)
sus_tourism_t	-0.0032**	-0.0025***	-0.0016	-0.0038***	-0.0031***	-0.0034*
	(2.3182)	(3.1733)	(1.0324)	(3.0470)	(3.6372)	(2.0634)
govern_t	-0.0008	-0.0019***	-0.0015	-0.0028	-0.0043***	-0.0009
	(0.6106)	(4.0203)	(1.0956)	(1.6273)	(3.4424)	(0.5652)
R-squared	0.337	0.696	0.376	0.433	0.643	0.334
SER	0.0005	0.0003	0.0005	0.0005	0.0004	0.0005

Notes: Asterisks ***, **, * denote statistically significant at the 1%, 5% and 10% level respectively. Figures in the parentheses are *t*-statistics. *SER* denotes standard error of regression.

Table 4. DOLS results of the impact of income, sustainable tourism and good governance on biodiversity loss

Variables	Voice & Accountability	Political stability	Government effectiveness	Regulatory quality	Rule of law	Control of corruption
Lags,Leads (-k,+k):	(0, 1)	(0, 1)	(0, 2)	(0, 2)	(0, 2)	(0, 1)
constant	0.6745***	0.6985***	0.6700**	0.7101***	0.6830***	0.6963***
	(148.53)	(193.61)	(58.062)	(2138.8)	(376.40)	(71.384)
income_t	0.0055**	-0.0011	-0.0011	0.0057**	0.0005	0.0051**
	(3.5746)	(1.3714)	(0.6363)	(62.098)	(0.8487)	(3.2262)
sus_tourism_t	-0.0094**	0.0008	0.0089	-0.0149**	0.0025	-0.0132**
	(2.9741)	(0.6839)	(1.8447)	(63.382)	(2.0502)	(2.8758)
govern_t	-0.0070*	-0.0040***	-0.0016	-0.0292***	-0.0119**	-0.0085*
	(2.0658)	(8.0069)	(0.4684)	(100.70)	(12.904)	(2.2331)
R-squared	0.832	0.938	0.957	0.999	0.996	0.745
SER	0.0004	0.0002	0.0004	0.0000	0.0001	0.0005
L_c statistics	0.054	0.131	0.025	0.046	0.055	0.080
	(>0.200)	(>0.200)	(>0.200)	(>0.200)	(>0.200)	(>0.200)

*Notes: Asterisks ***, **, * denote statistically significant at the 1%, 5% and 10% level respectively. Figures in the parentheses are t-statistics. Critical values for L_c statistics are given in [34]. SER denotes standard error of regression.*

Estimates for the FMOLS procedure is shown in Table 5. Results in Table 5 show that the L_c statistics clearly cannot reject the null of cointegration in all six equations estimated. Income is positive and statistically significantly different from zero at least at the 5 percent level. Sustainable tourism is statistically significantly different from zero at least at the 10 percent level and show negative sign – increase sustainable tourism reduce biodiversity loss. However, only political stability, regulatory quality and rule of law are statistically significantly different from zero at least at the 10 percent and show correct sign. Nevertheless, in general, the above results clearly suggest that sustainable tourism and good governance will result in lower deforestation rates and therefore help in reducing the loss in biodiversity in Malaysia.

4 Conclusion

The tourism sector is economically important because it is a source of foreign exchange, as well as job opportunities for the masses. Recent approach for tourism development is to balance between harvesting the benefits from tourism activities without degrading the environment and create unfails opportunities for the local communities. Policies targeted for sustainable tourism with the hope that boosting the tourism industry at the same time be able to mitigate the loss of biodiversity resulted from tourism activities. Nevertheless, a key element in the potential success of a country's development policies is dependent on the quality of the government or the practice of good governance.

In this study we investigate whether sustainable tourism and good governance practices by the government of Malaysia has any positive impact in reducing the rate of deforestation for the period 1996 to 2012. In this study we used a macro-level measures of governance indicators provided by the world bank - voice and accountability, political stability and absence of violence, government effectiveness, regulatory quality, rule of law, and control of corruption. Sustainable tourism was constructed as an index using three sustainability indicators - ratio of tourism expenditures to GDP, ratio of tourist arrival to population, and rainfall.

Table 5. FMOLS results of the impact of income, sustainable tourism and good governance on biodiversity loss

Variables	Voice & Accountability	Political stability	Government effectiveness	Regulatory quality	Rule of law	Control of corruption
$constant$	0.6798***	0.6863***	0.6831***	0.6824***	0.6815***	0.6819***
	(165.83)	(279.92)	(187.63)	(179.43)	(316.77)	(122.30)
$income_t$	0.0027**	0.0014**	0.0018**	0.0031***	0.0024***	0.0027***
	(2.8917)	(2.6000)	(2.2038)	(3.6297)	(5.1522)	(3.0696)
$sus\_tourism_t$	-0.0035**	-0.0021**	-0.0018	-0.0046***	-0.0027***	-0.0041*
	(2.2286)	(2.4743)	(1.1595)	(3.2390)	(3.6425)	(2.1646)
$govern_t$	-0.0006	-0.0021***	-0.0019	-0.0041*	-0.0049***	-0.0010
	(0.6084)	(4.2978)	(1.3458)	(2.0793)	(4.5463)	(0.5960)
R-squared	0.210	0.764	0.314	0.337	0.700	0.199
SER	0.0006	0.0003	0.0005	0.0005	0.0003	0.0006
L_c statistics	0.155	0.192	0.505	0.426	0.455	0.286
	(>0.200)	(>0.200)	(>0.200)	(>0.200)	(>0.200)	(>0.200)

*Notes: Asterisks ***, **, * denote statistically significant at the 1%, 5% and 10% level respectively. Figures in the parentheses are t-statistics. Critical values for L_c statistics are given in [34]. SER denotes standard error of regression.*

Since the time series data is short (17 observations) we employed the DOLS and FMOLS which is a more efficient estimator that corrects for simultaneity bias and small sample bias. Interestingly, our results suggest that sustainable tourism and good governance in Malaysia do contribute in mitigating biodiversity loss measure by deforestation rates. Among the contributing factors are voice and accountability, political stability, regulatory quality, rule of law and control of corruption.

References

1. R. Butler, Rainforest diversity – origins and implications, (2006). Retrieved 1/22/2014 from http://rainforests.mongabay.com/0301.htm.
2. R. Butler, Rainforest, (2014). Retrieved 1/22/2014 from http://rainforests.mongabay.com/
3. United Nations Environment Programme (UNEP), Environmental impacts of tourism – global level, (2014). http://www.unep.org/ Access 16/7/2014.
4. C. Christ, O. Hillel, S. Matus, J. Sweeting, Tourism and biodiversity: mapping tourism's global footprint, Washington, Conservation International and UNEP (2003)
5. L. Briguglio, M. Briguglio, Sustainable tourism in small islands: the case of Malta, Mimeo, (undated). Available at https://secure2.gov.mt/tsdu/file.aspx?f=1079
6. *World Commission on Environment and Development (WCED), Our common future, London*, Oxford University Press, (1987)
7. *United Nations World Tourism Organization (UNWTO), Indicators of sustainable development for tourism destinations: a guidebook, Madrid, World Tourism Organization* (2004)
8. K. Greenidge, N. Greenidge, Sustainable tourism development: the case of Barbados, Economic Review, **37**, 1&2, 83-125. (2011)
9. R. Butler, Tourism – an evolutionary approach, In J.G. Nelson, R.W. Butler and G. Wall (eds). Tourism and sustainable development: monitoring, planning, management, Waterloo, University of Waterloo, 27-44 (1993)
10. G. Koop, L. Tole, Is there an environmental Kuznets curve for deforestation? Journal of Development Economics, **58**,231-244 (1999)
11. M. Bhattarai, M. Hammig, Institutions and the environmental Kuznets curve for deforestation: a cross country analysis for Latin America, Africa and Asia, World Development, **29**, 6,995-1010 (2001)
12. N. Kishor, A. Belle, Does improved governance contribute to sustainable forest management? Journal of Sustainable Forestry, **19**,55-79(2004)
13. C. Umemiya, E. Rametsteiner, F. Kraxner, Quantifying the impacts of the quality of governance on deforestation, Environmental Science & Policy, **13**,695-701 (2010)
14. D. Kaufman, A. Kraay, M. Mastruzzi, Governance matters VII: governance indicators for 1996-2007, World Bank Policy Research June 2008, Washington, DC, The World Bank, (2008)
15. F. Neto, A new approach to sustainable tourism development: moving beyond environmental protection, Natural Resource Forum, **3**, 27, 212-222 (2003)
16. R. Nunkoo, H. Ramkissoon, Small island urban tourism: a residents' perspective, Current Issues in Tourism, **13**, 1, 37-60. (2009)
17. M.V. Reddy, Sustainable tourism rapid indicators for less-developed islands: an economic perspective, International Journal of Tourism Research, **10**, 557-576 (2008)
18. United Nations Environment Programme and World Tourism Organisation (UNEP-WTO), Making tourism more sustainable: a guide for policy makers, The United Nations Environment Programme, United Nations, Paris, (2005)
19. C.J. Hunter, Sustainable tourism as an adaptive paradigm, Annals of Tourism Research, **24**, 4, 850-867 (1997)
20. B. Wheeller, Sustaining the ego. Journal of Sustainable Tourism, **1**, 2, 232-239 (1993)
21. A. Torres-Delgado, J. Saarinen, Using indicators to assess sustainable tourism development: a review, Tourism Geographies, **16**, 1, 31-47 (2014)
22. E. Yunis, Indicators to measure sustainability in tourism, Paper presented at the 7th International Forum on Tourism Statistics, Stockholm, Sweden, (2004)
23. C. HwangSuk, E. Sirakaya, Sustainability indicators for managing community tourism, Tourism Management, **26**, 3, 431-445 (2005)
24. S.F. McCool, R.N. Moisey, N.P. Nickerson, What should tourism sustain? The disconnect with industry perceptions of useful indicators, Journal of Travel Research, **40**, 2,124-131 (2001)

25. F.J. Blancas, M. Gonzalez, M. Lozano-Oyola, F. Perez, The assessment of sustainable tourism: application to Spanish coastal destinations, Ecological Indicators, **10**, 2, 484-492 (2010)
26. A.F. Herrera-Ulloa, S. Lluch-Cota, H. Ramirez-Aguirre, S. Hernandez-Vazquez, A. Ortega-Rubio, Sustainable performance of the tourist industry in the state of Baja California SUR, Mexico, Interciencia, **28**, 5, 268-272 (2003)
27. S. Saleem, Biodiversity and economic growth, World Environment Day, June 2010, 111-118. (2010)
28. C.W.J. Granger, P. Newbold, Spurious regression in econometrics, Journal of Econometrics, **2**, 111-120 (1974)
29. J.H. Stock, M. Watson, A simple estimator of cointegrating vectors in higher order integrated systems, Econometrica, **61**, 783-820 (1993)
30. P.C.B. Phillips, B.E. Hansen, Statistical inference in instrumental variables regression with $I(1)$ processes, Review of Economic Studies, **57**, 99-125(1990)
31. P. Narayan, S. Narayan, Determinants of demand for Fiji's exports: an empirical investigation. The Developing Economies, **62**, 1,95-112 (2004)
32. D.A. Dickey, W.A. Fuller, Likelihood ratio statistics for autoregressive time series with a unit root. Econometrica, **49**, 1057-1077 (1981)
33. J.G. MacKinnon, Numerical distribution functions for unit root and cointegration Tests. Journal of Applied Econometrics, **11**,601–618 (1996)
34. B.E. Hansen, Tests for parameter instability in regressions with $I(1)$ processes, Journal of Business & Economic Statistics, **10**, 3,321-335(1992)

22

Rail travel: Conceptualizing a study on slow tourism approaches in sustaining rural development

Farah Atiqah Mohamad Noor[1], Vikneswaran Nair[2], Paolo Mura[3]

[1,2,3]School of Hospitality, Tourism and Culinary Arts, Taylor's University, 47500 Subang Jaya, Selangor Darul Ehsan, Malaysia

Abstract. Rail transportation in Peninsular Malaysia is a popular transportation mode for locals to return to their hometown but is not frequently used as the mode of transport when travelling for holidays. Rural towns in Peninsular Malaysia have immense opportunity to be promoted as a popular tourism destination without the need of intense modern development. Using train rather than taking a car or a bus would endorse the concept of slowness during travel enabling tourists to enjoy the time taken to travel rather than rushing to travel to a destination. Encouragement of travelling by rail to the rural towns will enable improved utilization of the existing rail network and further uplift the travel appeal to rural towns in Peninsular Malaysia. In order to promote the concept of slow tourism that would benefit the rural towns' sustainability, the perception of tourists on travelling slowly by train should first be understood and taken for consideration. A qualitative methodology of in depth interviews with domestic and international tourists whom have travel on trains to the rural towns will be conducted.

1 Introduction

Slow tourism is relatively a new concept and has only been studied over the last 30 years in comparison with other types of tourism that has been studied for over a century ago. Many researches that have been conducted on this topic spans on the likes of definition [1], Savelli's types of slow tourist [2] and how slow tourism works in a popular tourist destination such as Caribbean [3] . However, there are very few researches that are being conducted on the perception and mind set of tourists of a country to pursue slow tourism.

Rail sometimes serve mainly as a transportation corridor connecting rural areas, or urban settings and green strips and other times become the recreational ground for domestic and international tourists [4]. Railway lines in Peninsular Malaysia have existed for more than a century ago since the colonial times. Currently, the railway lines serve as an intercity transport between the bigger towns and rural towns of Peninsular Malaysia. Visiting rural towns in Peninsular Malaysia has been confined to travelling via a car and buses especially for the locals. Most of the locals only use intercity train when they are returning to their hometown but not travelling for holiday purposes.

There are numerous rural towns along the intercity train route in Peninsular Malaysia which offers the opportunity for rural tourism to be explored. This opportunity can be beneficial to develop rural towns as a growing tourism destination while maintaining the charm and uniqueness of a quaint town. The main idea for using rail travel as a gateway to rural tourism experience is adapting the concept of the slowness of travel that has been forgotten by many tourists nowadays.

The main purpose of conducting this study is to understand the willingness of tourists to travel slowly by choosing a transportation mode such as the intercity train to travel to rural towns in Peninsular Malaysia. The researcher wants to highlight rail travel as one of the attraction of the rural holiday experience rather than the full experience of the rural destination itself. In this study, the slow concept is highly regarding the transport mode chosen while on holiday. Comparing to the airplane, train is a more convenient and a practical transport to choose, especially for distances of less than 800 kilometres [2].

Taking Kuala Lumpur as the starting point to the rural towns for example, certainly the total area travelled from Kuala Lumpur to any of the rural towns will be lesser than the actual 700 miles (1126 km) length of the whole Peninsular Malaysia [5]. Aside from that, the environmental and sociocultural features of rural towns in Peninsular Malaysia can be feasibly preserved by focusing on promoting these towns through existing intercity rail transportation. Not to mention, this study can encourage tourists to feel that it is good to take their time during travelling to rural towns because only by slower pace that they get to appreciate the cultural heritage of Malaysians.

A rural town in the context of Peninsular Malaysia is the agricultural land of natural resource sector companies, especially in the plantation and mining sectors; with a low level of urbanization and having natural resource-based industries as the main income source [6]. In order to promote slow tourism via rail to the rural towns, the researcher would like to conceptualize this study to understand the possibility for rail travel to assist the development of rural towns throughout Peninsular Malaysia. Before this concept is rationalized, we must first realize the perception of a small number of tourists that travel using train to these rural towns along the intercity train route and also the locals who never travel with train for holiday purposes. Peninsular Malaysia is chosen in order to encourage the transfer of tourist displacement not just concentrated in Klang Valley but also in rural towns throughout Peninsular Malaysia.

2 Literature Review

Slow tourism concept derived from the Slow Food Italy as pioneered by Carlo Petrini in the 1980s. As a non-profit, member-supported, eco-gastronomic organization, The Slow Food movement established in 1989 aimed to decrease the eating trend of fast food and fast life as well as bringing back the local food traditions and people's interest in the food they eat, its origins and how our food options affect the rest of the world [7].

Slow City (CittaSlow) movement is a non-profit organization that appear from the principles of Slow Food movement which further emphasized the need to adopt the slowness of life against the fast pace of 21st century. Principles of the CittaSlow movement includes to maintain a calm and less polluted physical environments, conserve local aesthetic traditions and foster the crafts, cuisine and produce of the locals [8].

The slow concept has been further strengthened by Carl Honore and his hugely successful book, In Praise of Slowness where he talked about the current generation obsession with everything fast and trying to encourage the return to the original idea of slowness in life [9]. Using technology to create healthier environments, making citizens aware of the value of more leisurely life rhythms and sharing their experience to seek administrative solutions for better living are also the pledges of Slow City movement [8].

Through both Slow Food and Slow City movement, the birth of a new type of tourism called slow tourism has slowly encapsulated the belief that domestic, regional and international tourism could adapt to the approach of slow travel through transportation used, cuisine experienced and changing perception of travel values. Slow tourism puts itself in the alternative tourism genre by adopting 'soft growth' concept where advancing development (quality) instead of promoting physical growth (quantity) is emphasized [3].

Therefore, slow tourism is a type of tourism promoting equitable socioeconomics benefits to local communities, curbs environmental pressures, and fulfils the rising responsible tourism demand favoured by a more consciously motivated group of travellers [3]. Articles on slow tourism has been contributed by other authors such as authors of *Slow Travel and Tourism* [10], as well as Conway and Timms [3] whom studied slow tourism and applying it as the alternative tourism activity in Caribbean Islands. The table highlights certain dimensions of slow tourism based on a conceptual framework constructed by Lumsdon and McGrath [1]:

Table 1. Dimensions in Slow Tourism (Lumsdon & McGrath, 2011)

Dimensions in Slow Tourism	Sub-dimensions
Slowness and value of time	1,2,5,13,14,15,16,17
Locality and activities at the destination	4,5,18,19
Mode of transport and travel experience	3,6,7,8,9,10,11,20,21,22
Environmental consciousness	11,12,23

Literatures

Note: (1) Honoré [9]; (2) Krippendorf [11]; (3) Jain and Lyons [12]; (4) Matos [13]; (5) Woehler [14]; (6) Lumsdon and Page [15]; (7) Ceron and Dubois [16]; (8) Schiefelbusch, Schâfer and Müller [17]; (9) Halsall [18]; (10) Speakman [19]; (11) Mintel [20]; (12) Dickinson, Robbins and Lumsdon [21]; (13) Virilio [22]; (14) Andrews [23]; (15) Peeters [24]; (16) Adams [25]; (17) Klein [26]; (18) Pietryowski [27]; (19) Nilsson, Svard, Widarsson and Wirell [28]; (20) Dann [29]; (21) Elsrud [30]; (22) Barr, Shaw, Coles and Prillwitz [31], (23) Dolnicar, Crouch and Long [32].

According to the framework by Lumsdon and McGrath [1], the mode of transport and travel experience is the most significant dimension in slow tourism [12,15-20,29,30-31]. Slow travel is a journey involving conventional rail transport; without the inclusion of high speed trains [16]. Therefore, the initial concept of using rail travel to facilitate slow tourism can be an additional sub-dimension to the existing dimension of mode of transport and travel experience. The added dimensions can be demonstrated as per Table 2:

Table 2. Dimensions in Rail Travel as an Approach for Slow Tourism (Author's own)

Dimensions in rail travel as an approach for slow tourism	Sub-dimensions
Low carbon travel	1,2,3,4,5,6,7,8, 9,10
Enhancement of travel experience during on-board journey	11,12,13,14,15,16,17,18,19
Literatures	
Note: (1) Reis and Jellum [4]; (2) Givoni and Banister [33]; (3) Lumsdon and Dickinson [1]; (4) Wickizer and Snow [34]; (5) Georgic, Daniel, Roxana, and Stefania [35]; (6) Gardner [36]; (7) Vorster [37]; (8) Dickinson, Robbins, Filimonau, Hares, and Mika [38]; (9) Willard and Beeton [39]; (10) Markwell, Fullagar and Wilson [40]; (11) Rhoden [41]; (12) Prideaux [42]; (13) Chen, Shyr, Chen and Li [43]; (14) Jain and Lyons [12]; (15) Curtin [44]; (16) Lumsdon and McGrath [1]; (17) Watts [45]; (18) Jane [46]; (19) Sivilevičius, Maskeliūnaitė, Petkevičienė, and Petkevičius [47].	

In this case, low carbon travel and tourism as mentioned by Vorster [37] is a transformation from the current emissions-centric transportation, accommodation and concerning paradigm in tourism economy to a travel growth that promotes environmental and social conscience. Vorster [37] discusses low carbon land transport, as one of the sub-clusters of low carbon travel in which a shift to mass rail system from cars during travelling can contribute to a 30 per cent reduction of vehicle emission in the next decade.

Furthermore, Givoni and Banister [33] stated that rail transport is possibly 'greener' and environmental-friendly as it is proven that it consumes lesser energy than the other means of transport utilized for long-distance travel. Tourists who chose to travel slowly by utilizing rail would automatically participate in low carbon travelling whether they realize it or not.

Apart from that, rail travel can be experienced as an enhancement of travel especially during the on-board journey. Transport and travel experiences of tourists that are largely remembered, predominantly comprised of visual observation throughout the travelled train route such as the viewing of external objects including landscapes, human and animal life although the transport's interior was also recognized [41]. Train travel can encourage window gazing in which a person may observe harsh environments while being in the comfortness of a train carriage [29]. Therefore, the exterior landscapes, train interior and comfortness can be seen as the indicators for the enhancement of travel experiences if slow tourism is partake by utilizing rail transport.

The importance of finding out the perception of a small number of tourists who undertake rail travel is also because these tourists are aspiring slow tourists. It must be understood that a slow tourist is the advocate for low-impact travel styles and will deliberately avoid flying [35]. Rail transportation can be an alternative mode for the slow tourists to travel rather than flying. During the beginning of the slow tourism appreciation, it is always thought that cycling [40] or hitch-hiking [48] to a destination is the approach of slow mobility.

However, it is mentioned that rail which is the opposing travel mode of flying could also be part of the slow mobility in slow tourism [2]. Therefore, it is suitable for the Malaysian tourism authorities to promote the mobility of slow tourism through the existing rail transport technology in Peninsular Malaysia which is safe and reliable but is fairly considered to be under-used for undertaking tourism in rural towns.

More importantly, a perception study of slow tourism by rail to rural towns can facilitate towards the success of the cooperative effort between the Ministry of Tourism and Culture Malaysia, the Homestay Association of Malaysia, Keretapi Tanah Melayu Berhad and travel agents in Malaysia and Singapore which was launched in October 2010 [49].The launch was meant to market the Malaysia Rail Tourism packages combining the homestay experience at the rural destination by taking a train, providing tourists the chance to enjoy the scenic Malaysian landscape as part of their holiday experience [49].

This goes hand in hand with the integration of homestay program together with the rail travel packages which is able to display a look into the lives of Malaysian rural community and the traditional communal activities. Currently, the packages are heavily marketed for Singaporeans as the rail travel starts at Tanjong Pagar Railway Station, Singapore, but it could open up a new interest for tourists from other countries to experience the authenticity of rural towns in Peninsular Malaysia. Through this study, the tourism authorities can be provided with an understanding of the perception of tourists that travel on the train to these rural destinations for the future upgrade of the whole rail-homestay experiences.

Sustainability is the management of all viable resources according to economic, aesthetic and social needs while preserving the cultural integrity, important eco logical processes and biological diversity [2]. Tourism authorities will be able to adapt sustainability to rural towns by promoting tourism through rail travel and upholding the principle of slowness in travel by enjoying the rail ride without the worry of the extended time being used to pursue rail travel. United Nations of World Tourism Organization stated that the rural community can be sustained when the tourism products act harmoniously with the environment, community and local cultures so that they benefitted out of tourism development rather than suffer because of it [2].

The community will be able to profit from increased tourist arrivals and be employed in tourism jobs without the need of migrating to a bigger city. Moscardo and Pearce [50] suggest that the role of transport in tourism is divided to transport dominating the experience, transport as integrated element of experience, transport as functional link and transport as a significant constraint. This study correlates with that of Lumsdon and Page [15] whom stated the examples of transport commodities that fits the role of transport in tourism. Lumsdon and Page [15] cited intercity rail as the transport example of functional link that facilitates tourism.

However, intercity rail experience itself can prove to be an integrated element of the whole tourism experience as the journey itself focuses on passing by rustic views of rural towns in which it could not be experienced by other modes of transport efficiently in Peninsular Malaysia. Therefore, this study will address the research gap by understanding the perception of tourists who chose to travel with rail in Peninsular Malaysia rather than using other available transport modes.

3 Research Methodology

The chosen method to conduct this research is by using qualitative approach in order to achieve deeper understanding of the tourists' and locals' perception to use rail to visit rural towns in Peninsular Malaysia. Qualitative research is chosen because perception studies are usually subjective in nature due to varying opinions among individuals who might or might not be familiar with the research topic. The qualitative methodology can be used to further understand any phenomenon about which little is yet known [51].

They can also be used to gain new perspectives on things which are already known, or things that are hard to be conveyed quantitatively [51]. Slow tourism approach using rail travel to promote rural towns is relatively a new concept of tourism development and very few studies has been conducted on the mind set of locals of a country and international tourists whom are interested to pursue rural tourism in Peninsular Malaysia as the possibility to accept it as a touristic activity.

The type of qualitative research method adopted for this research will be in depth interviews with selected participants according to the targeted sample which is divided to three groups of ten people. In depth interviews is chosen due to the ability to extract as many information possible from an individual by soliciting their personal views through asking pre-determined open-ended questions. In this research, the sampling method opted is selective sampling which is defined as the selection of people according to the aims of the research using characteristic such as age, status, role in organization and stated ideology as starting points [52]. The researcher will be interviewing thirty individuals of which the first group is ten international tourists travelling on the intercity train to the rural towns from Kuala Lumpur. The second group will be ten Malaysian tourists whom have travelled before on the train to the rural towns for holiday purpose. The third group will be ten Malaysians whom have never travelled before on the train to the rural towns for holiday purpose. In order to find the first and second group sample, the researcher will travel on the day train to selected rural towns in Peninsular Malaysia. The international tourists will be randomly scouted on the train itself through the researchers' observation and their arrival destination while for the local tourists; the researcher will first ask them if they are travelling on the train for the purpose of holiday at the rural towns. Then, the researcher will ask for their permission to be interviewed on the train itself. On the other hand, in order to select the local tourists whom have never use rail to go for holiday at the rural towns, the researcher will do online search through posting the requirements on part time work web portals and provide monetary reward to those who fit the criteria as well as being able to be interviewed one on one on a predetermined time and date.

The qualitative data analysis method will be the documentation of the data obtained from the in depth interviews. Through documentation, data comes from the transcribed text of the interviews recorded in audiotapes [53] in which it contain the reconstructed original comments, observations, and feelings [53]. The next step will be to conduct thematic analysis which is to identify all data that relate to the already classified patterns, expanding the patterns, identify specific and corresponding pattern which are then combined into sub-themes [53]. After obtaining the sub -themes, it is easy to see the emerging patterns and then asking the respondents to give feedback based on the transcribed conversations [53]. The feedback obtained will be further used in the thematic analysis.

4 Expected Research Findings

The tourism activities in Malaysia are mainly concentrated in the bigger cities such as Kuala Lumpur, Penang, Melaka and Johor Bahru as well as the popular islands in the west coast and east coast of Peninsular Malaysia. There are other tourism opportunities that can be offered by rural towns should there be more researches conducted on exploring that possibility. Malaysian rural towns do not need major landscape restructuring in order to facilitate tourism but by using the existing facilities and identifying the touristic asset of the towns, it will be sufficient to encourage its growth of tourism. Not to mention, this research would be able to spread the concept of slow tourism approach in travelling by using rail, one of the slower vehicles in order to fully immerse in the Malaysian experience at a reasonable time. It will provide an understanding of travelling at a slower pace for better discovery of cultures and the rural tourism experience.

The conceptualization of this study will be able to facilitate towards the success of Tourism Malaysia's rail tourism packages. Tourism Malaysia has recently launched a number of rail travel packages that combine travelling by Keretapi Tanah Melayu (Malaya Train) to rural towns in peninsular Malaysia with homestay accommodation and participation in cultural activities. The program has been in running for less than two years and it will be interesting to find out the opinions of tourists whom have participated or are interested in the tours. By understanding their perception and satisfaction of the tours, the researcher will be able to identify the success and matters of improvement within the rail travel packages. Rail travel by using slow tourism approach would contribute to Malaysia's pledge towards becoming a sustainable tourism destination. The approach is useful in the long term environment preservation of Malaysian rural towns by encouraging rail travel instead of other less environmental-friendly vehicles such as airplane, buses and personal automobiles. Encouragement of traveling by rail to the rural towns will enable improved utilization of the existing rail network and further uplift the travel appeal to rural towns in Peninsular Malaysia.

5 Conclusion

Slow tourism is a bench of tourism that has not been widely studied especially in the Asian region. The current literatures of slow tourism mostly concentrate on the definition, characteristics and types of slow tourism rather than the perception of individuals to pursue slow tourism during their holidays. Therefore, there are only a few theories that can be used to provide a theoretical framework to this study. Nevertheless, it is hoped that by conceptualizing this study, it can be a stepping stone to a further interest of slow tourism in Asia. Perception studies of rail travel and the willingness of individuals to adapt slowness in their rural travel experiences will be the major drive of this study. As the proposed methodology will be interviews with the selected individuals, findings will be obtained after analysis of the interviews. The understanding of tourists' perception on choosing a slower transportation such as rail can be detrimental towards the success of applying the slow tourism concept by rail to visit rural towns. This research could also facilitate future studies by applying slow tourism approach in the time taken, cuisine experienced, attraction visited and accommodation chosen.

6 Acknowledgement

The funding for this project was made possible through a research grant obtained from the Malaysian Ministry of Education, under the Long Term Research Grant Scheme (LRGS), 2011. Reference no. JPT.S (BPKI) 2000/01/015JId.4 (67).

References

1. L.M. Lumsdon & P. McGrath, *Developing a conceptual framework for slow travel: a grounded theory approach.* Journal of Sustainable Tourism, **19**, 3, 265–279 (2011)
2. B.F. Timms & D. Conway (n.d.). *Slow Tourism at the Caribbean ' s Geographical Margins,* (Dodman 2009).
3. A.C. Reis & C. Jellum. *Rail Trail Development: A Conceptual Model for Sustainable Tourism.* Tourism Planning & Development, **9**, 2, 133–147 (2012)
4. F.W. Foxworthy. Commercial timber trees of the Malay Peninsula (1927)
5. A. Liu. *Tourism in rural areas: Kedah, Malaysia.* Tourism Management, **27**, 5, 878-889 (2006)
6. S. Heitmann, P. Robinson & G. Povey. *Slow Food, Slow Cities and Slow Tourism.* In P. Robinson, S. Heitmann, & and P. Dieke (Eds.), Research Themes for Touris. UK: CAB International. 114-127 (2011)
7. S. Pink, (2008, September). Mobilising visual ethnography: Making routes, making place and making images. In *Forum Qualitative Sozialforschung/Forum: Qualitative Social Research* , **9**, 3, (2008)
8. C. Honoré. *In Praise of Slowness. How a Worldwide movement is Changing the Cult of Speed.* San Francisco: HarperCollins (2004)
9. J.E. Dickinson & L. Lumsdon, L. *Slow travel and tourism.* Earthscan (2010)
10. J. Krippendorf. *The Holiday Makers.* London: Heinemann (1984)
11. G. Lyons, J. Jain & D. Holley. *The use of travel time by rail passengers in Great Britain.* Transportation Research Part A: Policy and Practice, **41**, 107–120 (2007)
12. R. Matos. *Can Slow Tourism Bring New life to Alpine Regions?.* In K. Weirmair, & C. Mathies (Eds.), The Tourism and Leisure Industry Shaping the Future. USA: Routledge. 93-104 (2004)

13. K.K. Woehler. Chapter 5. *The Rediscovery of Slowness, or Leisure Time As One's Own and As Self-Aggrandizement?*. 83-92 (2004)

14. L. Lumsdon & S.J. Page. *Progress in transport and tourism research: reformulating the transport-tourism interface and future research agendas.* Elsevier Science Ltd 1-27 (2004)

15. J.P. Ceron & G. Dubois. *Limits to tourism? A backcasting scenario for sustainable tourism mobility in 2050.* Tourism and Hospitality Planning & Development, **4**, 191–209 (2007)

16. M. Schiefelbusch, A. Jain, T. Schafer &D. Muller. *Transport and tourism: The roadmap to integrated planning developing and assessing integrated chains.* Journal of Transport Geography, **18**, 482–489 (2007)

17. D.A. Halsall. *Railway heritage and the tourist gaze: Stoomtram Hoorn-Medemblik.* Journal of Transport Geography, **9**, 151–160 (2001)

18. C. Speakman. *Tourism and transport: Future prospects.* Tourism and Hospitality Planning & Development, **2**, 129–137 (2005)

19. Mintel. Slow travel special report. London: Author. N (2009)

20. J.E. Dickinson, D.K. Robbins & L. Lumsdon. *Holiday travel discourses and climate change.* Journal of Transport Geography, **18**, 482–489 (2010)

21. P. Virilio. La Vitesse. *Paris: Éditions Flammarion* (1991)

22. C. Andrews. *Slow is beautiful: new visions of community, leisure and joie de vivre.* New Society Publishers (2006)

23. P. Peeters, P. *Mitigating tourism's contribution to climate change – an introduction.* In P. Peeters (Ed.), Tourism and climate change mitigation: Methods, greenhouse gas reductions and policies. Breda, The Netherlands: Stichting NHTV Breda. 11-26 (2007)

24. B. Adams. *Time.* Cambridge: Polity (2004)

25. O. Klein. *Social perception of time, distance and high-speed transportation.* Time and Society, **13**, 245–263 (2004)

26. B. Pietryowski, B. *You are what you eat: The social economy of the slow food economy.* Review of the Social Economy, **62**, 307–321 (2004)

27. J.H. Nilsson, A.C. Svard, A. Widarsson & T. Wirell (2007, September 27–29). Slow destination marketing in small Italian towns. Paper presented at the 16th Nordic Symposium in Tourism and Hospitality Research, Helsingborg, Sweden (2007)

28. G.M.S. Dann. *Travel by train: keeping nostalgia on track.* In A.V. Seaton (Ed.), Tourism: The state of the art. Chichester, UK:Wiley. 775-782 (1994)

29. T. Elsrud. *Time creation in travelling.* Time and Society, **7**, 309–334 (1998)

30. S. Barr, G. Shaw, T. Coles & J. Prillwitz. *A holiday is a holiday: Practicing sustainability, home and away.* Journal of Transport Geography, **18**, 474–481 (2010)

31. S. Dolnicar, G. Crouch & P. Long. *Environmentally friendly tourists:What do they really know about them?* Journal of Sustainable Tourism, **16**, 197–210 (2009)

32. M. Givoni & D. Banister. *Reinventing the wheel–planning the rail network to meet mobility needs of the 21st century.* TSU working paper, Ref. 1036 (2008)

33. B.J. Wickizer & A. Snow. *Rediscovering the Transportation Frontier: Improving Sustainability in the United States Through Passenger Rail.* Sustainable Dev. L. & Pol'y, 11, 12. (2010)

34. G. Georgic, B. Daniel, D.M. Roxana & B. Stefania (n.d.). *Slow Movement as an Extension of Sustainable Development for Tourism Resources : A Romanian Approach*, 595–605 (2004)

35. N. Gardner. a manifesto for slow travel, *25*(April) (2009)

36. S. Vorster. Travel and tourism (" travelism ") in the low-carbon economy : The role of public policy in accelerating decarbonisation over the next four decades, (October) (2012)

37. J.E. Dickinson, D. Robbins, V. Filimonau, A. Hares & M. Mika, M. *Awareness of Tourism Impacts on Climate Change and the Implications for Travel Practice A Polish Perspective.* Journal of Travel Research, **52**, 4, 506-519 (2013)

38. P. Willard & S. Beeton. *Low Impact Experiences: Developing Successful Rail Trail Tourism.* Tourism Planning & Development, **9**, 1, 5–13 (2012)

39. S. Fullagar, K. Markwell & E. Wilson (Eds.). *Slow tourism: Experiences and mobilities*. Channel View Publications. **54** (2012)

40. S. Rhoden. ©Association for European Transport and contributors (2006)

41. B. Prideaux. *Tracks to tourism: Queensland rail joins the tourist industry*. International Journal of Tourism Research, **1**, 2, 73–86 (1999)

42. C. Chen Wei, O.F. Shyr, C. Chen Huan & T. Li. *High Speed Rail Tourism and the Generation Y Market: Any Possibilities?*. International Journal Of Science In Society, **3**, 4, 71-80 (2012)

43. S. Curtin. *Wildlife tourism: the intangible, psychological benefits of human–wildlife encounters*. Current Issues in Tourism, **12**, 5-6, 451-474 (2009)

44. L. Watts, L. *The art and craft of train travel*. Social & Cultural Geography, **9**, 6, 711-726 (2008)

45. A. Jane, A. *All together onboard*. Travel Trade Gazette UK & Ireland, (3104), **46** (2014)

46. H. Sivilevičius, L. Maskeliūnaitė, B. Petkevičienė & K. Petkevičius. *The model of evaluating the criteria, describing the quality of organization and technology of travel by international train*. Transport, **27**, 3, 307–319 (2012)

47. M. O'Regan. *Alternative mobility cultures and the resurgence of hitchhiking*. Slow tourism: Experiences and mobilities. Bristol: Channel View, 128-142 (2012)

48. Media Release Malaysia Launches Rail and Homestay. (2010).

49. G. Moscardo & P.L. Pearce, *Chapter 2: Life Cycle, Tourist Motivation and Transport: Some Consequences for the Tourist Experience*. In Tourism & Transport, 29 (2004)

50. M.C. Hoepfl. Choosing qualitative research: A primer for technology education researchers (1997)

51. I.T. Coyne, I. T. *Sampling in qualitative research. Purposeful and theoretical sampling; merging or clear boundaries?*. Journal of advanced nursing, **26**, 3, 623-630 (1997)

52. J. Aronson. *A pragmatic view of thematic analysis*. The qualitative report, **2**, 1, 1-3 (1994)

23

Community Involvement in Tourism Development: A Case Study of Lenggong Valley World Heritage Site

Nur Zafirah A. Khadar [1], Mastura Jaafar [2], Diana Mohamad [3]

[1,3]Sustainable Tourism Research Cluster (STRC), Universiti Sains Malaysia, 11800 Penang, Malaysia
[2]School of Housing, Building and Planning, Universiti Sains Malaysia, 11800 Penang, Malaysia

Abstract. This paper examines the empirical relationship between the economic impact and community involvement in the Lenggong Valley. Recommendations for improvement in development effectiveness through the development of a community centre for economic and social activities, with specific attention given to types of activity and community involvement stimulating the economic development in the Lenggong Valley. Heritage tourism development is a tourism in which arts, culture and heritage form a key attraction for visitors and it can be represented as an area of significant economic benefit to heritage sites. The tourism industry in Hulu Perak became more widespread after Lenggong Valley is recognized as a World Heritage Site. There is shown a positive effect on the development and economic prosperity.

1 Introduction

In general, the heritage tourism offers a range of cultural heritage products, from visiting monuments to discovering unique lifestyles, as a that could serve in cultural and heritage tourism demand [1]. UNESCO defines heritage tourism as "to create a discerning type of tourism that takes account of other people's cultures" [2]. Culture and heritage tourism are internationally recognized for its financial potential in addition to contributing to sustainable tourism development. More importantly, the heritage tourism paradigm shift and transformation may serve as the local communities' economical gains platform. Indeed, culture and heritage tourism has been gaining importance recently not only for its' economic gains but due to more sustainable approaches.

As rural and regional economies go through difficult times of change, it may seem to some local communities that heritage can help in terms of economic gains. When what is old and valued in the community can no longer serve its original function, surely it can still attract funding and tourism as a part of cultural heritage. It is a well known fact that a natural link exists between cultural heritage tourism and regional development. Regional development is a key factor which contributes to the economic welfare of the host country.

In this study, we are focusing on Lenggong Valley that situated in the northern part of Perak, Malaysia, located 100 miles from the north of Ipoh; which is famous for heritage, culture and archaeological attraction [3]. UNESCO has gazetted Lenggong Valley Archaeological Heritage as one of the UNESCO World Heritage Site on 30th June 2012. The Lenggong Valley is one of Peninsular Malaysia's most important areas of archaeology, as excavations have revealed many traces of Malaysia's prehistoric.

Of interest, it is known for the evidence of ancient human activity on the Peninsula. The Lenggong Valley landscape has gone a very limited changes were to date, it remains surrounded by green vegetation and limestone hills. Apart from an open-air museum, the Lenggong Valley house legends, skeletons, cave drawings and precious finds such as jewellery, pottery weapons, and stone tools.

These attributes are envisaged as pull factors for business activities and thus, have an economic impact on and investment in Lenggong Valley. Traditionally, local communities in Lenggong valley are involved in the primary economic sectors, which are agriculture and fisheries [4]. Therefore, the study aims to examine and discuss the Lenggong Valley toward community involvement through economic impact in heritage tourism development activities.

2 Literature review

2.1 Economic impact from heritage tourism development

Heritage tourism encompasses elements of living culture, history, and natural history of a place that was intended to preserve and maintained for the future generation. More specifically, it focused upon experiencing cultural environments, including landscapes, the visual and the performing arts and special lifestyles, values, traditions, and events. Other than influencing the economic development, these elements contribute to present-future growth stability.

Heritage and culture play a crucial role in encouraging an excellent team play of resources management (cultural and natural) between community residents, organizations, civic institutions and governments; especially in rural settings. More importantly, these unique elements characterize the community and through this characterization, it draws community and visitors alike [5]. This facilities harmony and understanding among people, it supports culture and helps renew tourism [6]. Therefore, heritage tourism sustainable management seeks to achieve a balance between the preservation of heritage resources and providing economic development opportunities for the community.

Heritage tourism is one kind of prevalent special interest tourism (SIT) and usually related to the domains of cultural tourism and urban tourism [7]. Heritage tourism successfulness is calculated in the course of attractive heritage resources management and implementation of effective policy; by which, could establish through residents' tourism development supportiveness [8] have taken the local residents' attitude into account when examining the relationships between the locals' involvement towards development in heritage sites. Community participation in planning and development stages is also a fundamental necessity for sustainability of development [9], which in turn, is essential for finding a balance between economic prosperity, environmental protection and social equity and business opportunity [10].

Heritage tourism sustainable management seeks to achieve a balance between the preservation of heritage resources and providing economic development opportunities for the community. For the success of heritage tourism and its sustainability, it is important to understand community involvement impacts on the heritage tourism development. Pragmatic heritage tourism development benefits the community in terms of appreciation for and pride in their local city and its history.

The influence of a well-planned and well-managed local tourism programs extends to improving the local community economy and enhancing the quality of life. The benefits may include the potential for profitable domestic industries - hotels, restaurants, transportation systems, souvenirs and handicrafts and guide services.

3 Research Methodology

A self-administered survey was taken in June 2014 as the data collection instrument by this study. Targeting the local community that resides in 15 villages of the Lenggong Valley, this study has successfully retrieved 85 per cent usable questionnaires. Using a four-point Likert scale (1= strongly disagree, 4 = strongly agree), respondents were asked to rank their answers on 221 questions related to tourism development in the Lenggong Valley. The questions were based on a review of the literature questionnaire consisted of six parts; however, for the purpose of this study, only Part 1 and Part 6 were used that containts Part 1 - addresses the respondents' demographic information with 9 items – gender, age, race, experience in work, indigenous people , occupation, personal monthly income, education level and job profession of the community and Part 6 – perceptions of local community in social and economic impacts) [11].

4 Data analysis

The survey data was analysed in SPSS version 22 by using the summary of descriptive statistics of respondents' profile and paired sample t- test between respondents' profile and economic impacts of community involvement in Lenggong Valley. Descriptive statistics are used to describe the basic features of the data in a study. A paired sample t-test is used to determine whether there is a significant difference between the average values of the same measurement made under two different conditions. Both measurements are done on each unit in a sample, and the test is based on the paired differences between these two values. The usual null hypothesis is that the difference in the mean values is zero. The null hypothesis is:

H_o: There is a significant difference between a respondents' profile and economic impacts

H_1: There is no significant difference between a respondents' profile and economic impacts

4.1 Characteristics of respondents

Of 221 total respondents', 55.2 percent were female respondents and 44.8 percent were male respondents (Table 1). The respondent population is aged between 17 years old to 80 years old, with majority of respondents' fall into 17 -26 years old category (29 per cent). This followed by 53 to 62 years old (17.6 percent), 44 to 53 years old (17.2 percent). 26 to 35 years old (14.9 percent), 35 to 44 years old (14.5 percent), 62 to 71 years old (5.9 percent) and only 0.9 percent were aged between 71 to 80 years old. 43 percent respondents' were in others job profession followed by 21.3 percent in support of government and private sectors, 17.6 percent in an agriculture, 10 percent in food industries, 3.2 percent in handicraft field, 2.7 percent in transportation and another 2.3 percent in accommodation filed.

Moreover, 56.1 percent of the respondents' are Secondary School in Malaysian Certificate of Education (SPM) holder, 16. 7 percent possess a Secondary School in Lower Secondary Assessment (PMR), Primary School and College that have 9 percent, 5.4 percent with a Bachelor and 3.6 graduated from high school. This study found 33.5 percent respondents' with no monthly income and 29.9 percent with monthly income below RM 1,000. This is followed by 27.1 percent with monthly income between RM 1,000- RM 2,000 of income, 6.8 percent earned between RM 2,001- RM 3,000 monthly, 2.3 percent with monthly income between RM 3,001- RM 4,000 and 0.5 percent enjoy RM 4,001 - RM 5,000 of income.

Table 1. Respondents' Profile

Sample data (*n=221*)		
Variables	Frequency	(%)
Gender		
Male	122	55.2
Female	99	44.8
Age		
17-26	64	29.0
26-35	33	14.9
35-44	32	14.5
44-53	38	17.2
53-62	39	17.6
62-71	13	5.9
71-80	2	0.9
Job Profession		
Transportation	6	2.7
Accomodation	5	2.3
Food	22	10.0
Handcraft	7	3.2
Agriculture	39	17.6
Support	47	21.3
Others	95	43.0
Education Level		
Primary School	20	9.0
Secondary School (PMR)	37	16.7
Secondary School (SPM)	124	56.1
High School	8	3.6
College	20	9.0
Bachelor	12	5.4
Income		
Below RM 1,000.00	66	29.9
RM 1,000.00 - RM 2,000.00	60	27.1
RM 2,001.00 - RM 3,000.00	15	6.8
RM 3,001.00 - RM 4,000.00	5	2.3
RM 4,001.00 - RM 5,000.00	1	0.5
Without income	74	33.5

4.2 Paired sample T-Test between economic impacts and respondent characteristics

In this study, paired sample t-test was used to determine the relationship between economic impacts and characteristics of the respondents' that involved in heritage tourism development at Lenggong Valley, Perak. The dependent variables that have chosen were contributed to the National Income (GDP) [A], authorities often hold meetings with the local community to discuss the development of tourism in Lenggong [B], authorities are also encouraging local community involvement in tourism activities [C] and prices of goods and services increasing [D]. The independent variables include income [AI] , job profession [AII], age [BI] , gender [CI] and education level [CIII].

From Table 2 the first row observes the relationship between contribute to the National Income (GDP) [A] and income [AI] and job profession [AII]. It shows the [AI] t- statistics, t = 7.241, and p = 0.000 and for the [AII] shows the t-statistics, t = -11.961, and p = 0.000 i.e., a very small probability of this result occurring by chance, under the null hypothesis of no difference. Therefore, the null hypothesis is rejected for [AI] and [AII]. On the other hand, second row observation shows the relationship between authorities often hold meetings with the local community to discuss the development of tourism in Lenggong [B] and age [BI] and job profession [BII]. The results obtained [BI] where t- statistics, t = 4.376, and p = 0.000 and for the [BII] indicates t-statistics, t = -15.519, and p = 0.000. The null hypothesis is rejected for [BI] and [BII] given the significant relationship between the variables. Meanwhile, for the third row implies a relationship between authorities are also encouraging local community involvement in tourism activities [C] and gender [CI], age [CII], education level [CIII] and job profession [CIV] hence the results explained in the table for the [CI] t-statistics, t = 35.217, and p = 0.000, for the [CII] indicator, t- statistics, t = 6.188, and p = 0.000 followed by [CIII] indicator t-statistics, t = 6.996, and p = 0.000 and [CIV] indicator t-statistics, t = -14.405, and p = 0.000. Next, for the last row describe the relationship between the price of goods and services increasing [D] and income [DI] subsequently the result obtained [DI] as t-statistics, t = 4.000, and the p = 0.000.

Table 2. Paired sample T-test between variables

Paired Samples Test					
DV (Economic Indicators)	IV (Respondents Profile Indicators)	Mean	Std. Deviations	t	Sig. 2 tailed
Contribute to the National Income (GDP) [A]	Income [AI]	1.081	2.220	7.241	0.000**
	Job Profession [AII]	-1.416	1.760	-11.961	0.000**
Authorities often hold meetings with the local community to discuss the development of tourism in Lenggong [B]	Age [BI]	0.566	1.922	4.376	0.000**
	Job Profession [BII]	-2.090	2.002	-15.519	0.000**
Authorities are also encouraging local community involvement in tourism activities [C]	Gender [CI]	2.330	0.984	35.217	0.000**
	Age [CII]	0.769	1.848	6.188	0.000**
	Education Level [CIII]	0.747	1.587	6.996	0.000**
	Job Profession [CIV]	-1.887	1.947	-14.405	0.000**
Prices of goods and services increasing [D]	Income [DI]	0.633	2.354	4.000	0.000**

** Significant at the 0.05 level (2-tailed)

5 Discussion and conclusion

This study has investigated the community involvement that supports the economic impact by considering economic dependence, community attachment, the local authority's role and perceived tourism impacts to support heritage tourism development. According to the findings, it is learned that respondents' characteristics play significant role in improving the community involvement in Lenggong Valley. The heritage tourism will help to increase the local development in making the Lenggong Valley as an attractive historical site in Malaysia. The coming of foreign and local tourist would indirectly generate economic growth in the district of Lenggong Valley, hence can increase the revenue authorities and the income of the population. Most of the respondents agreed on the importance role of local authority and perceived by having a better plan, it would help the province to increase its tourism economically as well.

The improvement of agriculture and support fields could contribute to increase in Contribute National Income (GDP). This paper suggests the improvement in the form of training program to equip the respondents with skills, and hence can encourage supports towards community participation in heritage tourism development. Government may continue giving assistance by way of financial support in the development of tourism infrastructure. Besides that, the government may offer financial assistance for small entrepreneurs to produce products that can encourage local and international tourists to come and visit the Lenggong Valley, in fact, directly can increase economic impacts in tourism development [13]. Moreover, despite the negative significant results between job profession and GDP, it is within this paper interest to emphasize on job profession goods production relationship in terms of resources management as documented by [6].

On the other hand, potential to encourage participation in heritage tourism development as an entrepreneur, further result shows that the male respondents were more responsive especially those who are occupied in agriculture and support fields. This suggests the crucial role in implementing psychological perspective into heritage tourism development plan. In the context of encouragement for community participations results did not highlight a role played by education level. Therefore, complicated approach was deemed unnecessary in developing the promotional framework. Higher level of community attachment could be translated an effective resources investment and management, by which, directly influencing the tourism development support. In cases of income-prices of goods and services relationship, it was learned that increase in prices of goods and services could be accepted provided that the respondents' have substantial in monthly income.

6 Acknowledgement

This project was funded through a research grant from the Ministry of Higher Education, Malaysia under the Long-Term Research Cluster Grant Scheme 2011 [STRC Grant No. 1001/PTS/8660012].

References

1. K. Caton & C.A. Santos, *Heritage Tourism On Route 66: Deconstructing Nostalgia*, Journal of Travel Research, **45**, 4, 371–386 (2007)
2. UNESCO, (2005), "Cultural Tourism", http://portal.unesco.org/culture/en/ev.php-url_id=11408&url_do=do_printpage&url_section=201.html, Retrieved 01 March 2008.
3. M. Saidin, *Bukti Prasejarah Di Malaysia*. Dewan Bahasa dan Pustaka, Kuala Lumpur, Malaysia (2010)
4. M. Jaafar, A.A.A. Rashid, S.A. Maideen & S.Z. Mohamad, *Entrepreneurship In The Tourism Industry: Issues in Developing Countries*. International Journal of Hospitality Management, **30**, 827-835 (2011) http://dx.doi.org/10.1016/j.ijhm.2011.01.003
5. Silberberg, Ted. *"Cultural Tourism and Business Opportunities for Museums and Heritage Sites."* Tourism Management **16**, 5, 361-365 (1995)
6. G. Richards, *Production and consumption of European Cultural Tourism*. Annals of Tourism Research: Tillburg University Press (1996)

7.   C.F. Chen & F.S. Chen, *Experience Quality, Perceived Value, Satisfaction And Behavioral Intentions for Heritage Tourist,* Tourism Management, **31**, 29–35 (2009)

8.   N. Uriely, A.A. Israeli & A. Reichel, *Heritage Proximity and Resident Attitudes Toward Tourism Development,* Annals of Tourism Research, **29**, 3, 859–862 (2002)

9.   P. Dyer, D. Gursoy, B. Sharma & J. Carter, *Structural Modeling Of Resident Perceptions Of Tourism And Associated Development on The Sunshine Coast,* Australia :Tourism Management, **28**, 409–422 (2007)

10.   R. Isaksson & R. Garvare, *Measuring sustainable development using process models,* Managerial Auditing Journal, **18**, 8, 649–656 (2003)

11.   D.W. Ko & W.P. Stewart, *A Structural Equation Model Of Residents' Attitudes For Tourism Development,* Tourism Management, **23**, 521–530 (2002)

12.   A. Mathieson & G. Wall, *Tourism: Economics, Physical and Social impacts.* London: Longman (1982)

13.   K.L. Andereck, K.M. Valentine, R.C. Knopf & C.A. Vogt, *Residents' Perceptions of Community Tourism Impact,* Annals of Tourism Research, **32**, 4, 1056–1076 (2005)

14.   D. Gursoy, C. Jurowski & M. Uysal, *Resident Attitudes: A Structural Modeling Approach,* Annals of Tourism Research, **29**, 1, 79–105 (2002)

15.   D. Gursoy & D.G. Rutherford, *Host Attitudes Toward Tourism: An Improved Structural Model*, Annals of Tourism ResearchI, **31**, 3, 495–516 (2004

24

Local Sabahans' Satisfaction with Level of Access to Mount Kinabalu

Christy Bidder[1], Reni Cacillia Polus[2]

[1]Faculty of Hotel and Tourism Management, Universiti Teknologi MARA, 88997 Sabah, Malaysia

[2]Faculty of Hotel and Tourism Management, Universiti Teknologi MARA, 94300 Sarawak, Malaysia

Abstract. This study analyzes the local Sabahans' satisfaction with the level of access to Mount Kinabalu in Sabah, Malaysian Borneo. Specifically, it examines the number of complaints by local Sabahans regarding access and their perception of changes in accessibility to the mountain. Interviews with Sabah Parks and Sutera Sanctuary Lodges were conducted and questionnaires were distributed to local residents to collect data. The results show that there were intense complaints regarding the climbing cost and extensive waiting time to secure a confirmed booking at the outset of price increases. However, the researchers could not locate any recently published complaints. Respondents who have previously climbed Mount Kinabalu perceive the mountain to be less accessible for local Sabahans now due to a less affordable cost and a longer waiting time. Those who have not climbed Mount Kinabalu also think the climbing cost has become less affordable for local Sabahans, but they do not perceive that to be causing the mountain less accessible for local Sabahans.

1 Introduction

In some places, formerly public places (shorelines or forests) may become privatized at the expense of perceived or real access of the local residents. They may be displaced by visitors or priced out of regular use [1]. For instance, a quarter of Boracay Island in the Philippines has been sold to outside corporations resulting in a water supply crisis and limited infrastructure benefits for residents [2]. In Bali Indonesia, the major agricultural land and water supplies have been redirected for the use of large hotels and golf courses [2].

In Pangandaran Indonesia, a village beach land that was conventionally utilized for grazing, repairing boats and nets and holding festivals was bought by entrepreneurs for a five-star hotel [2]. Change in access by local residents is a specific subset of tourism impact on the host community. It may be closely related to the local residents' overall satisfaction with tourism development [1]. This particular investigation looks at local Sabahans' satisfaction with the level of access to Mount Kinabalu. This objective is based on one of the components, or indicators, of access suggested by WTO [1].

2 Literature Review

In many areas of the world, parks are typically owned and managed by the public sector, who is usually short on tourism competencies and professional expertise (e.g. in tourism economics, marketing, tourism management, and service quality). Moreover, the public sector is usually financially constrained and lacks the necessary resources to conserve nature and provide visitor facilities to attend to the increasing public demand [3-4]. Such shortages pave the way for the introduction of privatization in management of tourism resources. Often the private sector has much higher levels of tourism market expertise and resources (capital and manpower) than does the public sector. Thus, the former is much more capable of attracting visitors, servicing their needs and providing all of the tourism services [3].

The private sector often acts as a provider of tourism services including accommodation, restaurants, tour operations, waste collection, site maintenance and information provision, in the form of concessionaires [5]. In particular, the private sector is able to offer high standard tourism services to meet the demand and expectation of tourists [5]. Undoubtedly, the provision of a high quality tourism experience comes with higher costs. The profit earned from this experience is the incentive to achieve outstanding service and uphold the status of the destination. Additionally, with the private sector taking care of tourism facilities and services, the public sector can use its available human and financial resources to provide public services (i.e. nature conservation and welfare of local communities) [5].

However, the private sector is driven by profit. Thus, if it is not monitored, private operators with selfish personal agendas can cause overuse of tourism resources, thereby degrading the environment [3]. It is upsetting that in tourism public-private partnerships, the private sector seems to have acquired total domination [4]. Because of this, the governments are becoming weaker in their decision-making power, making way for the private sector to commandeer public agendas. The monopoly of a private tourism operator can often cause devastating consequences for local people and the environment [4].

In 1998, Sabah Parks (SP hereafter) privatized the accommodation and catering facilities in Kinabalu Park to Sutera Sanctuary Lodges (SSL hereafter). The rationale behind this privatization is to increase the number of visitors and improve tourism facilities and services in the park to meet visitor expectations. The program was also introduced to provide job opportunities for the local communities in a tourism-related business.

Furthermore, it was hoped that with the privatization, the administrative, manpower and financial responsibilities of SP would be lessened, thereby allowing it to focus on conservation efforts [7-8]. In 2007, SSL increased the cost of accommodations on Mount Kinabalu and other properties in Kinabalu Park. The cost of a dorm bed jumped from RM30 to RM188 (meals included). That was an increase of about 500%. In 2009, the cost of the package was further increased to RM330 per person [7, 8]. Prior to privatization, climbers had an option to bring their own food, thereby saving some cost [7].

It is imperative that those responsible for the planning of tourism work toward optimizing the welfare of local residents while keeping the costs of tourism development to a minimum [9]. Critical to the success and sustainability of the tourism industry is the support of destination communities for tourism [9-10], or what is termed as a 'happy host' [11]. Local communities will usually withdraw their support for tourism if they perceive the costs of tourism to prevail over the benefits, thereby jeopardizing the future success and development of the industry [12].

For-profit tourism undertakings may be hindered or terminated by excessive negative resident reaction toward tourism development [13]. Therefore, tourism planners must take into account the views of the local residents if the industry is to be sustainable in the long run [13].

3 Methods

To examine local Sabahans' satisfaction with the level of access to Mount Kinabalu, two indicators were analyzed: 1) number of complaints by local Sabahans regarding access; and 2) perception of change in accessibility. A survey was conducted to assess local Sabahans' perception of change in accessibility. Using convenient sampling method, self-administered questionnaires were distributed in local villages, educational institutions and shopping malls. Additionally, for the first indicator, secondary data sources (e.g. print and online articles) were used and interviews with both SP and SSL were conducted.

4 Results and Discussion

4.1 Profile of Respondents

Of the 300 questionnaires distributed, 263 questionnaires were returned. 14 incomplete questionnaires were excluded. Table 1 shows there were an almost equal number of male (49.2%) and female (50.4%) respondents. Almost half of the respondents (49.2%) were aged between 20 and 30 years. All of the respondents had completed some level of education: high school or equivalent (28.6%), some college (30.2%) and a Bachelor's Degree (23.8%). The majority of them (81%) were native Sabahans, Kadazandusun. Almost all of the respondents (92.3%) had a source of income with almost half of them (47.8%) earning less than RM2000 per month and 34.4% are earning between RM2001 and RM5000 per month. Only 38.6% of the respondents had previously climbed Mount Kinabalu.

Table 1. Profile of Respondents (n = 249).

	Items	%	Items		%
Gender	Male	49.2	Source of income	Yes	92.3
	Female	50.4		No	7.3
Age	< 20 years	5.6	Average monthly income	< RM1000	26.3
	20 – 30 years	49.2		RM1001 – RM2000	21.5
	31 - 40 years	27.4		RM2001 – RM3500	19.0
	41 - 50 years	12.5		RM3501 – RM5000	15.4
	> 51 years	5.2		RM5001 – RM7500	5.3
Highest level of education	High school or equivalent	28.6		RM7501 – RM10000	2.4
	Vocational or technical school	0.8		> RM10000	2.8
	Some college	30.2	Have you climbed Mount Kinabalu?	Yes	38.6
	Bachelor's Degree	23.8		No	61.4
	Master's Degree	13.7			
	Doctoral Degree	2.8			
Ethnicity	Malay	12.9			
	Chinese	5.6			
	Indian	0.4			
	Native Sabahans	81.0			

4.2 Number of Complaints Regarding Access

Following the increases in accommodation rates, complaints were lodged by various parties, including prospective climbers, repeat climbers as well as local and foreign tour operators. Many of them claimed that the price was drastic and unjustifiable. They criticized that the price increases had not translated into better maintenance of facilities: hot water still interrupted; electricity and plumbing leaks still happening. Some expressed their concerns that Mount Kinabalu might become out of reach for many Malaysians due to the astronomical accommodation rates.

They also questioned the inclusion of meals in the accommodation rates in the name of conservation. In their judgment, the packed lunch using polystyrene boxes and plastic bags were actually producing more rubbish on Mount Kinabalu [7-8]. Another major complaint centered upon the extensive waiting time to wrangle a spot to climb Mount Kinabalu. It would take several months in advance to acquire a confirmed booking. A Facebook petition called 'Mount Kinabalu – belongs to NO ONE else' was established and over 1000 people signed it [7-8]. However, the researchers failed to locate the petition as it has most probably been removed.

The researchers made an attempt to locate any recent complaints published online or in print, but none were discovered. A recent interview with SP and SSL disclosed that they have not received any formal complaints lately. The SSL representatives explained that the common complaint they do receive recently focuses on the shortage of hot water supply and electricity on Mount Kinabalu, which is rather beyond their control since it is not uncommon that hot water supply and electricity are scarce in high altitude places.

Commenting on the complaint regarding Mount Kinabalu being too expensive for local Sabahans to climb, the SP representatives expounded that the introduction of Sabahan rate (RM80 for accommodation and meals, excluding permit, insurance, porter and guide fee; offered on a 25-Sabahan-daily basis) has helped resolve the issue to a significant extent, although on rare occasions they do encounter local Sabahans who insist on paying the Sabahan rate even when the quota has already been reached.

The SSL representatives commented that most of the complaints were not made by Sabahans, and that they were lodged by those who were not well informed about the justification behind the increased accommodation rates. As indicated in Figure 1, over half of the respondents (51.04%) who have previously climbed Mount Kinabalu paid a total of less than RM200, and more than a quarter (36.46%) paid between RM201 and RM400.

The majority of them (75%) think the total cost was reasonable. When asked how much the climbing cost should be for Sabahans, 72.6% of all the respondents think it should be less than RM200, which is precisely what the Sabahan rate is offering. The Sabahan rate is limited to only 25 Sabahans daily. When this quota is reached, the next interested Sabahan climbers will have to pay the general Malaysian packages, cheapest of which is RM329.00 [14].

Commenting on the extensive waiting time to get a confirmed booking, the SP and SSL representatives justified that Mount Kinabalu has become a globally renowned tourist attraction; therefore it is expected that the demand to climb the mountain is increasing. Nevertheless, in the name of preservation and conservation, the limit on the daily number of climbers (192 climbers at a time) has to be maintained, hence the long waiting time. When queried how far in advance one is advised to make a reservation, the SP representatives explained that there really is no pre-determined time as to how far in advance one should make a booking, but it is highly recommended to book as far in advance as possible.

As shown in Figure 1, the waiting time to obtain a confirmed booking does not seem overly lengthy. Over half (59.38%) of respondents who have climbed Mount Kinabalu reported that it took them less 2 months to get a confirmed booking. In our viewpoint, such length of waiting time is not uncommon in eminent tourist destinations that do impose a limit on the daily number of visitors. For instance, prospective climbers of Mount Everest are advised to pick the date for their climb at least six months beforehand [15]. To trek the Inca Trail in Peru, one is recommended to make a booking as far in advance as possible as one knows the dates of his/her international flight [16].

4.3 Perception of Change in Accessibility

Accessibility is measured by two factors, namely climbing cost and waiting time to acquire a confirmed booking. As shown in Figure 2, nearly half of the respondents (43.75%) who have previously climbed Mount Kinabalu perceive the mountain to be less accessible for local Sabahans now because the present climbing cost is less affordable. Additionally, a rather high number of those respondents (32.29%) perceive Mount Kinabalu to be less accessible for local Sabahans now because it takes a longer time to get a confirmed booking.

For respondents who have not climbed Mount Kinabalu, nearly half of them (42.69%) do not know if Mount Kinabalu is now more or less accessible for local Sabahans in terms of climbing cost and waiting time. Nevertheless, about a quarter of those respondents (23.03%) feel that Mount Kinabalu is now more accessible because it now takes a shorter time to get a confirmed booking. Although more than a quarter of them (30.72%) perceive the climbing cost to be less affordable now, it does not seem to make them feel that Mount Kinabalu is less accessible for local Sabahans due to cost.

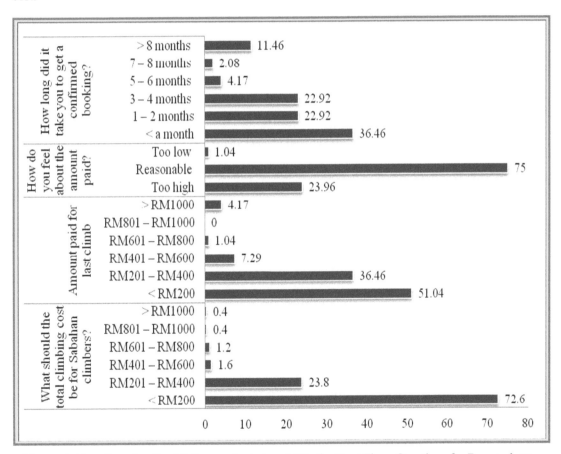

Figure 1. First Question for All Respondents (n = 249); the Next Three Questions for Respondents who have Previously Climbed Mount Kinabalu (n = 96)

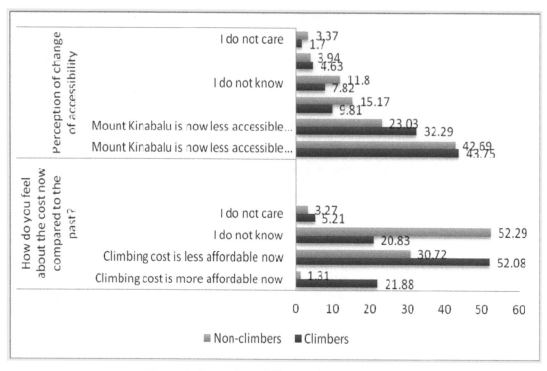

Figure 2. Perception of Changes in Accessibility

5 Conclusion

Local Sabahans' satisfaction with the level of access to Mount Kinabalu may be pictured as a calm lake that is extremely susceptible to the forming of ripples by the cast of a stone into it. Following closely the rise in accommodation rates in Kinabalu Park, the number of complaints lodged was intense. However, the 'storm' subsided with introduction of the more affordable Sabahan rate and improvement of visitor facilities and services on Mount Kinabalu. Complaint regarding access (climbing cost and waiting time to get a confirmed booking) seems to be minimal these days. But it does not necessarily mean all is fine and peaceful. While complaint may act as a warning system for emerging discontent, it neither monitors all opinions nor monitors any opinions continuously. Thus, it is crucial to assess the local reaction toward the satisfaction with level of access to Mount Kinabalu. Overall, local Sabahans perceive the access to Mount Kinabalu has changed. Those who have previously climbed Mount Kinabalu think the mountain is less accessible for local Sabahans now because the climbing cost is less affordable and it takes a much longer time to secure a confirmed booking. Those who have not climbed Mount Kinabalu share the opinion that the climbing cost has become less affordable, but they do not necessarily think of that as contributing to the less accessibility of Mount Kinabalu for local Sabahans. If care is not exercised to ensure a satisfactory level of access to Mount Kinabalu for local Sabahans or to ensure local Sabahans have a continued fair and equal access to Mount Kinabalu, a storm might just strike again.

6 Acknowledgements

We would like to express our heartfelt gratitude to Mr. Rodzan Pengiran Dahlan and Mr. Anthony Tinggi from Sabah Parks, and Mr. Henry Balenting and Mr. Adrian Alaska from Sutera Sanctuary Lodges for their valuable time and cooperation in providing the information required for the writing of this paper.

References

1. World Tourism Organization, *Indicators of sustainable development for tourism destinations: a guidebook* (World Tourism Organization, Madrid (2004)
2. http://www.odi.org/sites/odi.org.uk/files/odi-assets/publications-opinion-files/2861.pdf
3. http://www.ahs.uwaterloo.ca/rec/pdf/inttrends.pdf
4. www.twnside.org.sg/title/tourism.doc
5. http://hss.ulb.uni-bonn.de/2008/1288/1288.pdf
6. H.C. Goh, M.M. Yusoff, Int. J. Trade. Eco. Financ. **1**,2, 179-183 (2010)
7. http://www.newsabahtimes.com.my/nstweb/fullstory/25505
8. http://www.thestar.com.my/story.aspx/?file=%2f2009%2f1%2f31%2flifetravel%2f3107154&sec=lifetravel
9. R. Sharpley, Tourism Manage. **42**, 37-49 (2014)
10. C. Jurowski, D. Gursoy, Ann. Tour. Res. **31**,2, 296-312 (2004)
11. T. Snaith, A. Haley, Tourism Manage. **20**,5, 595-603 (1999)
12. R. Lawson, J. Williams, T. Young, J. Cossens, Tourism Manage. **19**,3, 247-256 (1998)
13. J. Williams, R. Lawson, Ann. Tour. Res. **28**,2, 269-290 (2001)
14. http://www.mysabah.com/download/mt-kinabalu-laban-rata-room-rates.pdf
15. www.ratestogo.com/blog/climbing-mount-everest/
16. http://www.perutreks.com/inca_trail_04d_faq.html

25

Costume Development Model for Tourism Promotion in Mae Hong Son Province, Thailand

A. Sarobol[1]

[1]Faculty of Humanities, Chiang Mai University, 50200 Chiang Mai, Thailand

Abstract. This research aims to study Pha Bong community's dressing style and to develop a new ethnic costume that shows their identity to promote tourism in the province. Pha Bong Community is a community in Maehongson Province where two ethnic groups, people of Tai Yai (Shan) and Sakor Karen, co-exist. The data collection methods include focus group and in-depth interview with target population, small group discussion and review of literature on costume development. The obtained data were then submitted to content analysis. First, it was found that they both have their own identity, resources, network marketing and inherited wisdom from their ancestors. Each group runs their business separately. Secondly, the research resulted in the creation of a new costume for the Pha Bong community created by members of two ethnic groups. This costume combines Karen symbol with Tai Yai (Shan) clothing style. The motif and pattern of the fabric identify community members' lifestyle, belief and value. It is recommended that development should be planned upon available resource and the need of the community. In addition, the community leader should encourage members to take parts in management and to cooperate for a sustainable development.

1 Introduction

Mae Hong Son is a province located in the northern part of Thailand. Being surrounded by mountains and forests and a home for multi cultures, the province is suitable for cultural tourism. Ban Pa Pu, located in Tambon Pha Bong, Muang district, Mae Hong Son Province, is a culturally blended community where Tai Yai(Shan) and Karen Sakor coexist. These two ethnic groups, living harmoniously and generously, have their own ethnic identity. Members of Karen Sakor join together when weaving. Tai Yai(Shan) team up for cooking and running homestay.

Each ethnic group has their unique traditional costume. In addition, Tambon Pha Bong has its own ethnic food and natural hot springs. This makes the community an ideal place for tourism. Institute of Tourism Authority of Thailand, Chiang Mai Provincial Health Office and the Faculty of Humanities, Chiang Mai University, have selected Pha Bong community to be a prototype community for Healthy-Based Tourism. Thus, the community members or the two ethnic groups were asked to look for a costume that represents their ethnic identity and that can be a symbol of Pha Bong community. This costume development would support tourism activities in Mae Hon Sorn province.

This research was conducted by using participatory process study (Atchara sarobol, 2006). Two ethnic groups exchanged their knowledge, cooperated and received shared benefits. They brainstormed together, collected information on resources, culture and community costumes via SWOT analysis which included in-depth interviews, focus group and participatory workshops led by people who had knowledge and experience from two ethnic groups. The objectives of the study were to study the identity of costumes in Pha Bong community and to develop a costume for Pha Bong community to promote tourism.

2 Methodology

This qualitative research study collected data from targeted samples. The samples consisted of four experts in local costume and 10 community members, drawn from two ethnic groups, who attended participatory workshops. The procedures were as follows:

1. Meetings with the villagers to do SWOT Analysis on the topics related to ethnicity, cultures, intellectual resources in their community.

2. Focus groups and participatory observation with the people who had knowledge and members of the two ethnic groups to get the villagers' costumes information and find the identity of villagers' costumes and develop their costumes symbol together.

3. Collecting historical information on villagers' costumes by in-depth interviews to get the meanings, the values, beliefs of patterned fabric in the community.

4. Participatory workshops on the topics related to the style of costume, yarn dyed woven from natural materials and creating symbolic garments with embroidery.

5. Review of the related literature.

3 Data Analysis and Discussion

It was found that the strengths of the Pha Bong Community were group management i.e., Karen Sakor's weaving group and Tai Yai (Shan)'s homestay group, their own identity (the Shan and Karen ethnic group, having raw materials, network, succession as well as network marketing. The weakness was that the lack of a database for tourism management operated by the community. The overall tourism management was split into parts. An opportunity for community to develop was collaboration between the two ethnic groups in designing costume. The challenge was identified as separate management by each ethnic group.

3.1 The Process to Find Identities and Clothing Styles of Pha Bong Community

The findings from the group discussion between members of the two ethnic groups and the researchers showed that the new dress pattern should blend the identity of each ethnic group together while keeping the unique symbol of each group. A Tai Yai(Shan) expert mentioned that Tai Yai(Shan) shirt looked like Lanna shirt. It had front crossing three-part sleeves with no arms. The arm or sleeve was attached to the shirt without stitching. The collar runs along the neckline and one edge goes down to touch the front flap. The sarong is a skirt with front fascia. As for Karens, their outstanding symbol is the unique pattern whose meanings were influenced by beliefs of their ancestors.

Karen experts said that the White Karen (Sakor group) had an ancient belief that the pattern on Karen's clothes came from the pattern of a big snake skin.   Four popular patterns for weaving and embroidery were Yo-ho-gue, Gue-pe-pe-lo, Chui-ko-law, and Tee-kha. Only one pattern "Gue-pe-pe-lo" was selected because it was associated with good fortune. This pattern displays round flowers. The perfect pattern has eight flowers with the connecting lines between them and embroidered at the cuffs in combination with other elements. The fabric used was the hand-woven cloth with the loom and dyed yarn from natural tree bark found in the wild in season.

Figure 1. The Tai Yai(Shan) women dress   **Figure 2.** The "Gue-pe-pe-lo" pattern

3.2 Dressing Style of Pha Bong Community

Pha Bong community costume style reflects Tai Yai (Shan) characteristics. The shirt was front crossed, 3-part sleeves. The original Tai Yai(Shan) shirt did not have arms and used the strap hand-weaving cloth of the Karen with embroidery around the neck and flap with the original Karen's pattern "Gue-pe-pe-lo". Long sarong was seam sewing with waistband, front flap like that of the Tai Yai(Shan). At the bottom of sarong was made of the same design of "Nam Lai" like Karen's sarong. The sarong was made from the strap hand-woven cloth, dyed with natural raw materials available in the community.

After the group discussion, the women's group members agreed to join the workshop on natural dyes and workshop on symbolic garments' embroidering. The knowledge was transferred from the experts in each ethnic group. The Karen experts trained Tai Yai participants on how to dye yarn. The woven fabric by the Karen were sewn by Tai Yai group members into garments such as cotton shirt and sarong. The women from both ethnic groups exchanged their knowledge on garments' embroidery.

3.3 Workshop on Natural Dyeing fabric embroidery.

Figure 3. Demonstration of natural dyeing steps

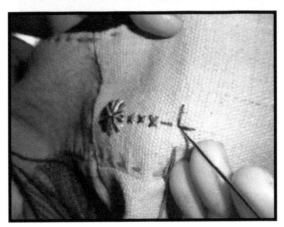

Figure 4. Workshop on fabric embroidery

Figure 5. The clothing style of the Pha Bong Community, combining Shan and Karen identity

4 Discussion

At Pha Bong Community, Mae Hong Son province, the community members had developed the costume design with mixed symbols of the two ethnic groups. This was to combine clothing style of the Tai Yai(Shan)'s and the "Gue-pe-pe-lo" pattern of Karen embroidery along the shirt and "Lai Nam Lai" pattern at the bottom of the sarong to show the identity of the community. Both traditional dress of ethnic Tai Yai(Shan) and original pattern of ethnic Karen truly reflect the wisdom of dressing that has been handed down from their ancestors, from generation to generation. The costume reflects a hidden belief that has a lot of value to the mind of the community's members who took part in developing the prototype costume, by using available materials in the community and exchanging local wisdom. This is counted as creating a new identity for the community to promote tourism. This collaboration is consistent with the concept that the members must participate in thinking, analyzing, and operating as well as enjoying the benefits together. It also supports the identity concept of the members in using the symbol of each ethnic group to determine the identity of the garment. Even though it is a reproduction under a different context (with some modification), the symbol remains the same. The product reflects self-reliance as it is produced by using raw materials available in the community and through exchanging local wisdom. This is in accordance with the concept of community tourism by Sin Sarobol (2003), "the CBT is tourism by residents who own resources, make us of the available resources as a cost factor or travel arrangements appropriately accordingly. The resource may include nature, cultural traditions, lifestyle, production methods as well as selling products with its own identity such as handicrafts and textile.

5 Recommendation

The development of the clothing patterns should be in the community with the available raw materials, skills related to textile production, community-based tourism management, network, and with the need to wear a costume for everyday life purpose or for special occasions. This can be further developed as a souvenir reflecting a unique sense of community which promotes local tourism.

References

1. B. Ornkhan and S. Srichamnong, Participatory Procedure, Chiang Mai: B.S. Printing [Thai] (2001)
2. Y. Santasombat, Lak Chang: A Recreation of Tai Identity in Taikong, Bangkok: Amarin Printing and Publishing Limited, [Thai] (2000)
3. S. Salobol, *Tourism by Community*, Chiang Mai: Wanida Press, [Thai] (2003)
4. Office of the National Research Board,Guidelines for the People to Participate in Rural Development. Bangkok. Kurusapha Printing, [Thai] (1995)
5. A. Fuengfoosakul, Identity, Bangkok: Tiger Printing, [Thai] (2003)
6. A. Sarobol, Participation of Doi Tao Community in Developing the Wisdom on Textile, Doctoral dissertation, Academic Disciplines on Rural Planning and Development Graduate School, Mae Jo University, [Thai] (2006)
7. T. O'riordan, Globalism, Localism and Identity, London: Earthscan Publications Ltd,(2001)
8. United Nation Development Programe, UNDP guidebook on Participation, The concept of Participation in Development, (online) http://www.undp.org/essopp/paguide1.html.
9. http://www.taiyai.org/index.php?name=suites&file=readsuites&id=1

26

Factors Affecting Tourist Satisfaction: An Empirical Study in the Northern Part of Thailand

Suthathip Suanmali[1]

[1]School of Management Technology, Sirindhorn International Institute of Technology, Thammasat University, Pathumthani 12000, Thailand

Abstract. In 2015, the ASEAN Economics Community (AEC) will be fully implemented, and, to pave the way for Thailand to be the tourism hub of Southeast Asia, it is important to study factors affecting tourist satisfaction. The emphasis of this study is on a northern province in Thailand, Chiang Mai, where there are many natural and cultural attractions. The significant factors are identified using statistical techniques. The data is obtained from a satisfaction survey as it was developed and distributed randomly to foreign tourists who visit Chiang Mai. The quantitative data is then analyzed using factor analysis and multiple regression analysis to identify significant factors. The result indicates that the most significant factor affecting the overall satisfaction is the cost of staying, and other significant factors are hospitality, attractions and accessibility, and infrastructure. In addition, policy recommendations are presented in the paper.

1 Introduction

Thailand is a destination with many iconic tourist attractions, such as mountains, islands, culture and traditions, architectures, the way of life, and foods. The tourism industry plays a vital role as an industry of Thailand. It is extremely essential to Thailand's economy. According to the statistical data from the Ministry of Tourism and Sports shows that the revenue received from the tourism industry in 2012 was 983,928.36 million Baht, increased by 26.76% from 2011. The number of international tourist arrivals in Thailand in 2012 was 22,353,903 people. The value of the tourism industry has increased by 16.24% from 2011. The average expenditure is 4,392.81 Baht person per day, with revenue of 983,928.36 million Baht. The average growth rate for the years 1987-2012 has increased by 7.72%.

In 2015, the ASEAN Economic Community will be implemented. This will strongly affect Thailand's tourism industry. Dr. Suthawan Chirapanda, Principle of School of Business, University of the Thai Chamber of Commerce has forecasted the number of tourists visiting Thailand at around twenty million people and forecasted that Thailand will rank as the second country in Asia that tourists choose to visit. This is also due to the fact that Thai people radiate warmth like no other.

The international community has long regarded Thais as people whom are friendly, welcoming, and good in services. In terms of liberal arts, Thailand is also considered as a forerunner in attractiveness because of the exoticness in designs and patterns. There are plenty of tourist attractions, such as Chiang Mai, Phuket, Krabi, Pattaya, etc. The strength of Thailand is further augmented due to its geographical location, since it is the center of ASEAN. Provinces that contribute highly to the tourism industry's income for Thailand are Phuket, Bangkok, Krabi, Chonburi, and Chiang Mai.

According to the 2013 Travelers' Choice Destinations award, Chiang Mai (Thailand) is ranked in 24th place in the World and in 5th place in Asia. Chiang Mai is a cultural and natural wonderland with ethnic diversity, a multitude of attractions, and the welcoming hospitality of Thailand. Chiang Mai is the largest and most culturally significant city in northern Thailand and is one of the oldest cities in Thailand and has a small-town, old-world attitude completely different from the hustle and bustle of Bangkok. Chiang Mai is a place where both backpackers and luxury tourists can enjoy the ultimate Thailand holiday.

To conclude, the AEC will be implemented shortly and Thailand is aimed to be the hub of tourism. It is important to study factors affecting tourist satisfaction. The emphasis of this study is on Chiang Mai, on nature and entertainment attractions. A satisfaction survey is developed and distributed randomly to tourists who visit Chiang Mai.

2 Literature Review

Leading researchers have recognized the important of tourism products: "Misunderstanding of the tourism product is often a constraint in a smoothly functioning tourism system". Tourism product development includes information services, transportations, accommodations, and attraction [1].

The tourism product is described as a series of determinants from variable destinations, which produce an output for tourists. The model consists of a hierarchy of five elements: the physical plant, service, hospitality, freedom of choice, and involvement. As described in this research, the physical plant is the core of the tourism product, which includes the natural resources, fixed properties (such as accommodations), accessibility, acceptable environmental quality, good weather, and appropriate numbers of other tourists [2]. The input of services makes the physical plant useful for tourists, and refers to the performance of specific tasks designed to meet the needs and wants of tourists. Hospitality is the attitude and style in which those specific tasks are performed, for example, a warm and friendly smile by local residents welcoming new arriving tourists. The latter two elements of the model directly involve the tourist as part of the product, which seems logical if tourism is to be considered as an experience. Freedom of choice means that the tourist is entitled to have choices and opinions in order for the experience to be satisfactory. The encapsulating shell of the tourism product is involvement. Successful participation in the tourism product hinges on an acceptable physical plant, good service, hospitality, and freedom of choice. Discomfort with an element will hinder tourist involvement with the tourism product, consequently limiting the quality of the tourism experience. A positive experience with all five elements ensures quality and a satisfying tourism product.

In addition, the research on marketing in travel and tourism. There are five sectors in the in the overall product, which are *Hospitality sector, Attractions and events sector, Transportation sector, Travel organizers' and intermediaries' sector,* and *Destination organization sector* [3]. Hospitality is an expression of welcome by local residents to tourists arriving in their community (i.e. hotels, guest houses, apartments, and condominiums). The attraction and event sector can be defined as theme parks, museums and galleries, national parks, heritage sites and centers, and festival and events. The transportation sector includes airlines, shipping lines, railways, bus operators, and car rental operators. Travel organizers and intermediaries sector contains travel e-mediaries, tour operators, tour wholesalers, retail travel agents, and conference organizers. Destination organization sector consists of National tourist offices (NTOs), Destination marketing organizations (DMOs), regional tourist offices, and tourist associations.

Furthermore, the formulation of the components of tourism products is *Attractions, Accessibility, Amenities, and Networking*. An attraction is a place where attract tourists such as natural, cultural or man-made (festivals or performing arts). Accessibility is the ease of obtaining or achieving organizational goals such as tourism with travel agents. Amenities are facilities for tourists to obtain pleasure. In this case, amenities can be accommodation, cleanliness, and hospitality. Networking is the cooperation by local, national, or international organizations to produce tourism products [4-5].

Customer satisfaction is essential to any business preposition and the same can be said for tourism products. The essence for the success of Chiang Mai tourism industry is definitely tourist satisfaction.

Tourist satisfaction is important for successful destination marketing because it influences the choice of destination, the consumption of products and services, and the decision to return. Satisfaction is basically the comparison of the customer's expectation before and after consumption. Tourist satisfaction is the difference between tourist's expectations and the actual perceived value [6]. It is important to identify and measure consumer satisfaction with each attribute of the destination because satisfaction or dissatisfaction with one of the attributes leads to satisfaction or dissatisfaction with the overall destination [7-8]. To conclude, satisfied tourists not only will revisit the place, but also will recommend it to others. Besides, increasing the level of satisfaction will reduce the number of tourists' complaints. On the other hand, tourist satisfaction will not be achieved unless the tourists feel that the quality received is greater than the money paid. So, the measurement of overall satisfaction with service quality is an important point of our study. Based on our review on literatures and the characteristics of Chiang Mai, there are six attributes related to this study. The summary of the attributes and their definitions are summarized in Table 1. In addition, the comparison of attributes used in this study and other studies is shown in Table 2.

Table 1. Summary of Chiang Mai Tourism Product

Indicator	Item	Definition
Hospitality	Tangible Intangible	The tangible and intangible elements affect tourists' satisfaction: for example, variety of food or warm and welcoming atmosphere.
Attraction	Cultural Natural Recreation and Activities	An attraction refers to a place that appeals to tourists that visit Chiang Mai. An attraction can be attractive in many ways. For example, photographers are able to take photographs of panoramic scenery in Chiang Mai.
Accessibility	Transportation Basic Medical - Treatments/Hospital Authorities	Accessibility is defined by the ability to provide appropriate visitor access into a destination, and travel throughout the destination.
Infrastructure	Water supply Electricity Communication Public lavatory Safety facilities	Infrastructure is the basic physical needs of the city, for example, transportation, communication, sewage, water, and electricity. Infrastructure projects may be funded publicly or privately.
Environment	Climate condition Air quality Noise Natural resources Cleanliness Personal safety and security	Environment can be defined as the surroundings, which includes climate conditions, and environmental conditions such as air quality, cleanliness, and feelings towards the destination.
Cost	Cost of Accommodation Cost of Transportation within Chiang Mai Cost of Food and Beverages Other Expenses	The expenses that will be taken into account by tourists while staying in Chiang Mai.

3 Methodology

3.1 Method of Approach and Data Collection

Two research methods are employed in this study. One is documentary research from literature surveys, journals, articles, and previous research works. These data are collected from research published in credible international journals.

Table 2. Comparison of Main Sectors

Main Sector	The Impact of Service Quality on Tourist Satisfaction in Jerash	The Tourism Product	Factors Affecting Tourists Satisfaction: A Case Study in Chiang Mai
Hospitality		✓	✓
Attraction and Event	✓	✓	✓
Accessibility	✓		✓
Infrastructure	✓	✓	✓
Environment		✓	✓
Cost of Staying			✓

Second is survey research. Surveys are done by means of questionnaire surveys for only foreign tourists who visit Chiang Mai during the time of research. The survey is conducted in such a way that we hand out questionnaires to tourists for them to complete. This takes place at different places of attractions such as temples, heritage sites, and natural attractions. Simultaneously, interviews are administered to business owners in the tourism industries, and travel agencies. Topics addressed are the effect of AEC on Chiang Mai's tourist sector, the interviewee's point of view on the future of Chiang Mai, and the interviewee's point of view on determinants influencing the tourism industry of Chiang Mai overall.

3.1.1 Population and Sample

The population is foreign tourists that visited Chiang Mai in the year 2013, and the sample is foreign tourists who visit Chiang Mai that are selected randomly. Specific groups of samples are identified from the current group of tourists. The Yamane sampling technique is utilized.

3.1.2 Materials

Instruments used to collect and record data for this study are open-ended interview questions and survey questionnaires (closed questionnaires, 5-point Likert scale, and open-ended questions for instance suggestions and recommendations). Survey questionnaires attempt to address the overall satisfaction of tourism is Chiang Mai, for example, hospitality - variety of food and beverage in Chiang Mai, attraction - varieties of natural such as national parks and trekking, accessibility - availability of information and document about Chiang Mai (map and traffic sign), Infrastructure - local transportation service, Environment - overall cleanliness of Chiang Mai, Cost of Staying -overall cost of your stay in Chiang Mai.

3.1.3 Procedure

Data related to the overall satisfaction of tourists who visit Chiang Mai in 2013 is obtained from self-administered questionnaires. Each category is measured by using a 5-point Likert scale ranging from one to five. 1 stands for very dissatisfied, 2 stands for dissatisfied, 3 stands for neutral, 4 stands for satisfied, and 5 stands for very satisfied. The collected data were analyzed using Statistical Package for Social Science (SPSS) version 6.0. Factor analysis was utilized to determine the underlying structure of the original 26 determinants toward tourist satisfaction. Lastly, multiple regression analysis was employed to investigate determinants, which affect the level of satisfaction of tourists in Chiang Mai. Multiple regressions is a statistical tool that enable us to determine how multiple independent variables are related to a dependent variable. In this research, 26 determinants are developed to identify the level of satisfaction of each determinant whereas overall satisfaction is referred to as dependent variable. Factor analysis is employed to reduce the dimensions of independent variables [9]. Significant factors affecting tourist satisfactions in Chiang Mai are identified using multiple regression analysis.

4 Results

4.1 Descriptive Statistics

The total number of respondents is 445. However 309 of them are usable (69.44%). Among the 309 respondents, there are 156 male and 153 female. In male respondents, there are 39 (25%) who have visited Chiang Mai before. On the other hand, 117 (75%) males have visited Chiang Mai for the first time. Out of 153 females, 32 (20.9%) of them have visited Chiang Mai before, and the remaining 121 females have visited Chiang Mai for the first time. Therefore 71 tourists are repeat visitors. The majority of tourists, more than half of our samples, are from Europe.

4.2 Factor Analysis and Multiple Regression

The result of factor analysis is summarized in Table 3. Determinants (26) can be grouped into five factors: *Hospitality, Attraction and Accessibility, Cost of Staying, Environmental Factor, and Infrastructure.*

Table 3. Result of Factor Analysis

Factor	Mean	Std. Deviation	Factor Loading	Variance Explained (%)
FACTOR 1: Hospitality (X_1)				15.912
Appealing accommodation facilities	4.20	0.738	0.458	
Variety of food and beverage	4.31	0.740	0.784	
Quality of food and beverage	4.27	0.697	0.748	
Willingness of staff to help tourists	4.34	0.765	0.788	
Warm and welcoming of local people	4.44	0.703	0.716	
FACTOR 2: Attraction & Accessibility (X_2)				14.262
Variety of cultural attractions	4.36	0.731	0.587	

Variety of natural attractions	4.33	0.781	0.585	
Local products	4.10	0.848	0.517	
Availability of information and documents	3.96	0.908	0.654	
Convenience to travel	4.14	0.820	0.572	
Accessibility to basic medical treatment	3.99	0.866	0.784	
Accessibility to local authorities	3.84	0.891	0.664	
FACTOR 3: Cost of Staying (X_3)				13.493
Price of accommodation	4.18	0.778	0.727	
Price of food and beverages	4.36	0.733	0.775	
Price of local transportation	4.03	0.883	0.487	
Price of products	4.17	0.724	0.514	
Overall cost of your stay in Chiang Mai	4.24	0.706	0.644	
FACTOR 4: Environmental Factor (X_4)				12.060
Quality of water supply	3.72	0.943	0.441	
Availability of clean public toilets	3.36	1.021	0.567	
Climate conditions	4.22	0.746	0.517	
Air quality	3.70	1.040	0.808	
Level of noise	3.60	0.954	0.774	
Personal safety and security	4.21	0.750	0.609	
Overall cleanliness	3.86	0.911	0.770	
FACTOR 5: Infrastructure (X_5)				7.007
Local transportation services	3.96	0.893	0.591	
Availability of high speed internet and Wi-Fi	3.90	0.910	0.743	
Total Variance Explained				62.734

There are many assumptions for multiple regression analysis. However, some of the more frequently violated assumptions are reviewed here briefly. First, regression works best when there is a lack of multicollinearity, which is shown by the variance inflation factor (VIF). VIF should not exceed 10 [10]. Second, standard multiple regressions can only accurately estimate the relationship between dependent and independent variables if the relationships are linear in nature [11]. To determine the importance of each factor to tourist satisfaction in Chiang Mai, the multiple regression analysis was conducted based on earlier findings of the factor analysis. The overall tourist satisfaction was the dependent variable. All variables were entered at the same time. Referring to Table 4, the results of the multiple regression analysis indicates that all five factors significantly influence tourist satisfaction in Chiang Mai. Cost of staying turns out to be the most important factor, followed by *Hospitality, Environment, Attraction and Accessibility*, and *Infrastructure* in that order.

Table 4. Regression Results: Factors Affecting Tourist Satisfaction in Chiang Mai

Factor	Unstandardized Coefficients	Standardized Coefficients	t-value	VIF
Factor 1: Hospitality	0.278	0.262	5.806[***]	1.710
Factor 2: Attraction and Accessibility	0.140	0.144	3.149[***]	1.743
Factor 3: Cost of staying	0.314	0.336	7.390[***]	1.730
Factor 4: Environmental factor	0.156	0.171	4.094[***]	1.464
Factor 5: Infrastructure	0.101	0.122	2.992[***]	1.394
Adjusted R^2 = 0.633				
Durbin-Watson = 1.981				

*p < 0.10,**p < 0.05, and ***p < 0.01

The Durbin–Watson (DW) is always between 0 and 4 and the values of 1.5 < DW< 2.5 show that there is no auto-correlation in the data [12], and all VIF values in this study are less than 10. Furthermore, the normal P-Plot in this study is shown below in Figure 1 as the data are plotted against a theoretical normal distribution in a way that the points should form an approximate straight line. Departures from this straight line indicate departures from normality [13]. Data collected in this study indicate a relative normal distribution.

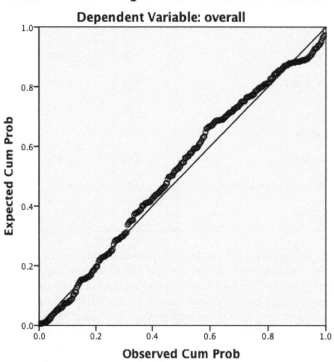

Figure 2. Normal P-Plot of Regression Standardized Residual Dependent Variable: Overall

5 Discussions

Cost of Staying includes price of accommodation, food and beverage, transportation, products, and overall cost of stay. The cost of staying in Chiang Mai is fairly low, compared to similar attractions in other provinces. If the price of staying increases, the satisfaction of tourists will decrease. Hospitality is the second significant factor that affects tourist satisfaction. Thai people have friendly and welcoming characteristics and personality - known worldwide as the land of smiles. Tourists deeply witness and feel impressed by such matters of Thai culture. In addition, this inspires tourists to return to Chiang Mai in the future. Beyond the friendly and welcoming personality and instincts of Thai people, local food in Chiang Mai from small restaurants to luxury and decorative cuisines is unarguably unique and diverse. From the comment of surveys, one of the respondents said, "My favorite thing about Chiang Mai is the people. The people here are kind and helpful. I hope the people keep their warm and open hearts".

The environmental factors of Chiang Mai, geographically situated on highlands, create distinct and unique scenery for the eyes of tourists who are touched by what they have witnessed. The weather and climate in Chiang Mai is therefore pleasant to the people due to the geography of this province, making the place a perfect place for tourism all seasons round. As for tourists who love nature and natural attractions, Chiang Mai is an undeniably choice for such tourists.

Attraction and Accessibility of Chiang Mai has become a major factor that influences visitation of tourists in Chiang Mai. Chiang Mai, a heritage city which has existed for as long as seven centuries, has continued its rich and unique culture which is passed on from generations and is still maintained for the present. Most of the culture can be viewed from architecture such as temples and festivals. In addition, travelling to Chiang Mai is very easy because of the convenient transportation and travel routes to Chiang Mai due to international airports, which operates direct flights from aboard such as Seoul (South Korea), Singapore, China, Hong Kong, and Amsterdam (Netherlands). Domestically, diverse types of public transports are available from other provinces to Chiang Mai, for example, five trips by trains from Bangkok to Chiang Mai daily, and over 100 trips by public buses from Bangkok to Chiang Mai.

6 Conclusion

In conclusion, this study provides information that can be useful in the tourism industry to improve service quality in Chiang Mai. In preparation for the AEC, policies should be improved and developed to attract and satisfy tourists. Finally, this study indicates the most influential factor, which is *Cost of Staying*. The tourism authority of Thailand introduces new policies to prepare for the upcoming AEC. Those policies do not cover all factors, especially *Cost of Staying,* which should be the main concern for policy makers. All results obtained in this study is restrict to current information only. This study focuses only on factors that increase tourists' satisfaction.

This study can provide policy recommendations to government agencies. Controlling the standard of the price to be the same for both Thai and foreign tourists can raise the level of satisfaction among tourists. Besides this factor, conserving tourism resources (cultural and natural) and improving cleanliness of public toilets for both free and charge toilets can help in assisting the ability (of Chiang Mai) in the tourism industry to compete with other nations in the AEC. Methods of conserving tourism resources are: educating local people for the protection and judicious use of natural resources, stopping over utilization of natural resources, making habits for waste disposal, increasing the number of dustbin, and prohibiting heritage sites.

As suggested earlier, all policies recommended to government might not be doable because there are numerous limitations. For instance, competition within the private sector, amount of budget received from government are insufficient for development. There is also lack of consistency of developing government policy plan, and lack of short term and long- term planning. Furthermore, there is lack of implementation of policy in a systematical approach. Hence, government will have to play their role as supporters in terms of policies and fundamental infrastructure. This is to increase opportunities and abilities of the private sector to enhance the limitations of capabilities to compete in the tourism economy. Simultaneously, the private sector will have to cooperate and collaborate with government.

7 Acknowledgement

This research is partially supported by Sirindhorn International Institute of Technology. I would like to acknowledge Buddhapoom Maneechote, Paramee Chaisompongpun, Pawara Boonsorn, Paweena Jonngarmnent, and Tanattha Rakbamrung for their assistance in collecting the data.

References

1. C.A. Gunn, *Tourism Planning, 2ⁿᵈ Edition*, New York, Taylor and Francis (1988)
2. Smith, S.L.J. The Tourism Product, Annals of Tourism research. http://ftur.uh.cu/intra/ftp/Materiales%20docentes/4to%20a%F1o/Asignatura%20Ocio/Tema%20IV/(%20GOLF)/CD%20%20Golf%20y%20AAVV/Viajes%20y%20Productos/The%20tourism%20product.pdf (1994)
3. V. Middleton, A. Fyall, M. Morgan, A. Ranchhod *Marketing in Travel and Tourism*, Butterworth-Heinemann, Routledge; 4ᵗʰ edition (2009)
4. R. D. Mason, *Engineering Statistics for Business and Economics, 9ᵗʰ Edition*, Jakarta, Grants (2000)
5. Poerwanto, Geography of Tourism in Dictates Education, Ministry of Education and Culture, University of Jember (2000)
6. M. Kozak, M. Rimmington, *Tourist satisfaction with Mallorca, Spain, as an off-season holiday destination,* Journal of Travel Research **38**, 260-269 (2000)
7. Pizam, Y. Neumann, A. Reichel, *Dimensions of Tourist Satisfaction with a Destination*, Annals of Tourism Research, 314-322 (1978)
8. Parasuraman, V.A. Zeithaml, L.L. Berry, *A Conceptual Model of Service Quality and Its Implications for Future Research,* Journal of Marketing **49**, 41-50 (1985)
9. A.Crossman, *Principle Components and Factor Analysis*, http://sociology.about.com/b/2012/01/13/statistics-spotlight-principal-components-and-factor-analysis.htm, accessed December 23 (2013)
10. M. Kutner, C. Nachtsheim, and J. Neter *Applied Linear Regression Models, 4ᵗʰ Edition*, New York, McGraw-Hill/Irwin (2004)
11. J.W. Osborne, E. Waters Four Assumptions of Multiple Regression That Researchers Should Always Test, *North Carolina State University and University of Oklahoma Practical Assessment, Research, and Evaluation* **8** (2002)
12. G.D. Garson, *Testing Statistical Assumptions*, Blue Book Series (2012)
13. J.M. Chambers, W.S. Cleveland, B. Kleiner, and P.A. Tukey, Graphical Methods for Data Analysis, *Wadsworth International Group* (1983)

Permissions

The contributors of this book come from diverse backgrounds, making this book a truly international effort. This book will bring forth new frontiers with its revolutionizing research information and detailed analysis of the nascent developments around the world.

We would like to thank all the contributing authors for lending their expertise to make the book truly unique. They have played a crucial role in the development of this book. Without their invaluable contributions this book wouldn't have been possible. They have made vital efforts to compile up to date information on the varied aspects of this subject to make this book a valuable addition to the collection of many professionals and students.

This book was conceptualized with the vision of imparting up-to-date information and advanced data in this field. To ensure the same, a matchless editorial board was set up. Every individual on the board went through rigorous rounds of assessment to prove their worth. After which they invested a large part of their time researching and compiling the most relevant data for our readers.

The editorial board has been involved in producing this book since its inception. They have spent rigorous hours researching and exploring the diverse topics which have resulted in the successful publishing of this book. They have passed on their knowledge of decades through this book. To expedite this challenging task, the publisher supported the team at every step. A small team of assistant editors was also appointed to further simplify the editing procedure and attain best results for the readers.

Apart from the editorial board, the designing team has also invested a significant amount of their time in understanding the subject and creating the most relevant covers. They scrutinized every image to scout for the most suitable representation of the subject and create an appropriate cover for the book.

The publishing team has been an ardent support to the editorial, designing and production team. Their endless efforts to recruit the best for this project, has resulted in the accomplishment of this book. They are a veteran in the field of academics and their pool of knowledge is as vast as their experience in printing. Their expertise and guidance has proved useful at every step. Their uncompromising quality standards have made this book an exceptional effort. Their encouragement from time to time has been an inspiration for everyone.

The publisher and the editorial board hope that this book will prove to be a valuable piece of knowledge for researchers, students, practitioners and scholars across the globe.

List of Contributors

Rosazman Hussin
The Ethnography and Development Research Unit, Faculty of Humanities, Arts and Heritage, Universiti Malaysia Sabah, 88400 Kota Kinabalu, Sabah, Malaysia

Suhaimi Md. Yasir
Seaweed Research Unit, Faculty of Science and Natural Resources, Universiti Malaysia Sabah, 88400 Kota Kinabalu, Sabah, Malaysia

Velan Kunjuraman
The Ethnography and Development Research Unit, Faculty of Humanities, Arts and Heritage, Universiti Malaysia Sabah, 88400 Kota Kinabalu, Sabah, Malaysia

Hamimah Talib
Faculty of Science and Natural Resources, Universiti Malaysia Sabah, 88999 Kota Kinabalu, Sabah, Malaysia

Jennifer Chan Kim Lian
Faculty of Business, Economics and Accountancy, Universiti Malaysia Sabah, 88999 Kota Kinabalu, Sabah, Malaysia

Timothy Ajeng Mereng
Faculty of Science and Natural Resources, Universiti Malaysia Sabah, 88999 Kota Kinabalu, Sabah, Malaysia

David Yoon Kin Tong
Faculty of Business, Multimedia University, 75450 Melaka, Malaysia

Dong-Won Ha
Department of Tourism, Hanyang University, Seoul, South Korea

Seung-Dam Choi
Department of Tourism, Hanyang University, Seoul, South Korea

Yeon-Kyung Kwon
Department of Tourism, Hanyang University, Seoul, South Korea

Hyun-Jung Kim
Department of Tourism, Hanyang University, Seoul, South Korea

A.S. A. Ferdous Alam
Institute for Environment and Development (LESTARI), Universiti Kebangsaan Malaysia (UKM), 43600 UKM Bangi, Selangor, Malaysia

Er A. C
Faculty of Social Sciences and Humanities (FSSK), Universiti Kebangsaan Malaysia (UKM), 43600 UKM Bangi, Selangor, Malaysia

Halima Begum
Faculty of Social Sciences and Humanities (FSSK), Universiti Kebangsaan Malaysia (UKM), 43600 UKM Bangi, Selangor, Malaysia

Shida Irwana Omar
Sustainable Tourism Research Cluster, Universiti Sains Malaysia, 11800, Penang, Malaysia

Gelareh Abooali
School of Housing, Building and Planning, Universiti Sains Malaysia, 11800, Penang, Malaysia

Badaruddin Mohamed
Sustainable Tourism Research Cluster, Universiti Sains Malaysia, 11800, Penang, Malaysia
School of Housing, Building and Planning, Universiti Sains Malaysia, 11800, Penang, Malaysia

Diana Mohamad
Sustainable Tourism Research Cluster, Universiti Sains Malaysia, 11800, Penang, Malaysia

Troy P. Tuzon
Faculty of the College of International Tourism and Hospitality Management, Lyceum of the Philippines University Laguna, Calamba City, Laguna, Philippines

Lira Jane A. Hilao
Students of the College of International Tourism and Hospitality Management, Lyceum of the Philippines University Laguna, Calamba City, Laguna, Philippines

Irish Renerie D. Marana
Students of the College of International Tourism and Hospitality Management, Lyceum of the Philippines University Laguna, Calamba City, Laguna, Philippines

Kevin N. Villalobos
Faculty of the College of International Tourism and Hospitality Management, Lyceum of the Philippines University Laguna, Calamba City, Laguna, Philippines

Enrico Garcia
Faculty of the College of Arts and Sciences, Lyceum of the Philippines University – Laguna, Calamba City, Laguna, Philippines

Merlita C. Medallon
Research Director, Lyceum of the Philippines University – Laguna, Calamba City, Laguna, Philippines

M. Mohamad
Faculty of Business Management and Accountancy, Universiti Sultan Zainal Abidin, Kuala Terengganu, Malaysia

N. I. Ab Ghani
Faculty of Business Management and Accountancy, Universiti Sultan Zainal Abidin, Kuala Terengganu, Malaysia

Jin-OK Kim
Division of Tourism, Hanyang University, 222 Wangsimni-ro, Seongdong-gu, Seoul 133-791, South Korea

Jin-Eui Lee
Division of Tourism, Hanyang University, 222 Wangsimni-ro, Seongdong-gu, Seoul 133-791, South Korea

Nam-Jo Kim
Division of Tourism, Hanyang University, 222 Wangsimni-ro, Seongdong-gu, Seoul 133-791, South Korea

Mastura Jaafar
School of Housing Building and Planning, Universiti Sains Malaysia, 11800 Penang, Malaysia

Mana Khoshkam
School of Housing Building and Planning, Universiti Sains Malaysia, 11800 Penang, Malaysia

Munira Mhd Rashid
School of Housing Building and Planning, Universiti Sains Malaysia, 11800 Penang, Malaysia

Norziani Dahalan
School of Distance Education, Universiti Sains Malaysia, 11800 Penang, Malaysia

Kee Mun Wong
School of Business and Accountancy, University of Malaya, 50603 Kuala Lumpur, Malaysia

Peramarajan Velasamy
Research and Informatics Department, Malaysia Healthcare Travel Council, 59000 Kuala Lumpur, Malaysia

Tengku Nuraina Tengku Arshad
Research and Informatics Department, Malaysia Healthcare Travel Council, 59000 Kuala Lumpur, Malaysia

Norziani Dahalan
School of Distance Education Universiti Sains Malaysia, Pulau Pinang, 11800, Malaysia

Mastura Jaafar
School of Housing Planning Universiti Sains Malaysia, Pulau Pinang, 11800, Malaysia

Siti Asma' Mohd Rosdi
School of Housing Planning Universiti Sains Malaysia, Pulau Pinang, 11800, Malaysia

Shardy Abdullah
School of Housing, Building and Planning, Universiti Sains Malaysia, 11800 Penang, Malaysia

Arman Abdul Razak
School of Housing, Building and Planning, Universiti Sains Malaysia, 11800 Penang, Malaysia

Mastura Jaafar
School of Housing, Building and Planning, Universiti Sains Malaysia, 11800 Penang, Malaysia

Tania Maria Tangit
Faculty of Hotel & Tourism Management, Universiti Teknologi MARA, Sabah, Malaysia

Ahmad Khairuman Md Hasim
Faculty of Hotel & Tourism Management, Universiti Teknologi MARA, Sabah, Malaysia

Akmal Adanan
Faculty of Hotel & Tourism Management, Universiti Teknologi MARA, Melaka, Malaysia

Dewi Mulia

Main Rindam
Centre for Distance Education, Universiti Sains Malaysia, 11800 Penang, Malaysia

Kim-Kathrin Kunze
Department of Marketing, University of Siegen, 57068 Siegen, Germany

Hanna Schramm-Klein
Department of Marketing, University of Siegen, 57068 Siegen, Germany

Mastura Jaafar
School of Housing, Building and Planning, Universiti Sains Malaysia, 11800 Penang, Malaysia

Mana Khoshkam
School of Housing, Building and Planning, Universiti Sains Malaysia, 11800 Penang, Malaysia

Jamal El-Harami
Al-Zaytooneh University of Jordan, Amman, Jordan

Suthathip Suanmali
Transportation Research Center, Sirindhorn International Institute of Technology, Thammasat University, Pathum Thani 12000, Thailand

Kasidis Chankao
Transportation Research Center, Sirindhorn International Institute of Technology, Thammasat University, Pathum Thani 12000, Thailand

Veeris Ammarapala
Transportation Research Center, Sirindhorn International Institute of Technology, Thammasat University, Pathum Thani 12000, Thailand

Nor Hasliza Md Saad
School of Management, Universiti Sains Malaysia, 11800 Penang, Malaysia

Siti Nabiha Abdul Khalid
Graduate School of Business, Universiti Sains Malaysia, 11800 Penang, Malaysia

Norliza Zainol Abidin
Graduate School of Business, Universiti Sains Malaysia, 11800 Penang, Malaysia

Norhafiza Md Sharif
School of Distance Education, Universiti Sains Malaysia, 11800, Penang, Malaysia

Ku Azam Tuan Lonik
School of Distance Education, Universiti Sains Malaysia, 11800, Penang, Malaysia

Badariah Din
College of Law, Government and International Studies, Universiti Utara Malaysia, 06010 UUM Sintok, Kedah, Malaysia

Muzafar Shah Habibullah
Faculty of Economics and Management, Universiti Putra Malaysia, 43400 UPM Serdang, Selangor, Malaysia

W.C. Choo
Faculty of Economics and Management, Universiti Putra Malaysia, 43400 UPM Serdang, Selangor, Malaysia

Farah Atiqah Mohamad Noor
School of Hospitality, Tourism and Culinary Arts, Taylor's University, 47500 Subang Jaya, Selangor Darul Ehsan, Malaysia

Vikneswaran Nair
School of Hospitality, Tourism and Culinary Arts, Taylor's University, 47500 Subang Jaya, Selangor Darul Ehsan, Malaysia

Paolo Mura
School of Hospitality, Tourism and Culinary Arts, Taylor's University, 47500 Subang Jaya, Selangor Darul Ehsan, Malaysia

Nur Zafirah A. Khadar
Sustainable Tourism Research Cluster (STRC), Universiti Sains Malaysia, 11800 Penang, Malaysia

Mastura Jaafar
School of Housing, Building and Planning, Universiti Sains Malaysia, 11800 Penang, Malaysia

Diana Mohamad
Sustainable Tourism Research Cluster (STRC), Universiti Sains Malaysia, 11800 Penang, Malaysia

Christy Bidder
Faculty of Hotel and Tourism Management, Universiti Teknologi MARA, 88997 Sabah, Malaysia

Reni Cacillia Polus
Faculty of Hotel and Tourism Management, Universiti Teknologi MARA, 94300 Sarawak, Malaysia

A.Sarobol
Faculty of Humanities, Chiang Mai University, 50200 Chiang Mai, Thailand

Suthathip Suanmali
School of Management Technology, Sirindhorn International Institute of Technology, Thammasat University, Pathumthani 12000, Thailand

Fatan HamamahYahaya
School of Distance Learning Education Universiti Sains Malaysia 11800, Minden, Penang, Malaysia

Sakinah Abu Bakar
School of Distance Learning Education Universiti Sains Malaysia 11800, Minden, Penang, Malaysia

Norziani Dahalan
School of Distance Learning Education Universiti Sains Malaysia 11800, Minden, Penang, Malaysia

Omar and Nazirah MdYusof
School of Distance Learning Education Universiti Sains Malaysia 11800, Minden, Penang, Malaysia

Azizi Bahauddin
School of Housing, Building and Planning Universiti Sa ins Malaysia

Aldrin Abdullah
School of Housing, Building and Planning Universiti Sa ins Malaysia

Nor Zarifah Maliki
School of Housing, Building and Planning Universiti Sains Malaysia

Fatan Hamamah Yahaya
School of Distance Education Universiti Sains Malaysia 11800 Penang

Lightning Source UK Ltd.
Milton Keynes UK
UKHW050146180222
398830UK00002B/31